T. S. ELIOT   GUIDE
FOR THE PERPLEXED

THE GUIDES FOR THE PERPLEXED SERIES

Continuum's Guides for the Perplexed are clear, concise and accessible introductions to thinkers, writers and subjects that students and readers can find especially challenging. Concentrating specifically on what it is that makes the subject difficult to grasp, these books explain and explore key themes and ideas, guiding the reader towards a thorough understanding of demanding material.

Related titles include:
Beckett: A Guide for the Perplexed Jonathan Boulter
Deleuze: A Guide for the Perplexed Claire Colebrook
Derrida: A Guide for the Perplexed Julian Wolfreys
Existentialism: A Guide for the Perplexed Steven Earnshaw
Literary Theory: A Guide for the Perplexed Mary Klages
Tolstoy: A Guide for the Perplexed Jeff Love

T. S. ELIOT: A GUIDE FOR THE PERPLEXED

STEVE ELLIS

continuum

Continuum International Publishing Group

The Tower Building	80 Maiden Lane
11 York Road	Suite 704
London SE1 7NX	New York NY 10038

www.continuumbooks.com

British Library Cataloguing-in-Publication Data
A catalogue record for this book is available from the British Library.

ISBN: 978-1-8470-6016-7 (hardback)
          978-1-8470-6017-4 (paperback)

Library of Congress Cataloging-in-Publication Data
Ellis, Steve, 1952-
T. S. Eliot: a guide for the perplexed / Steve Ellis.
         p. cm.
Includes bibliographical references and index.
ISBN 978-1-84706-016-7
ISBN 978-1-84706-017-4
1. Eliot, T. S. (Thomas Stearns), 1888-1965–Criticism and interpretation.
2. American poetry–20th century–History and criticism. I. Title.

PS3509.L43Z67178 2009
821'.912–dc22
2009012171

Typeset by Newgen Imaging Systems Pvt Ltd, Chennai, India
Printed and bound in Great Britain by CPI Antony Rowe, Chippenham, Wiltshire

To my Eliot students, past, present and future

I am not sure . . . that we can judge and enjoy a man's
poetry while leaving wholly out of account all of
the things for which he cared deeply, and on behalf of
which he turned his poetry to account.
—T. S. Eliot, *The Use of Poetry and the
Use of Criticism*, p. 87

CONTENTS

ACKNOWLEDGEMENTS

Excerpts from 'Journey of the Magi', 'A Song for Simeon', 'Animula', 'Marina', 'Sweeney Agonistes' and Choruses from *The Rock* in *Collected Poems 1909–1962* by T. S. Eliot, copyright 1936 by Harcourt, Inc.. and renewed in 1964 by T. S. Eliot, reprinted by permission of Houghton Mifflin Harcourt Publishing Company.

Excerpt from *The Family Reunion*, copyright 1939 by T. S. Eliot and renewed 1967 by Esme Valerie Eliot, reprinted by permission of Houghton Mifflin Harcourt Publishing Company.

Excerpt from *The Cocktail Party*, copyright 1950 by T. S. Eliot and renewed 1978 by Esme Valerie Eliot, reprinted by permission of Houghton Mifflin Harcourt Publishing Company.

The author would like to thank Faber and Faber Ltd for permission to reprint excerpts from 'Rhapsody on a Windy Night', 'Gerontion' and 'Ash-Wednesday' in *Collected Poems 1909–1962* by T. S. Eliot.

ABBREVIATIONS AND EDITIONS OF ELIOT'S WORKS USED IN THE TEXT

ASG   *After Strange Gods: A Primer of Modern Heresy.* The Page-Barbour Lectures at the University of Virginia 1933 (London: Faber, 1934)

CP   *The Complete Poems and Plays* (London: Faber, 1969)

FLA   *For Lancelot Andrewes: Essays on Style and Order* (1928), new ed. (London: Faber, 1970)

ICS   *The Idea of a Christian Society* (London: Faber, 1939)

NDC   *Notes Towards the Definition of Culture* (1948), new ed. (London: Faber: 1962)

OP   *On Poetry and Poets* (London: Faber, 1957)

SW   *The Sacred Wood: Essays on Poetry and Criticism* (1920), 7th ed. (London: Methuen, 1950)

SE   *Selected Essays*, 3rd ed. (London: Faber, 1951)

SP   *Selected Prose*, ed. Frank Kermode (London: Faber, 1975)

TC   *To Criticize the Critic and Other Writings* (1965), new ed. (London: Faber, 1978)

UP   *The Use of Poetry and the Use of Criticism: Studies in the Relation of Criticism to Poetry in England* (1933), new ed. (London: Faber, 1964)

VMP   *The Varieties of Metaphysical Poetry . . .*, ed. Ronald Schuchard (London: Faber, 1993)

WLF   *The Waste Land: A Facsimile and Transcript of the Original Drafts Including the Annotations of Ezra Pound*, ed. Valerie Eliot (London: Faber, 1971)

INTRODUCTION: ELIOT'S POETRY AND THE USE OF ELIOT'S CRITICISM

Good commentaries can be very helpful: but to study even the best commentary on a work of literary art is likely to be a waste of time unless we have first read and been excited by the text commented upon even without understanding it.
—*'A Note of Introduction' to* In Parenthesis, *by David Jones, p. viii*

T. S. Eliot is one of the most celebrated twentieth-century poets and one whose work is perceived as extremely challenging in several respects; as he himself noted in his essay 'The Metaphysical Poets', 'it appears likely that poets in our civilization . . . must be *difficult.* Our civilization comprehends great variety and complexity, and this variety and complexity, playing upon a refined sensibility, must produce various and complex results' (*SE* 289). Added to this sense of poetic responsibility to a complex contemporary civilization is a difficulty for today's readers that Eliot probably didn't envisage: the widespread unfamiliarity with the Christian belief and culture that his work becomes increasingly steeped in.

This *Guide for the Perplexed* on Eliot then is justified in addressing the work of a poet practically synonymous with perplexity, but it does not attempt to explain every literary allusion in his work, nor even the majority of these. For those readers requiring a step-by-step explication of Eliot's work, there are already a sufficient number of Reader's Guides and Study Notes which serve this function (and some of the best starting points are highlighted in this volume's Further Reading section and Bibliography). Eliot repeatedly warned that 'explanation' and 'understanding' are not the same thing, and that in his own experience as a reader 'too much information about the origins of the poem may even break my contact with it' (*OP* 110–2).

Instead, I take a broader approach by offering Eliot's own prose writings, which are extensive, as an illuminating means of access to his poetry. As a major critic, as well as poet, Eliot was highly conscious of the challenges his poetry set, of its relation and difference to the work of previous poets and of the ways in which the activity of reading was problematized by his work. I also discuss a series of key and recurring literary relationships acknowledged in his prose writing – to writers such as Dante, Shakespeare, Marvell, Baudelaire and Conrad, bearing in mind his declaration that 'in my earlier criticism, both in my general affirmations about poetry and in writing about authors who had influenced me, I was implicitly defending the sort of poetry that I and my friends wrote' (*TC* 16). This defence is indeed, as we shall see, sometimes 'implicit' rather than declared.

One difficulty in adopting an 'Eliot as commentator on Eliot' approach is our modern scepticism about authorial 'intention' and dismissal of the author-figure as the privileged source of meaning or interpretation. But Eliot's relation as a critic to his poetry was far from authoritative or proprietorial; that is, he never claimed any 'ownership' of it. 'What a poem means is as much what it means to others as what it means to the author', he noted in 1933 (*UP* 130), and he reiterated the point ten years later: 'the reader's interpretation [of a poem] may differ from the author's and be equally valid – it may even be better. There may be much more in a poem than the author was aware of' (*OP* 31). The necessary difficulty of modern poetry stimulates and justifies a plurality of interpretation, given that no one reading is likely to encompass the variety and complexity the modern poem embodies. While Eliot felt the poet had a duty to register this complex modernity, that is, a duty to his own historical situation, there is also a duty to tradition, a tradition that has not passed down all modes of thought and feeling as of equal value but comprises a particular heritage that Eliot sympathized with. At this point of intersection between a tradition that is exclusive, and a modernity the poet must adopt an inclusive attitude towards, Eliot's early writing lies; the result is the pervasive dialogue in that writing between the 'one' and the 'many', the unifying centre and multi-voicedness, the 'ideal' and the 'actuality'.

As Eliot's career developed, the commitment to the first-named in each of these pairs gained in strength, and the opposition was reformulated as that between order and chaos, or orthodoxy and an unwelcome liberalism, his affiliations underlain by his formal conversion to Christianity in 1927. Eliot's poetry increasingly centralizes and excludes the range of diverse voices he has hitherto embraced, and the 'mind of Europe' he felt it was a poet's task to give voice to (*SE* 16) becomes less diverse and multiple, practically boiling down to the 'classic standard' represented by the line of communication running from Virgil to Dante, and from Dante on to modern Europe. 'The maintenance of the standard', he argues in a key essay of 1945, 'is the price of our freedom, the defence of freedom against chaos' ('What is a Classic?', *OP* 70). In 1934 he had described 'the struggle of our time' as that seeking 'to concentrate, not to dissipate', and 'to renew our association with traditional wisdom' (*ASG* 48). In the poetry from the mid-1920s onwards we have a parallel 'concentration': the diction becomes 'purified', more severely homogeneous, excluding, for example, the foreign language quotations, the dialects, the mixed discourse effects (song, jazz, nursery rhyme) that culminated in *The Waste Land*; the imagery too becomes more ascetic and restrained, indeed to the point where several readers of Eliot have claimed a loss of poetic power in his later career.

One of the key debates in Eliot criticism is how far this 'mature' (in Eliot's term) insistence on orthodoxy, standards and 'traditional wisdom' is already present in the early work, work which seems to offer a far greater welcome to different experience, different philosophical positions and linguistic and cultural variety. The importance of 'tradition' of course is present from the outset in Eliot's most famous early essay, 'Tradition and the Individual Talent' of 1919, and a good number of critics would accept, in Ronald Schuchard's words, that 'Eliot's classical, royalist, and religious point of view was already formulated' a long time before his much-quoted profession of that position in 1928 in the Preface to *For Lancelot Andrewes*.[1] Kenneth Asher has also argued that 'from beginning to end, Eliot's work, including both the poetry and the prose, was shaped by a political vision inherited from French reactionary thinkers'.[2] I agree that such a point of view informs his criticism and poetry both early and late, but its features are obscured by the plethora of diverse experience, reference and sensation Eliot was also keen to record in his early poetry. His famous comment on Joyce's use of myth in *Ulysses* (1922) as 'a way of controlling, of ordering, of giving a shape and a significance to the immense panorama of futility and anarchy which is contemporary history' ('*Ulysses*, Order, and Myth', *SP* 177) is relevant to *The Waste Land* of the same year in both the ambition of the poem's panoramic scope and its use of ordering and controlling mechanisms to address an 'anarchy' the poem also bears witness to. The debate over how far Eliot is a celebrant of modernity's 'variety and complexity', as opposed to a writer bent on critique and 'control' of it, is fuelled by Eliot's belief in poetry's necessary immersion in the 'new' and its imperative to record a hectic modern civilization. In 'Tradition and the Individual Talent' he argues that for poetry to aspire to be traditional in the sense of evading its specific historical moment would be an empty conformism: 'to conform merely would be for the new work not really to conform at all; it would not be new, and would therefore not be a work of art' (*SE* 15). 'Tradition', as Eliot makes clear, has a much more searching import, being the full realization of that historical intersection noted above, with the poet's living 'in what is not merely the present, but the present moment of the past' (p. 22). Only thus might a new and exciting poetry be produced, yet that poetry might still convey in large part the futility and 'horror' of the contemporary, to quote from *The Waste Land*'s abandoned epigraph, and thus anticipate some of his later, explicitly right-wing thinking.[3]

These ideas and the critical debate relating to them will be developed in the following chapters, but I want to preface them by emphasizing what I see as an underlying consistency of outlook in Eliot's writing, not only between the poetry and prose, but between the poetry leading up to and including *The Waste Land*, and that which follows, even though stylistically the later poetry is very different. As early as 1916 we find Eliot pointing out a modern 'Reaction against Romanticism':

> the beginning of the twentieth century has witnessed a return to the ideals of classicism. These may roughly be characterized as *form* and *restraint* in art, *discipline* and *authority* in religion, *centralization* in government (either as socialism or monarchy). The classicist point of view has been defined as essentially a belief in Original Sin – the necessity for austere discipline.[4]

Though such a 'belief' seems to me to operate unmistakably throughout Eliot's prose and poetry, its outline, as noted above, emerges more clearly as his career progresses. In the early poetry the element of 'primitivism' which is such an important part of the tradition – 'Poetry begins . . . with a savage beating a drum in a jungle, and it retains that essential of percussion and rhythm; hyperbolically one might say that the poet is *older* than other human beings' (*UP* 155); 'even the most primitive feelings should be part of our heritage' (*ICS* 62) – is forcefully exploited and enjoyed, and can be related to Eliot's powerful attraction to the music of jazz and Stravinsky, the 'vitality' of the English working-class music hall and some forms of erotic writing. In the later work primitivism is largely of value in the spur it provides for spiritual values to wrestle with and overcome it, but in its battle with classical form and restraint in the early writing it is embraced more keenly, as we shall see. The response to the primitive part of 'our heritage' also survives within the later religious insistence on the value of blasphemy and diabolism as an indication that the soul is spiritually 'alive': 'it is better, in a paradoxical way, to do evil than to do nothing: at least, we exist' (*SE* 429). What is more worrying to Eliot, and what his work constantly diagnoses, is an enfeebled and mechanized modernity where the 'darker' aspects of sexuality and spirituality alike have been reduced to a 'listless apathy' ('Marie Lloyd', *SE* 458–9), the world of the 'hollow men', of the crowd of the living dead flowing over London Bridge in *The Waste Land*. The 'Marie Lloyd' essay ends in fact with Eliot's diatribe against 'forcing' modern civilization upon native peoples (here the Melanesians) which will result in their being 'deprived . . . of all interest in life. They are dying from pure boredom' (*SE* 459). A profound attraction–repulsion ambivalence towards the 'primitive' prompts the extensive use of the 'double' figure in much of Eliot's work, but respect for the 'darker' aspects of being never becomes an absolute, as evident in his qualified tribute to D. H. Lawrence in 1934: 'in contrast to Nottingham, London or industrial America, his capering redskins of *Mornings in Mexico* seem to represent Life. So they do; but that is not the last word, only the first' (*ASG* 60).

This book follows in its four chapters the course of what Eliot indicates as the gradual purging and 'purification' (*OP* 260) of his poetry, the thinning out of its multiple voices, the movement towards a barer and more ascetic style, the consolidation of the 'mind of Europe' around fewer key points and the strengthening of the religious-classicist programme. But the latter I argue was always an important feature of his work. From 'The Hollow Men' of 1925 onwards, Eliot's religious agenda becomes clearer, and the poetry and drama more approachable without extensive reliance on the criticism, though I continue to discuss this in the later chapters. Indeed, there is a sense that the closely interrelated parts of poems like 'Ash-Wednesday' and the *Quartets* are now acting as commentary upon each other, sometimes explicitly. I want to guard, however, against the idea that one can simply see the later poetry as primarily an expression of Eliot's 'beliefs'. He was insistent that 'poetry is not a substitute for philosophy or theology or religion'; its 'function is not intellectual but emotional', and to use it as a vehicle for 'thinking' is not at all the poet's 'job' (*SE* 137–38, 136). Where a poet does in Eliot's eyes use poetry to air his 'thoughts', as with some of the poems of Shelley, or Blake's longer philosophical works, Eliot is scathing, and traditions of Victorian moralizing or 'rumination' are likewise famously attacked (*SE* 288). On the other hand, what Eliot saw as the reaction to Victorianism in the development of so-called pure poetry (*poésie pure*) at the end of the nineteenth century seemed to him just as alarming an extreme. Thus I. A. Richards's enthusiastic claim that *The Waste Land* had effected 'a complete severance between his poetry and *all* beliefs' was rebutted several times by Eliot: 'I think that either Mr Richards is wrong, or I do not understand his meaning', though in line with Eliot's belief in the rights of the reader he acknowledges 'I am no better qualified to say No! [to Richards] than is any other reader' (*UP* 130).[5]

The relationship between poetry and 'belief' caused Eliot a good deal of head-scratching, especially in the late 1920s and early 30s when his own religious, social and cultural beliefs became more emphatic. During this period he declares his main concern as a critic is with 'the relation of poetry to the spiritual and social life of its time and of other times', and while poetry's 'integrity' has still to be preserved, and it has to be guarded from illicit moralizing functions, it 'certainly has something to do with morals, and with religion, and even with politics perhaps, though we cannot say what'. If there is no conclusion to this argument, we can at least 'agree upon a point from which to start'.[6] This point is the insistence on prioritizing an immediate response to or enjoyment of poetry over the gradual process of 'understanding' it, a point illustrated in Eliot's remark that 'I was passionately fond of certain French poetry long before I could have translated two verses of it correctly' (*SE* 237). This remark, as well as the epigraph to this Introduction, should remind the reader of this Guide that Eliot's poems can and should be read and reread first if it, or indeed any book on Eliot, is going to be serviceable.

I offer therefore an Eliot-centred approach to the 'understanding' of his poetry without of course insisting that this is the 'correct' way the poetry is to be understood, and the Further Reading chapter of this volume gives some information about the (especially recent) critical debate on Eliot. Having a separate chapter here means that the critical debate is not allowed to overwhelm the primary texts in the body of the Guide, which, given the amount that has been written on Eliot, it could well do. The exception to this arrangement is in my discussion of *The Waste Land* in Chapter 2, given that Eliot's own commentary on the poem in the notes he published with it has been and continues to be actively and directly engaged with by many critics. It has seemed sensible therefore to bring the primary and secondary writing together here.

Unlike some recent surveys or student-orientated books on Eliot, this Guide does not concentrate on *The Waste Land* to the exclusion, practically, of everything else, not only because of the enormous interest and value of the rest of Eliot's work but also in the belief that the whole of that work provides a fundamental context for reading any one item.[7] In his major essay on Dante Eliot noted disapprovingly how 'the effect of many books about Dante is to give the impression that it is more necessary to read about him than to read what he has written', whereas reading Dante's various works for the light they throw on each other 'can be more useful than a dozen commentaries' ('Dante', *SE* 276). This Guide remains of course a commentary on Eliot rather than an anthology of his writing, but the featuring of his own prose keeps that writing to the fore, and could be said to mitigate the addition of yet another book on him. The quotation from the Dante essay also requires that the writing and not the 'man' be the point at issue: in the limited space available to me I have not provided a biography, which is available from countless sources elsewhere, but have gone straight to that writing. As Eliot's associate and collaborator Ezra Pound succinctly put it in a memorial volume published after his death, 'Am I to write "about" the poet Thomas Stearns Eliot? or my friend "the Possum"? Let him rest in peace. I can only repeat, but with the urgency of 50 years ago: READ HIM'.[8]

CHAPTER 1

THE EARLY POETRY AND PROSE

In an ideal state of society one might imagine the good New growing naturally out of the good Old, without the need for polemic and theory; this would be a society with a living tradition.
— *'Reflections on* vers libre*', TC 184*

THE NEWNESS OF ELIOT

In 1936 W. B. Yeats had this to say about Eliot in a radio broadcast on 'Modern Poetry':

> in the third year of the War came the most revolutionary man in poetry during my lifetime, though his revolution was stylistic alone – T. S. Eliot published his first book. No romantic word or sound, nothing reminiscent, nothing in the least like the painting of Ricketts [the 'traditional high breeding' of which Yeats had previously discussed in the broadcast] could be permitted henceforth. Poetry must resemble prose, and both must accept the vocabulary of their time; nor must there be any special subject-matter. Tristram and Isoult were not a more suitable theme than Paddington Railway Station. The past had deceived us: let us accept the worthless present.
>
> > The morning comes to consciousness
> > Of faint stale smells of beer
> > From the sawdust-trampled street
> > With all its muddy feet that press

> To early coffee-stands . . .
> One thinks of all the hands
> That are raising dingy shades
> In a thousand furnished rooms.

We older writers disliked this new poetry, but were forced to admit its satiric intensity.[1]

The idea of T. S. Eliot as 'revolutionary' on the evidence of his first book *Prufrock and Other Observations* (1917) conceals various debts to nineteenth-century predecessors we shall remark on, but Yeats's comment effectively registers the shock of Eliot's emergence, as well as the sense that his work is a watershed after which nothing 'henceforth' could be the same. In this estimation Yeats is setting up an antithesis between poets of an 'old' and 'new' dispensation that enforces his own tragic self-image, in the 1930s, as one of a dying breed of 'last romantics' who 'chose for theme / Traditional sanctity and loveliness', as his poem 'Coole Park and Ballylee, 1931' puts it.[2] Eliot's work is seen as inaugurating a prevailing anti-romanticism (that is even 'anti-poetic' in its prose-like qualities), involving a disillusioned commitment to the contemporary in both diction and subject, however 'worthless' the contemporary is. The sordid qualities of the present, instanced by lines from Eliot's poem 'Preludes' (*CP* 22), are taken as representative of Eliot's work as a whole.

Although Yeats gives a narrow and partisan picture of Eliot here, there is no doubt that many readers, including Eliot himself, saw the novelty and impact of his work as stemming in part from its uncompromising immersion in modern urban experience.[3] In a late essay looking back over his career Eliot described his early work's exploitation of 'the poetical possibilities, never developed by any poet writing in my own language, of the more sordid aspects of the modern metropolis', and of his discoveries that 'the sort of experience that an adolescent had had, in an industrial city in America, could be the material for poetry; and that the source of new poetry might be found in what had been regarded hitherto as the impossible, the sterile, the intractably unpoetic' (*TC* 126). Eliot stresses this innovatory position in the poetry of 'my own language' while noting that the impetus to tackle this new subject-matter came from reading nineteenth-century French poets like Baudelaire and Laforgue, who will be discussed further below. The real interest of Yeats's comment for me, however,

9

lies in the two assertions that Eliot's 'revolution was stylistic alone', and that his work eschewed 'any special subject-matter. Tristram and Isoult were not a more suitable theme than Paddington Railway Station'. The statements are connected: in spite of Yeats's concentrating on Paddington (and its environs of coffee-stands and dingy rooms) there is a sense that Eliot's work is indifferent, so to speak, to subject, grasping impartially at both urban sterility as well as, say, the story of Tristram and Isoult; and this omnivorous 'indifference' towards subject necessarily focuses attention on questions of style in Eliot's work.

For a figure like Yeats, committed to the theme of 'Traditional sanctity and loveliness', Eliot's modernity was an abdication of the proper role of the poet to choose subjects that would 'elevate a rhyme', as the 'Coole Park' poem later puts it, and to work in a diction commensurate with such subjects. In *A Vision* Yeats represents the modern movement in the arts generally as the refusal of such a role and vocation, a 'general surrender of the will', leading to the following results:

> synthesis for its own sake, organisation where there is no masterful director, books where the author has disappeared, painting where some accomplished brush paints with an equal pleasure, or with a bored impartiality, the human form or an old bottle, dirty weather and clean sunshine.[4]

It is not that Eliot's work rejects, in fact, poetry's traditional dignities – Tristan and Isolde figure in *The Waste Land* after all (ll. 31–42); what is truly shocking is that it accords such material no more importance than the 'intractably unpoetic' elements that exist alongside it. In a well-known passage from 'The Metaphysical Poets' essay of 1921 Eliot does indeed salute precisely the type of poetic 'synthesis' Yeats complains of:

> when a poet's mind is perfectly equipped for its work, it is constantly amalgamating disparate experience; the ordinary man's experience is chaotic, irregular, fragmentary. The latter falls in love, or reads Spinoza, and these two experiences have nothing to do with each other, or with the noise of the typewriter or the smell of cooking; in the mind of the poet these experiences are always forming new wholes. (*SE* 287)

Here we have, in fact, the 'recipe' for an Eliot poem, in which the smell of cooking (or other, often unpleasant, smells the early poetry is full of) is just as critical an ingredient as falling in love or referring to the poet's intellectual interests; indeed, it is in the contrast and interplay between such multifarious 'low' and 'high' discourses as they circulate within the arena of the poem that the poem's power and innovatory status principally lies.

In what is probably Eliot's best-known essay, 'Tradition and the Individual Talent' of 1919, he emphasizes this latter point:

> the mind of the mature poet differs from that of the immature one . . . not [by] being necessarily more interesting, or having 'more to say,' but rather by being a more finely perfected medium in which special, or very varied, feelings are at liberty to enter into new combinations. (*SE* 18)

And again:

> the poet's mind is in fact a receptacle for seizing and storing up numberless feelings, phrases, images, which remain there until all the particles which can unite to form a new compound are present together. (*SE* 19)

The value of the ensuing poetic 'compound', Eliot adds, has nothing to do with the 'importance' of the material that goes into it but lies at the level of the compositional process itself: 'it is not the "greatness", the intensity, of the emotions, the components, but the intensity of the artistic process, the pressure, so to speak, under which the fusion takes place, that counts' (*SE* 19). And the poet's necessary receptivity to the 'numberless' components that make up a poem, including what might seem totally 'unpoetic' ones, implies an attentiveness to the 'very great number of experiences which to the practical and active person would not seem to be experiences at all' (*SE* 21).

This latter comment occurs in the essay just after Eliot has dismissed Wordsworth's 'emotion recollected in tranquillity' as the 'formula' for poetic composition, and Yeats's comments have already suggested Eliot's assault on Romantic traditions that seems to be confirmed in the 'Tradition' essay.[5] The poet does not need the qualification of having 'more to say' than the non-poet, or having more 'interesting', significant or profound thoughts and emotions to communicate via the poetry – it is not the 'greatness' of the components that counts, we are told. This dismissal of what Eliot saw as the myth of experience – that to be a poet you must have 'lived' (that is loved, suffered or thought) deeply – questions a prevailing Romantic assumption. Thus to contemplate one's own death (as in Keats's 'Ode to a Nightingale') or the death of others (Tennyson's *In Memoriam*), or one's own growth and decay as a poet (Wordsworth's *Prelude*), or one's situation as a parent (Coleridge's 'Frost at Midnight', Yeats's 'A Prayer for My Daughter'), or as a lover (as in Hardy's 'Emma' poems of 1912–13, written at about the same time as 'Prufrock' – 'Woman much missed, how you call to me, call to me . . .' ('The Voice')) – all this 'personal' work establishes the confessional, autobiographical 'I', however much adapted or fictionalized in the poems in question, at the centre of the poetic process. Eliot's resistance to a tradition of writing that validates the significantly 'personal' in this way is consistent, as we shall see, with his later religious and cultural commentary and expressions of belief, and his many attacks on the modern obsession with 'personality'. Already in an early essay like 'Tradition and the Individual Talent' he is arguing that the importance and value of a poem has nothing to do with the poet's personal experience in the accepted sense, and that the poet who has a shallow emotional life – 'his personal emotions . . . may be simple, or crude, or flat' (*SE* 20–1) – can yet produce complex and potent poetry. The essay ends by insisting that 'to divert interest from the poet to the poetry is a laudable aim' and that, in a celebrated formulation, 'poetry is not a turning loose of emotion, but an escape from emotion; it is not the expression of personality, but an escape from personality' (*SE* 21–2).

Where then, put simply, does an Eliot poem 'come from', if not from 'deep' within the self, a provenance suggested by so much poetry? We have already seen that it comes from seemingly incidental or insignificant occurrences which 'to the practical and active person would not seem to be experiences at all', like the smell of cooking, but Eliot also insists that the material of poetry can come to the author second-hand: 'emotions which he has never experienced will serve his turn as well as those familiar to him' (*SE* 21). The implication is that such experiences derive predominantly from the poet's reading: 'we shall often find that not only the best, but the most individual parts of his work may be those in which the dead poets, his ancestors, assert their immortality most vigorously' (*SE* 14). Eliot also suggests that language itself, as the poet works with it on the page, triggers various associations and images – what Eliot calls localised 'feelings' rather than the 'structural emotion' of the whole – that often simply 'come' in the process of composition and that contribute powerfully to the final effect. In short, we return to the idea of a poet's mind being a 'finely perfected medium in which special, or very varied, feelings are at liberty to enter into new combinations', and thus to the poet's need to be responsive to the whole range of experience, however trivial it might seem, and wherever it might come from in life or literature, as a rationale of composition that is opposed to what Eliot calls a 'semi-ethical criterion of "sublimity"' that only admits into poetry the deeply felt, the 'personally' undergone (*SE* 19).

For Eliot then poetry should efface the private and personal, be 'an escape from personality'. His use of the word 'medium' in the quotation above is a very interesting one, especially when he also speaks of the 'best' parts of a poet's work being those in which 'the dead poets, his ancestors, assert their immortality most vigorously'. The Eliot poem becomes a mouthpiece through which the dead speak, as well as a 'medium' in another sense where numberless particles have united to form a new 'compound'.[6] This might well endorse Yeats's talk of the 'surrender of the will' in modern art, in so far as the poet's mind, open and receptive to everything, is waiting for that moment when the final element enters to crystallize the whole (to continue the chemical analogy for the production of poetry which Eliot uses throughout the essay). Eliot indeed talks of the poet's 'passive attending upon the event', though he hastens to add that this is 'not quite the whole story', and that 'there is a great deal, in the writing of poetry, which must be conscious and deliberate' (*SE* 21). But although this latter comment indicates the discipline and craftsmanship required in the practice of writing, 'Tradition' ends by affirming Eliot's fundamental point that the poet proceeds by 'surrendering himself' to impersonal forces from the past and the present that, as it were, speak through him (*SE* 22), just as earlier in the essay he discussed this 'self-sacrifice' in terms of giving voice to something called 'the mind of Europe – the mind of his own country – a mind which he learns in time to be much more important than his own private mind' (*SE* 16–17). To be acutely aware of the present and the past, to access a 'historical sense [that] compels a man to write not merely with his own generation in his bones' but with what we might call the DNA of the 'whole of the literature of Europe' going back to Homer (*SE* 14), and of 'the rock drawing of the Magdalenian draughtsmen' (*SE* 16), is to lay the 'individual talent' at the service of 'tradition'.

ELIOT AND THE EUROPEAN TRADITION

The attack on what Eliot saw as the 'prejudice' (*SE* 14) – and a specifically English prejudice at that, as we shall see – that poetry is synonymous with the original and individual expression of profound personal experience also led him to castigate poetic 'eccentricity', which is 'to seek for new human emotions to express . . . The business of the poet is not to find new emotions, but to use the ordinary ones' (*SE* 21). In the essay 'Andrew Marvell' of 1921, Eliot quotes the argument of Marvell's 'To his Coy Mistress' – a poem he constantly refers to in his own early poetry – to the effect that pleasures must be seized before life's brief opportunities are over and remarks that 'the theme is one of the great traditional commonplaces of European literature' (*SE* 295). It is, of course, none the worse for that, and in tracing the theme back through poets like Horace and Catullus Eliot claims that 'a whole civilization resides in these lines' (*SE* 295). In giving voice to that civilization, Marvell's 'best verse' shows itself to be 'the product of European, that is to say Latin, culture' (*SE* 293), but in its handling 'the wit of Marvell renews the theme . . . in the variety and order of the images' (*SE* 295). Poetry should in this way aim at 'renewing' tradition, not dispensing with it. But the great European exemplar, throughout Eliot's career, is the Italian poet Dante Alighieri (1265–1321), the poet he regarded as 'the most persistent and deepest influence upon my own verse' (*TC* 125), and it is no accident that the final essay in Eliot's first book of criticism, *The Sacred Wood* (1920), is a discussion of Dante, nor that this essay follows on immediately from an essay on Blake, a key figure of English Romanticism.[7] The contrast between the two is summed up in the declaration that 'Dante is a classic, and Blake only a poet of genius' (*SW* 158), and Dante is a classic because his work gives voice to an entire religious, cultural and philosophical 'civilization', to reimport the term from the Marvell essay, in which medieval Catholicism and classical learning and literature (especially that bequeathed by Virgil

and Aristotle) come together. In his longest essay on Dante, dating
from 1929, Eliot will again insist that Dante's work gives us 'the mind
of Europe' rather than his own 'private mind' and that even where
that work speaks of Dante himself this is not to be confused with the
self-absorption of the Romantic tradition:

> Dante, I believe, had experiences which seemed to him of some
> importance; not of importance because they had happened to him
> and because he, Dante Alighieri, was an important person who
> kept press-cutting bureaux busy; but important in themselves; and
> therefore they seemed to him to have some philosophical and
> impersonal value. (*SE* 272–3)

The key word is again 'impersonal'. In *The Sacred Wood*, although
Eliot does praise Blake's genius as a 'terrifying' determination to see
the world anew, 'unclouded by current opinions' (*SW* 155), such cultural 'nakedness' ran the risk evident in his longer and more philosophical works which

> illustrate the crankiness, the eccentricity, which frequently affects
> writers outside of the Latin tradition . . . What his genius required,
> and what it sadly lacked, was a framework of accepted and tradi-
> tional ideas which would have prevented him from indulging in a
> philosophy of his own, and concentrated his attention upon the
> problems of the poet. (*SW* 157–8)[8]

And for Eliot, this 'eccentricity' is a recurrent feature, almost itself a
tradition, in English writing:

> We have the same respect for Blake's philosophy . . . that we
> have for an ingenious piece of home-made furniture: we admire the
> man who has put it together out of the odds and ends about the
> house. England has produced a fair number of these resourceful
> Robinson Crusoes; but we are not really so remote from the Con-
> tinent, or from our own past, as to be deprived of the advantages
> of culture if we wish them. (*SW* 156)

This idea of Blake as 'uncultured', cut off or islanded from European
(or to be more specific Latin, or what Eliot calls elsewhere in the
essay 'Mediterranean', *SW* 156) traditions, is later associated with a

Protestant nationalism (*SW* 157) that emphasizes the political and individual rights and responsibilities of the individual.[9] Eliot always thinks in terms of centres and peripheries, and increasingly so as his career progresses, identifying the former with the cultural and religious heritage of Greece and Rome which, the further it is strayed from, the greater the danger of 'eccentricity' in the writer in question.[10] His country of origin is significant here. Like many American writers keen to cross the Atlantic – Henry James, Edith Wharton, Ezra Pound – Eliot had an attachment to English literature and the English language that was always only part of a much wider sense of the European heritage, particularly its classical, Italian and French components, and the education he received at Harvard enforced and extended this 'Continental' consciousness. Thus his bachelor's programme between 1906 and 1909 combined courses on English, German, comparative and classical literature, as well as history and philosophy courses and the study of various European languages. A year's MA course and then a year studying in France continued this notably catholic education before Eliot returned to Harvard and enrolled for a Ph.D. on the work of the English philosopher F. H. Bradley, a subject showing that Eliot's Europeanism does not simply relate to literary discourse: many years later he argued that Bradley 'was fighting for a European and ripened and wise philosophy, against an insular and immature and cranky one' ('Francis Herbert Bradley', *SE* 449). The doctorate was completed in April 1916, by which time Eliot had settled in England and abandoned any thoughts of an academic career. And in religion, Eliot's embracing of an Anglo-Catholic faith can be seen as a similar positioning between England and the Continent, although his religious allegiance does lie squarely with the Church of England. Eliot in fact increasingly embraces the fundamental idea of 'Europe' through a highly conscious sense of Englishness and English identity in the desire to mediate between the 'mind' of the former and 'the mind of his own country' (*SE* **16**).[11] We shall explore this fully in later chapters, but in returning here to the formulation from 'Tradition and the Individual Talent' we note that though such 'talent' must be at the service of tradition, without it tradition cannot survive at all, so that Eliot can find room, especially in the early writing, to salute the (misdirected) individualism of Blake, or, in the Marvell essay, that of John Donne, a writer who fascinated the early Eliot against his better judgement that Marvell was the more orthodox European (*SE* 292–3).[12]

'The main current' of the European tradition, Eliot argues, 'does not at all flow invariably through the most distinguished reputations' (*SE* 16), and in suggesting its passage from medieval Italy to Renaissance England to nineteenth-century France Eliot's criticism disposed of a number of these 'reputations', including those of Milton, Wordsworth and Tennyson. Although Eliot had doubts which grew upon him about the religious sincerity of Donne, unfavourably comparing the element of 'self-expression' in his sermons with the 'escape from personality' exhibited in those of Donne's contemporary Lancelot Andrewes, who is 'wholly absorbed in the object' (*FLA* 25), Eliot was insistent in his early writing that Donne and his fellow Metaphysical poets belonged to 'the main current'. They can be said to anticipate Eliot's own poetics in 'possess[ing] a mechanism of sensibility which could devour any kind of experience' (*SE* 287) and thus introducing into their work that striking variety of discourses – scientific, technical, lyrical – that links falling in love with images of globes, maps, mathematical compasses (as in Donne's famous 'A Valediction: Forbidding Mourning') and insect life ('A Flea'). For Eliot the 'line' of the Metaphysical poets passes to nineteenth-century French poets like Baudelaire and Laforgue, who exploit a similarly varied range of emotional and intellectual experience to produce effects resembling the Metaphysical 'conceit'. Thus we arrive at the statement 'our civilization comprehends great variety and complexity, and this variety and complexity, playing upon a refined sensibility, must produce various and complex results' (*SE* 289). After the Metaphysicals, a sense of this complexity starts to be lost in English poetry as it puts itself at the service of more limited moral, satirical, didactic or philosophical ends, to arrive at what Eliot calls the 'ruminations' of Tennyson and Browning. That integration of mind and senses, *feeling* one's thought 'as immediately as the odour of a rose', which Eliot finds in Donne (*SE* 287), is lost as the poetic sensibility becomes 'dissociated', in Eliot's famous formulation (for more on the 'dissociation of sensibility', see below, pp. 53–4).

A poetry that adequately reflects the complexity of civilization aims to keep all its balls in the air at any one time, so to speak, and will not drop any of these in pursuing a narrower agenda of confession, exhortation or polemic. In discussing and attempting to define the quality of 'wit' in Marvell's poetry, Eliot notes the detached 'inspection and criticism of experience' that is a feature of wit, as well as the 'recognition, implicit in the expression of every experience, of other kinds of experience which are possible' (*SE* 303). Wit is 'absent', Eliot argues, 'from the work of Wordsworth, Shelley, and Keats, on whose poetry nineteenth-century criticism has unconsciously been based', and is indeed one of the prime casualties of the dissociation; nor is it to be confused with eighteenth-century irony or satire which 'lack wit's internal equilibrium', its impersonal 'urbanity' (*SE* 304). An 'alliance of levity and seriousness (by which the seriousness is intensified)' is also suggested as a feature of this difficult-to-define quality (*SE* 296), emphasizing how wit remains alive to an unexpected variety of tones and responses and seeks to balance these rather than becoming immersed in an exclusive 'seriousness' or earnestness that would banish from poetry a whole range of effects. One might not share Eliot's dismissal of Wordsworth, Shelley and Keats, but it is difficult to think that anyone would call their work 'witty', however this term is defined; and the element of wit in Eliot's own work is related to that receptivity to every different kind of experience we noted above, and to forming new 'wholes' out of that variety. When Tennyson's Ulysses, in the poem of that name, addresses his crew with the words 'My mariners . . . you and I are old', the address is a preface to the famous exhortation to use the remainder of life in the valiant quest 'To strive, to seek, to find, and not to yield':[13] the eponymous hero of Eliot's 'Prufrock' voices a similar realization, 'I grow old . . . I grow old . . .', but the words are immediately followed by a line – 'I shall wear the bottoms of my trousers rolled' – typical of the poem's manipulation and juxtaposition of 'levity and seriousness' as a whole, as it veers between the twin questions 'Do I dare / Disturb the universe?' and 'Do I dare to eat a peach?' (*CP* 14, 16). This nimble skipping around between positions permits in 'Prufrock' the effects of wit that Eliot denies are available to poetry that restricts itself to the 'elevated' subject, and that does not recognize the poetic potential of the 'smell of cooking' and the like:

> For I have known them all already, known them all –
> Have known the evenings, mornings, afternoons,
> I have measured out my life with coffee spoons. (*CP* 14)

If the Marvell essay confesses that wit is an extremely elusive quality, the reader of Eliot's poetry may complain that Eliot's own elusiveness, the refusal to commit to any one stance, or tone or discourse, intensifies the problems of interpretation, an issue we discuss below.

Wit 'implies a constant inspection and criticism of experience', a detachment that 'is not cynicism, though it has a kind of toughness which may be confused with cynicism by the tender-minded' (*SE* 303). In espousing this position and others we have touched on, and emphasizing the limitations of Romantic poetry, Eliot felt that his work participated in the wider cultural movement he identified in his statement of 1916, quoted in my Introduction, which exemplified 'The Reaction against Romanticism'. The political and religious positions outlined in this statement derive from a variety of writers and thinkers, and are declared openly in Eliot's later work, but already in 1916 he can be seen as identifying with the 'classicist point of view' promoted by the poet and philosopher T. E. Hulme, whom Eliot was probably personally acquainted with.[14] In the debate between 'Romanticism and Classicism', to quote the title of a lecture Hulme gave (probably in 1912), the antithesis was characterized thus:

> here is the root of all romanticism: that man, the individual, is an infinite reservoir of possibilities . . . One can define the classical quite clearly as the exact opposite to this. Man is an extraordinarily fixed and limited animal . . . It is only by tradition and organisation that anything decent can be got out of him . . . To the one party man's nature is like a well, to the other like a bucket . . . One may note here that the Church has always taken the classical view since the defeat of the Pelagian heresy and the adoption of the sane classical dogma of original sin.[15]

In the final paragraph of his 1930 essay on Baudelaire Eliot quotes an extract from Hulme which is practically identical in outlook to this statement (*SE* 430), and one could argue that for all its complexity his poetry is underwritten by this simply and categorically expressed 'dogma' (and well before his formal entry into the Anglican Church in 1927) in that the scenario of a 'waste land', inhabited by corrupt and sterile protagonists, is omnipresent in his work.[16] Even so, with his insistence on detachment and impersonality, Eliot wanted to guard against the idea that his early poetry at any rate can be seen as the expression of a set of 'beliefs': 'the poet can deal with philosophic ideas, not as a matter for argument, but as a matter for inspection' (*SW* 162; compare the poet's 'constant inspection of experience' in the Marvell essay above). As late as his conversion year, 1927, Eliot is still denying that Dante, for example, necessarily believed the scholastic ideas which he

> merely made use of . . . for the purpose of making poetry. The poet makes poetry, the metaphysician makes metaphysics, the bee makes honey, the spider secretes a filament; you can hardly say that any of these agents believes: he merely does. (*SE* 138)

This homely and rather glib comparison between poet and bee nevertheless indicates how much Eliot continued to resist the idea that poetry should convey a 'message', or be the vehicle for 'great' thoughts; how it is rather a kind of collage of ideas, sensations and experiences in a constant interplay that refuses to settle to any finality. Nevertheless, 'poetry can be penetrated by a philosophic idea' even if it is not the simple expression of it (*SW* 162), and the 'classicist' idea of human corruptibility and sinfulness is powerfully present in the early poems. By the end of the 1920s, Eliot seems more willing to accept, however, that the poet 'means what he says' (*SE* 269).

Unlike his compatriot and collaborator Ezra Pound, who moved from London to settle first in France, then in Italy, Eliot was to establish a permanent base in England and in the world of English letters, but his writing, like Pound's, can be seen as a shock to English insularity, a challenge to cultural self-sufficiency, and to that complacent infatuation with a native line of writing that Eliot sensed in operation around him in the country he had moved to. In 1918 he declares 'because we have never learned to criticize Keats, Shelley, and Wordsworth (poets of assured though modest merit), Keats, Shelley, and Wordsworth punish us from their graves with the annual scourge of the Georgian Anthology'.[17] This of course made Eliot's poetry extremely challenging for readers comfortable with, say, the Keats–Shelley aftermath, since its range of reference spans so many literatures (and, as we have seen, shares a poetic mix or medium with various 'impressions and experiences [which] combine in peculiar and unexpected ways' *SE* 20). Eliot was well aware of this challenge, and while we can say his work exposes the disadvantages of a limited education he was also insistent that it could speak to those outside an educational elite. In 'Tradition and the Individual Talent' he argues that the poet can access 'the mind of Europe' by other means than simply wading through an endless pile of books, and that the required poetic 'knowledge' is not to be confused with erudition, or pedantry or 'whatever can be put into a useful shape for examinations': 'some can absorb knowledge, the more tardy must sweat for it. Shakespeare acquired more essential history from Plutarch than most men could from the whole British Museum' (*SE* 16–17). It is not that the poet, nor the poet's readers, need 'know' everything; the mind of Europe has both its 'essential' and eccentric components, and Eliot's poetry, as we shall see, makes notable use of religious and philosophical 'commonplaces' handed down through the ages, as the Marvell essay might suggest. In his claim that 'I myself should like an audience which could neither read nor write' (*UP* 152), Eliot also indicates that there are ways of responding to poetry that are far different from recognizing and 'understanding' its cultural referents. The different musical and rhythmical components of the work – the use of nursery rhyme, popular song and jazz elements in *The Waste Land*, for example – are a reminder that poetry asks us to respond in many different ways, intellectual, sensory, emotional, and that its appeal is linked to the survival within us of our 'primitive' feelings: 'poetry begins, I dare say, with a savage beating a drum in a jungle, and it retains that essential of percussion and rhythm; hyperbolically one might say that the poet is *older* than other human beings' (*UP* 155). At the opening of the Dante essay of 1929, Eliot tackles this question of how much you need to 'know' in order to enjoy a given poem, and notes, as we have seen, how 'I was passionately fond of certain French poetry long before I could have translated two verses of it correctly'. It is possible, indeed necessary, for 'some direct shock of poetic intensity' to be produced in a reader who may yet remain uncertain of the work's 'meaning', though Eliot then asks the reader not to remain indifferent to establishing that meaning as fully as possible – 'nothing but laziness can deaden the desire for fuller and fuller knowledge'. But the paramount thing for Eliot in first encountering a poem is 'enjoyment' rather than 'understanding': 'it is better to be spurred to acquire scholarship because you enjoy the poetry, than to suppose that you enjoy the poetry because you have acquired the scholarship' (*SE* 237–8).

'RHAPSODY ON A WINDY NIGHT'

Having outlined some of Eliot's early critical positions, I shall now explore four poems – 'Rhapsody on a Windy Night', 'Gerontion', 'Sweeney Erect', 'The Love Song of J. Alfred Prufrock' – to see how useful these positions are as tools of investigation. 'Rhapsody' has been seen by the critic John Paul Riquelme as a work that undermines the Romantic 'descriptive-meditative crisis lyric': the poet at midnight, in the company of the moon, experiences the profound emotional enrichment that comes through the bond with Nature or with the poet's own offspring, as in Coleridge's 'Frost at Midnight' (a poem whose notable successors include Yeats's 'A Prayer for my Daughter', published four years later than 'Rhapsody').[18] The night-time experience of Eliot's poem, however, seems to provide no such 'enrichment', with its seedy urban scenario of brothels and gas-lamps, where even the moon is diseased and 'washed-out'. 'Rhapsody' uses such a setting to prompt the memory of the protagonist to bring forth further images of desolation and sterility that confirm the present moment. Memory is no blessing nor 'escape' from the urban scene, as it is say in Wordsworth's 'Tintern Abbey'; a key word in 'Rhapsody', 'twists' or 'twisted', describes both the eye of the prostitute under the street-lamp and the 'crowd of twisted things' the memory 'throws up', including a rusty spring and an old crab, to culminate in 'The last twist of the knife' in the final line.

'Rhapsody' seems to put into operation the statement in 'Tradition and the Individual Talent' about the poet's mind being a 'receptacle' for 'seizing and storing up numberless feelings, phrases, images' (*SE* 19):

Half-past two,
The street-lamp said,
'Remark the cat which flattens itself in the gutter,
Slips out its tongue
And devours a morsel of rancid butter'.
So the hand of the child, automatic,
Slipped out and pocketed a toy that was running along the quay,
I could see nothing behind that child's eye.
I have seen eyes in the street
Trying to peer through lighted shutters,
And a crab one afternoon in a pool,
An old crab with barnacles on his back,
Gripped the end of a stick which I held him.

Although these various images are united in suggesting a world governed by gross or mechanized instinct (anticipating the 'automatic hand' of the typist in part III of *The Waste Land*), the poem can indeed be seen as a 'medium . . . in which impressions and experiences combine in peculiar and unexpected ways' (*SE* 20). In particular, the lines on the crab bear no obvious relation with what has gone before, and it is up to each reader to assess their significance. For me they enforce the picture of an ageing, entropic universe, where forms like rusty springs grimly endure when 'the strength has left', and where the movements of claws as well as hands are triggered by blind, instinctual drives. The lines on the crab might indeed represent a very minor 'experience' which 'to the practical and active person' would be no experience at all, but which are here powerfully enlisted as one of the unexpected components making up the amalgam of the poem.

The poem seems among other things a transcript of the narrator's memory, or 'reminiscence', which figures as a 'receptacle' for a 'crowd of twisted things' that surface in an involuntary way as any order to that memory becomes 'dissolved' in the nocturnal walk. The poem might illustrate another complaint by Yeats about the modern movement that the writer is left 'helpless before the contents of his own mind'.[19] But alongside this theme of dissolution we note as elsewhere in Eliot how carefully patterned and structured the poem is, as with the culmination in the 'last twist' noted above, or in the fantastic conceit of seeing the moon as a prostitute, prompted by the correspondence between the 'wink' of her 'feeble eye' and the twisted eye of the woman in the second stanza (via the child's eye and other peering eyes of stanza four). This outrageous piece of 'wit' debunks the vestal moon of romantic tradition, just as other sites of innocence and inspiration (the child, the wind, music itself in the 'rhapsody' of the title) are subject to a sordid reappraisal; in Riquelme's words, we have Eliot's 'virtually systematic scarification of all the major Romantic images conventionally interpreted as signs of affirmation and fulfillment' (*Harmony of Dissonances*, p. 45). The final lines of the poem rescue the memory from its disordered lunar enchantment and re-establish it at the service of stability and routine: 'Here is the number on the door. / Memory! / You have the key', but this return to the world of order and the normality of brushing teeth is no refuge from the nocturnal flight but, as with the prison-key of line 413 of *The Waste Land*, suggests entry into a deathly regimentation:

'. . . The little lamp spreads a ring on the stair.
Mount.

The bed is open; the tooth-brush hangs on the wall,
Put your shoes at the door, sleep, prepare for life.'

The last twist of the knife.

'Mount' suggests the ascent of a scaffold (as it does in part III of 'Portrait of a Lady'), even if it is only (but very effectively) the tooth-brush that 'hangs', and indeed the final line suggests that to participate in daily existence is to meet with execution; the simple but highly resonant 'The bed is open', like a coffin, also suggests the vampiric state of being staked down in the intervals of these nocturnal excursions. Both suggestions enforce the idea of daily existence as a living death, an idea that receives its clearest expression in part I of *The Waste Land*, with its time-bound urban workers: 'A crowd flowed over London Bridge, so many, / I had not thought death had undone so many' (ll. 62–3). In his notes to the latter poem, Eliot indicates that the second line here is a translation from Dante's *Inferno* (3. 56–7), where Dante sees the vast crowd of 'neutrals' in Hell, who, he tells us, couldn't be said to be alive even when they were living (3. 64), but Eliot also has in mind the potent lines from Baudelaire's 'Les sept vieillards' he singles out for special attention in a late essay: 'Fourmillante cité, cité pleine de rêves, / Où le spectre en plein jour raccroche le passant!' (*TC* 127) and which he cites in the same notes.[20]

The Waste Land crowd, filing automaton-like towards its nine-to-five employment ('With a dead sound on the final stroke of nine') picks up the theme presented in 'Rhapsody' of clock-time as captivity and constraint. Throughout Eliot's work, the inhibiting power of time as conventionally measured for economic and social purposes is played off against the experience of time in the individual consciousness as fluid and indivisible, ideas that Eliot derived from the French philosopher Henri Bergson (1859–1941), whom he heard lecture during his year studying in France in 1910–11.[21] What Bergson called 'real duration' ('durée réelle') is an authentic experience of time which, as with all our sensations, is misrepresented by measuring and recording mechanisms, including the mechanism of language itself; certain psychic states like dream or trance are a means of access to such experience. But although Eliot is happy to join Bergson in exposing the inadequacy and reductiveness of 'bourgeois' notions of time, he hardly shared the celebration of time *per se* as an ultimate reality reinvigorated by directly experiencing it through non-rational means. The world into which the consciousness escapes between the measuring street-lamps in 'Rhapsody' dissolves 'clear relations' and divisions as we have seen, including those between past and present, memory and actuality, but it remains a sordid, nightmarish world that is a questionable refuge from the diurnal. Whereas Bergson, 'in affirming the reality of time rather than of eternity', was challenging among other things 'the classical Christian legacy',[22] Eliot comes increasingly to see time in both its bourgeois and Bergsonian aspects as 'unreal' when contrasted with that very legacy. The 'dead sound on the final stroke of nine' indicates a realm beyond measured time that evokes the theology Bergson rejects, in gesturing to the 'ninth hour' when Christ died on the cross (Mt. 27. 45–6, Jn 15. 33–4, Lk. 23. 44).

'Rhapsody on a Windy Night' may not be as challenging as other early poems by Eliot, in that it has no esoteric vocabulary and little direct literary allusion, with no epigraph and just one line in a language other than English (an adaptation of lines in Laforgue's 'Complainte de cette bonne lune'). 'The mind of Europe' may not be as forcibly on display here as elsewhere in Eliot, but the poem partakes of timeless literary 'commonplaces' of disillusion, of existence as a fallen life-in-death, just as it subverts equally perennial images of hope and renewal. What is novel and striking about the poem is, to adapt Eliot's words on Marvell, how it 'renews' these themes 'in the variety and order of the images', and how it locates them historically through the use of everyday referents – cigarettes, cocktails, tooth-brushes. At the same time it exhibits Eliot's characteristic referring to such mundane details in a formal, Latinate vocabulary that is appropriate to the detached 'inspection' of experience the classicist aims at:

> 'Remark the cat which flattens itself in the gutter,
> Slips out its tongue
> And devours a morsel of rancid butter.'

For Yeats, as we have seen, Eliot's revolution was 'stylistic alone', the imputation being that he was not saying anything new, but saying the old in a new way. We return to this claim at the end of the chapter.

'GERONTION'

'Gerontion' (the Greek for 'little old man') was written several years later than 'Rhapsody', appearing as the first poem in the *Poems* of

1920, and its significance for Eliot is shown by the fact that he pondered using it as a prelude or preface in printing *The Waste Land* a few years later (*WLF* 127). Here Eliot explicitly makes use of what we have seen Hulme refer to as 'the sane classical dogma of original sin', the poem suggesting that human beings live in the realm of a 'History' that deceives, misleads and endlessly disappoints; a place of 'vanities' figured as a labyrinth (the image recurs in Eliot's later work, notably 'Burnt Norton' and *The Family Reunion*) and gendered as 'she', a tease and temptress (the response to women in Eliot's work is considered at various points below). This unstable and alienating temporality is also a place of paradox where moral outcomes are bewildering and unpredictable: 'Unnatural vices / Are fathered by our heroism', and so forth. The idea of existence as living death is refocused here as existence as punishment, with clear indications of the exile into 'History' and temporality from the prelapsarian (that is, before the biblical 'Fall' of man) garden, the section of the poem just referred to being framed by the lines 'After such knowledge, what forgiveness?', and 'These tears are shaken from the wrath-bearing tree'.[23]

In Eliot's terms, rather than expressing any personal 'belief', the poem can be regarded as taking a traditional idea of the Fall (and its connotations) that has resurfaced powerfully in his own day – 'the beginning of the twentieth century has witnessed a return to the ideals of classicism . . . The classicist point of view has been defined as essentially a belief in Original Sin' – and acting as mouthpiece (or 'medium') for this confluence between an immemorial dogma and a topical disillusion (images of violence pervading the poem can be understood in the context of the First World War). This religious positioning, further distanced from the poet himself through the use of a persona, Gerontion, becomes a framework supporting the dazzling and curious series of images and figures wherein, Eliot would argue, the power of the poem lies, rather than in its 'thought':

> What will the spider do,
> Suspend its operations, will the weevil
> Delay? De Bailhache, Fresca, Mrs Cammel, whirled
> Beyond the circuit of the shuddering Bear
> In fractured atoms.

In this vision of despair the human 'family' proceeds to its final destruction, the exotic, individualistic names (as earlier in the poem with Mr Silvero and so forth), emphasizing different and separate nationalities united only in their isolation and ultimate doom. The earlier reference to these nationalities in the context of Holy Communion ('To be eaten, to be divided, to be drunk / Among whispers . . .') ironically enforces this sense of isolation and division, suggesting, as in *The Waste Land*, humanity's betrayal ('flowering judas') of Christ on behalf of various occult and illicit practices involving 'shifting . . . candles' and 'walk[ing] all night in the next room'. But again the poem is extremely indirect and cryptic in the way these effects are conveyed: 'Fräulein von Kulp / Who turned in the hall, one hand on the door' is a deliberate mystery, as is the significance of what she is doing, and each reader is allowed full scope to register just how furtive, sinister or pathetic she is.

At any rate, cosmopolitanism – 'Hakagawa, bowing among the Titians' – is no refuge or resource, just as the savage use of the wandering Jew motif:

> My house is a decayed house,
> And the Jew squats on the window sill, the owner,
> Spawned in some estaminet of Antwerp,
> Blistered in Brussels, patched and peeled in London,

suggests a malaise that is universal. 'House' is used throughout 'Gerontion' with different metaphorical associations. Given the biblical ideas of fall and exile underlying the poem, Gerontion's identification in the opening lines as 'an old man in a dry month . . . waiting for rain' has clear connotations of the 'old Adam', yet unredeemed by Christ's sacrifice, living under the old Jewish law or dispensation figured here as a derelict house and landlord.[24] Gerontion in fact, in line with one of Eliot's favourite motifs expressed most clearly in the later poem 'The Hollow Men' of 1925, is in a kind of limbo, caught in a betwixt and between state without any positive affiliation, home or sense of belonging beyond 'a rented house'. The other figures in the poem also turn out, in the final lines, to be merely 'Tenants of the house' too, rootless, adrift, cast out beyond the stars, the house now figuring as Gerontion's own consciousness, his 'dry brain in a dry season', thus emphasizing his identity as an Everyman figure who comprises multitudes. The epigraph to the poem, taken from Shakespeare's *Measure for Measure* (3. 1. 33–4), as well as the opening lines, emphasize this state of limbo which can only define itself in terms of its exclusions, with no 'positive' definition, 'nor youth nor age', leading to the 'neither . . . Nor . . . Nor' of lines 3–5 which denies this limbo any sense of action or potency.

In the famous episode of the Harrowing of Hell, Christ rescues the Jews of the old dispensation from limbo after his death, as Eliot would have read, for example, in Dante (*Inferno* 4. 52–63). Gerontion is aware of this rescue, but despairs that he is worthy of it, having lost the original, unfallen, closeness to God ('I that was near your heart') through the exile, and believing that the effects of time-as-punishment, that is, growing old, now render him an unpalatable morsel of flesh for 'Christ the tiger':

> I have lost my sight, smell, hearing, taste and touch:
> How should I use them for your closer contact?

'The tiger springs in the new year. Us he devours'. The inversion of the Christian communion here, in which the congregation eat the divine body, anticipates Eliot's later post-conversion body of work where Christianity is no soft option, so to speak, but an awesome and terrifying relationship with God. At this stage, however, the speaker of 'Gerontion' remains 'undevoured', shrivelled and stringy, perpetually in a 'dry season'. He rehearses the possibility that 'We have not reached conclusion, when I / Stiffen in a rented house', that is, that there may be something beyond death (the *double entendre* here of copulating with a prostitute using sexual sterility and the brothel setting as a metaphor for the 'waste' of existence, an omnipresent device in Eliot), but Gerontion has no faith that there is any return to the divine realm for such as he and the hordes of humanity he represents.

As we saw above, Eliot denies that a poem is important in so far as it delivers a significant 'message', or has 'more to say' than other works, and although I've concentrated in discussing 'Gerontion' so far on aspects of what it might be said to 'say', Eliot himself would identify the 'poetry' with issues of treatment – 'the intensity of the artistic process' – rather than with the significance or profundity of the poet's world view (*SE* 19); with the 'how', rather than the 'what'. To repeat his comment on Blake, 'what his genius required . . . was a framework of accepted and traditional ideas which would have prevented him from indulging in a philosophy of his own, and concentrated his attention upon the problems of the poet' (*SW* 157–8). Here 'the problems of the poet' are something other than the 'ideas' a poem incorporates, these last best deriving from tradition (and what, we might ask, is more traditional than the idea of original sin?). 'Poetry is not a substitute for philosophy or theology or religion . . . it has its own function' (*SE* 137–8), and that function is to raise common and even commonplace ideas and emotions to levels of intensity and renewal by allowing 'impressions and experiences [to] combine in peculiar and unexpected ways' (*SE* 20), thus 'making the familiar strange' (*SE* 301):

> The goat coughs at night in the field overhead;
> Rocks, moss, stonecrop, iron, merds.
> The woman keeps the kitchen, makes tea,
> Sneezes at evening, poking the peevish gutter.
>   I an old man,
> A dull head among windy spaces.
>
> Signs are taken for wonders. 'We would see a sign!'
> The word within a word, unable to speak a word,
> Swaddled with darkness. In the juvescence of the year
> Came Christ the tiger . . . .

And it is aided in doing these things, of course, by a facility with language that can deploy devices like assonance ('sneezes'/'peevish') and alliteration to best effect. We have seen Eliot maintain that the poet hardly needs to 'believe' in the ideas the poem makes use of, and even if the poet does believe in such ideas, 'I deny . . . that the reader must share the beliefs of the poet in order to enjoy the poetry fully' ('Dante', *SE* 269). In the early twentieth century, the question of 'belief' itself has become deeply problematic in any case; what can be straight-forwardly 'believed' any longer?:

> it appears likely that poets in our civilization, as it exists at present, must be *difficult*. Our civilization comprehends great variety and complexity, and this variety and complexity, playing upon a refined sensibility, must produce various and complex results. The poet must become more and more comprehensive, more allusive, more indirect, in order to force, to dislocate if necessary, language into his meaning. (*SE* 289)

Simple 'meanings' are no longer possible, and where there is a 'meaning' to express the poet must proceed indirectly, alluding rather than stating. This indirection opens up freedoms for the reader which Eliot recognized and welcomed in the way they pluralize the business of interpretation. Thus we noted Eliot's observations in the Introduction: 'what a poem means is as much what it means to others as what it means to the author' (*UP* 130); again, 'the reader's interpretation [of a poem] may differ from the author's and be equally valid – it may even be better' (*OP* 31).

We also noted that, in his desire to rescue poetry from the 'ruminations' of the Victorians, and suggest that it is something much more than the 'ideas' it contains, Eliot resisted the opposite extreme of espousing a doctrine of 'pure poetry', or 'art for art's sake', hence his dissent from I. A. Richards's statement that *The Waste Land* effects 'a complete severance between [Eliot's] poetry and *all* beliefs' (above, p. 6); he indeed labelled this judgement 'incomprehensible' (*SE* 269).[25] In taking a series of positions for his work that he suggests have always been dear to the 'mind of Europe' – *carpe diem*, Original Sin, 'all is vanity' / 'there is no new thing under the sun' (Eccl. 1.2, 9), 'the Catholic philosophy of disillusion' (which is 'antiromantic') ('Dante', *SE* 275) – Eliot simultaneously demotes such ideas, at least in his early poetry and criticism, by suggesting that they need not command the assent of either poet or reader. They act as the poem's necessary matrix, or 'scaffold', or general ambience ('poetry can be penetrated by a philosophic idea', *SW* 162) but within this ambience of decay, disillusion and 'waste' it is the strange and startling local components, like the old crab and Fräulein von Kulp, that resonate to the point of making Eliot's 'sterile' vision paradoxically fresh and vibrant. 'The chief use of the "meaning" of a poem, in the ordinary sense', Eliot writes, 'may be . . . to satisfy one habit of the reader, to keep his mind diverted and quiet, while the poem does its work upon him: much as the imaginary burglar is always provided with a bit of nice meat for the house-dog' (*UP 151*). And yet, as Eliot's own beliefs became clearer and more explicit – 'classicist in literature, royalist in politics, and anglo-catholic in religion' – as he declared in 1928 (Preface, *FLA* 7), he certainly wanted his work to be in some way at the service of such beliefs. The statement quoted above, 'I deny . . . that the reader must share the beliefs of the poet in order to enjoy the poetry fully', is flatly contradicted within two pages of the same essay: 'actually, one probably has more pleasure in the poetry when one shares the beliefs of the poet' ('Dante', *SE* 271), and the idea that the poet himself needn't assent to the ideas he makes use of is here also queried (*SE* 269). This whole extended footnote to the Dante essay shows Eliot's perplexities in this matter, as does the later *The Use of Poetry and the Use of Criticism* (1933). 'Gerontion' certainly seems to me a rather different poem to the earlier 'Prufrock', and notably less 'witty' (which as we have seen involves the ability to negotiate nimbly between different tones and positions). Gerontion as a persona has reached the stage of 'growing old' too, as Prufrock, but this is no matter for levity, and the way the poem looks forward to *The Waste Land*, 'The Hollow Men' and to Eliot's latest works suggests its Christian scheme is more than just a bit of 'nice meat' to satisfy the reader's habit of looking for meaning 'in the ordinary sense'. We return to some of these issues in later chapters.

'SWEENEY ERECT'

'Sweeney Erect' is the next-but-one poem after 'Gerontion' in the *Poems* (1920) volume, and it confirms the tone of the volume as a whole as much harsher and more caustic than the *Prufrock* volume of 1917. Images of human brutality and primitiveness, particularly evident in the depictions of sexuality, pervade the collection, and the ape-like and brothel-frequenting Sweeney is a dominant persona, rather than the dandy figure Eliot used in several earlier poems. We shall discuss issues of verse form below, but the use of quatrains (rhyming four-line stanzas) throughout *Poems* (1920) represents Eliot's (and Pound's) feeling that, in the words of the latter, 'the dilutation of vers libre . . . had gone too far' and that 'rhyme and regular strophes' were now needed.[26] This more ordered, disciplined verse contributes to the effect of distancing the protagonists of the poems from the reader, whereas the freer and more fluid verse of the *Prufrock* volume often traced an individual consciousness, in (problematic) interaction with others ('Let us go then, you and I'), that offered a more intimate tone. In several of the *Poems* of 1920 the angle of view by contrast is one of looking down disdainfully on humanity as a primitive species of microbe, insect or animal to which we are reminded at several points we all still belong, as with the protagonist's unwilling sense of kinship with the disgusting waiter in 'Dans le Restaurant': 'De quel droit payes-tu des expériences comme moi?' (*CP* 51).[27]

This 'low life' is evident in 'Sweeney Erect', where the protagonist and his associates are portrayed as particularly sordid and uncouth (with *Sweeney Agonistes*, written a few years later (see below, pp. 68–9), Eliot arguably gives voice to the contrary aspect of his repulsion-attraction complex with regard to 'primitivism'). In the poem the depiction of Sweeney with his 'razor' draws on the villainous barber of legend, Sweeney Todd, and both he and the prostitute, who is 'epileptic', are described in a series of brutal images – 'Gesture of orang-outang', 'This withered root of knots of hair' – that suggest Mrs Turner's 'house' is as much zoo as brothel, confirmed by the final entry of Doris 'padding on broad feet'. The stanza in parentheses,

(The lengthened shadow of a man
Is history, said Emerson
Who had not seen the silhouette
Of Sweeney straddled in the sun.),

affirms the idea that rather than having progressed from the ape – as the evolutionary category of man as *homo erectus,* with his gradually more upright shadow, would claim – man is irredeemably bestial. Thus the title of the poem not only ironizes Emerson's ideas (and we know from 'Gerontion' how Eliot responds to 'history'), but suggests human sexuality, in Sweeney's 'erectness', as the particular site or symptom of the bestial state (an idea continued into *The Waste Land*). All this seems clear enough, and the poem is arguably less challenging (certainly less 'indirect') than others by Eliot, the main difficulty perhaps residing in the opening ten lines which give a series of classical references that abruptly switches, in mid-stanza, to the hideous modern scene at line 11. The relation of a contemporary degradation to this European literary backcloth is, as elsewhere in Eliot, a question the poem poses.

The references in the opening lines, in fact, are all to stories of betrayal, deception and violence in classical literature, Theseus's desertion of Ariadne, Odysseus's tricking his way into Nausicaa's confidence and his blinding of the cyclops Polyphemus, two of the stories involving men preying on women. In this sense a context is set up for Sweeney's conduct that suggests that the long temporal vistas behind the present moment merely reiterate the bestial theme, just as later in *The Waste Land* the central figure of Tiresias will make no distinction between ancient Thebes and modern London in his registering of loveless sexual intercourse (ll. 243–6). The link between 'classicism' and 'Original Sin' is here affirmed, in the sense that when Eliot refers in his poetry to classical literature and mythology he pays particular attention to the (sexual) violence this literature is often imbued with; thus the murder of Agamemnon features in 'Sweeney Among the Nightingales' (*CP* 56–7) and, crucially, Tereus's rape of Philomel in *The Waste Land*, 'by the barbarous king / So rudely forced'. Later, in his play *The Family Reunion* (1939), Eliot will rewrite Aeschylus's story of murder and vengeance (in the *Oresteia*) for modern times. Eliot's sense of the classical tradition is hardly one of nobility and 'culture' in the customary sense, and certainly not as a source of that 'sweetness and light' which famously for Matthew Arnold in the nineteenth century could address the defects of modern civilization.[28] And yet, of course, to talk of Theseus and Ariadne on Naxos sounds far more imposing and dignified than to talk of Sweeney and his partner in a modern brothel, and here Eliot shows a characteristic attention to the aesthetic transformation of stories of ineluctable human depravity and to their place in our heritage. The story of Philomel is a key instance: raped by Tereus, her tongue cut out to prevent her disclosing the crime, she is transformed in Ovid's *Metamorphoses*, to which Eliot refers in *The Waste Land* notes (*CP* 77), into a nightingale whose melodious voice becomes the time-honoured symbol of the poet's own craft. Poetry, music, art, has always relied and thrived on stories involving human baseness and tragedy for its material – indeed, where would our Western traditions of 'culture' be without these stories? Eliot then would certainly agree with Walter Benjamin's famous dictum that 'there is no document of civilisation which is not at the same time a document of barbarism', or, as Yeats put it in one of his greatest poems, 'Meditations in Time of Civil War', that the glories of art are a compensatory reflex of human violence and bitterness.[29]

It is not then that the classical past, or any past indeed, mediated through literary or cultural tradition, is any more glorious or 'heroic' than our present; 'history', as *The Waste Land* will confirm, always tells the same (postlapsarian, i.e., after the 'fall') story, but the opening of 'Sweeney Erect', with its imperatives 'Paint me' and 'Display me', suggests the power of 'paint' and artifice to transform brute fact into august heritage. Language, art, are verily a cosmetic, a theme at the heart of part II of *The Waste Land*, where actual cosmetics – 'In vials of ivory and coloured glass' – strive to transform the wretched

Belladonna figure into Cleopatra, as the opening line of the scene suggests, in conspiracy with an elevated poetic language that draws on Shakespeare, Pope, Virgil, Ovid and so forth to describe her and her surroundings. But in spite of such cosmetics, verbal and otherwise, Belladonna is viewed as fundamentally akin to the Cockney Lil who succeeds her in the poem, 'antique' and sterile – 'all the women are one woman', Eliot tells us in the notes (*CP* 78), the difference between them, as between past and present, being a question of rhetoric – the power of art to inflate and transform. This is also expressed in the recurring reference in *The Waste Land* to the line from Ariel's song in *The Tempest*, 'Those are pearls that were his eyes' (ll. 48, 125). Here bodily corruption and decay are metamorphosed in Ariel's lines into something 'rich and strange', corpse becomes precious artwork, eyes become pearls. Eliot's early poetry can be seen then, at one and the same time, as a celebration of the transforming powers of language, song, paint and the whole cultural panoply, while attending to the grim state of what it is that is thus transformed, human life in all its sordidness, vanity and decay. The dramatist Webster, he tells us in 'Whispers of Immortality' (*CP* 52–3), always 'saw the skull beneath the skin', and the same might be said of Eliot.

As we shall see, in his later poetry, and even in *The Waste Land* itself, Eliot addresses this disjunction between the magnificence of language and the debasement of subject through a programme of disciplining and constraining the former, developing a conspicuously 'purged' discourse for a body of work that deals centrally with ideas of moral purgation, or purification. The exotic names and quotations from foreign languages, the more flamboyant images – 'Daffodil bulbs instead of balls / Stared from the sockets of the eyes!' ('Whispers of Immortality') – tend to disappear. One feature of diction that does remain constant, however, is Eliot's fondness for a Latinate vocabulary, instanced in lines from 'Sweeney Erect' like 'deprecate the lack of taste', or 'Mrs. Turner intimates'. Here, the use of these verbs, which the prostitutes themselves would never use or recognize of course, emphasizes the condescending tone of the poem as a whole, its 'inspection' of a primitive behaviour that lies beyond the pale of education, or 'civilised' consciousness. The final 'padding' entry of Doris into the poem sums up this ironic play between sophistication and bestiality, since the name itself, here appearing in all its modern mundaneness, was originally that of a figure from Greek mythology, thus bringing the end of the poem back round to the beginning.[30] If this is a touch of 'wit', it is heavily sardonic, and as remarked above rather different in its effects from that found in Eliot's first volume, *Prufrock and Other Observations* (1917).

'THE LOVE SONG OF J. ALFRED PRUFROCK'

The celebrated opening poem of the *Prufrock* volume, 'The Love Song of J. Alfred Prufrock', is an appropriate curtain-raiser for all of Eliot's early work, and littered, like *The Waste Land,* with references to Dante, Shakespeare, Marvell, Donne and many more. It differs from several of its successors however (though not from 'Portrait of a Lady', 'Conversation Galante' and 'A Cooking Egg') in the ironic tone and stance it owes to the poetry of Jules Laforgue, Eliot's great discovery around 1908, when he read about him in Arthur Symons's 1899 work *The Symbolist Movement in Literature*. Laforgue 'was the first to teach me how to speak, to teach me the poetic possibilities of my own idiom of speech' (*TC* 126). Symons described Laforgue's poetry, which saw 'the possibilities for art which come from the sickly modern being, with his clothes, his nerves', as indeed 'an art of the nerves': in it there is 'all the restlessness of modern life . . . It is distressingly conscious of the unhappiness of mortality, but it plays, somewhat uneasily, at a disdainful indifference'. And it meets the distresses of life with an impeccable, 'gentlemanly', set of manners, a self-conscious 'mask' which it never permits itself 'the luxury of dropping'.[31]

That encounter between a sensitive, nervy, acutely self-aware consciousness and an alienating social world is territory which is common to both Laforgue and Eliot, particularly as it is played out in relations between the sexes, though as several commentators have remarked, the state of conflict is more marked and intense in Eliot's work. The inhibiting routines, rituals and clutter of social life, 'the cups, the marmalade, the tea, / . . . the porcelain' are at enmity with an outrageous inner world that imaginatively consorts with the profound experience of those like Hamlet, or Lazarus, or that listens to 'the mermaids singing', and that toys with some momentous irruption of this latter realm into the former: 'Do I dare / Disturb the universe?' Eliot takes the time-honoured convention of the 'love song', reaching back to Marvell's 'To his Coy Mistress', referred to more than once in the poem, and which, as we have seen, itself resumes 'a whole civilization', as a loose structure on which to assemble a spectacular array of ideas, images and references. The situation of lover approaching mistress veritably implodes with the weight of concerns brought to bear on it, a sense once more of the weariness and vanity of life, of life as furtive role-play, of 'time' as a crippling medium in which human beings yet have to live. The 'overwhelming question' the lover seeks the courage of putting to the mistress is therefore not the familiar, romantic one of love song, but something far more cataclysmic, and indeed beyond formulation altogether. As Eliot was later to put it in his discussion of *Hamlet*, 'the intense feeling, ecstatic or terrible, without an object or exceeding its object, is something which every person of sensibility has known', a feeling which the poet strives to keep 'alive' instead of trimming down or putting 'to sleep' as society requires (*SE* 146).

'There will be time, there will be time / To prepare a face to meet the faces that you meet . . .' The lines anticipate those from one of 'Prufrock''s companion poems, 'Preludes', which remark on 'the other masquerades / That time resumes . . . ' (*CP* 22). One of the constants of Eliot's work is a sense of 'waste sad time', as the conclusion to 'Burnt Norton' puts it, or *The Waste Land*'s 'dead sound on the final stroke of nine': time as trap, time as prison, time as punishment or exile. But the Laforguean tone of 'Prufrock' differs from these later works in permitting a sophisticated comic irony in its treatment, an irony directed as much at its protagonist as at the world he grapples with: 'I shall wear white flannel trousers, and walk upon the beach'. If the epigraph to the poem, from Dante's *Inferno*, invites us to think of him as an inhabitant of Hell, this is, as Hugh Kenner suggested long ago, 'a quiet *fin-de-siècle* inferno . . . a genteel accumulation of stage effects, nothing quite in excess . . . this man's doom is an endless party-going'.[32] It is of course part of the 'wit' of the poem to replay the Dantesque scenario in this frivolous key, though this is not to lessen that sense of social entrapment the poem conveys. The use of a bathetic dialogue that offsets a discourse of the momentous is the key feature, perhaps, that Eliot takes from Laforgue, and this is quintessentially on show in a poem Symons quotes in his essay on him, 'Autre complainte de Lord Pierrot', where the impassioned declarations of the poet's mistress run up against the elegant and absurd stone-walling of the poem's speaker:

'Ah! tu ne m'aime pas; tant d'autres sont jaloux!'
Et moi, d'un oeil qui vers l'Inconscient s'emballe:
'Merci, pas mal; et vous?'[33]

This dandyism, where an impeccable demeanour confronts all the emotional or philosophical challenges thrown at it, is a constant element in the *Prufrock* volume, though the quest to 'remain self-possessed', as the protagonist of 'Portrait of a Lady' puts it, is for Eliot's speakers a more embattled one (*CP* 20).

BAUDELAIRE AND BEYOND

In an essay written near the end of his life, Eliot went as far as to say that he owed more to Laforgue 'than to any one poet in any language' (*TC* 22), and direct echoes of the French poet are plentiful in the early work. In the case of Baudelaire, however, Eliot suggested that 'a great poet can give a younger poet everything that he has to give him, in a very few lines. It may be that I am indebted to Baudelaire chiefly for half a dozen lines out of the whole of *Fleurs du Mal*' (*TC* 126–7); in fact that debt is then 'summed up' in two lines alone, those quoted above (p. 24). The more urgent and impassioned encounters in Baudelaire's poetry between the flâneur-protagonist and the spectral, the diseased and the damned evoked an ambivalent response in Eliot. As his sense of the modern urban inferno became less 'genteel' in poems after the *Prufrock* volume, leading up to *The Waste Land*, the French poet of the 'Unreal City', acknowledged in the note to *The Waste Land* (I. 60), became more of a resource. Later, in Eliot's essay on Baudelaire of 1930, Baudelaire's depictions of evil and damnation are saluted as preferable to 'the ennui of modern life' because they give 'some significance to living' (*SE* 427). An earlier essay on Baudelaire from 1927, arguing for him as 'essentially a Christian', is another important tribute (*FLA* 77). If Laforgue could say nothing about these levels of spiritual experience, however, there was still much in Baudelaire, beyond 'key' lines, that Eliot couldn't respond to in his own early work: he declares in an essay of 1920 that the latter poet 'more often failed than succeeded', and that 'there is nothing permanently interesting about his diabolism'.[34] Certainly, the lurid, pestilential city of *Les Fleurs du mal*, with its 'femmes damnées' ('doomed women') and 'cortège infernal' of 'monstres' ('satanical procession' of 'freaks'), should be distinguished even from the crowd of living dead who inhabit *The Waste Land* (*Complete Verse*, pp. 216, 179). Thus Eliot's *femmes fatales*, whether in 'Portrait of a Lady' or 'A Game of Chess', are desiccated and pathetic rather than voluptuous and animalistic like those of Baudelaire, and in fact Eliot's characteristic personae – the 'hollow men' – are inhabitants not so much of hell as of a limbo of inertia and evasion where damnation (itself a 'form of salvation' as we shall see, *SE* 427) is denied them.[35] In this sense Eliot's protagonists throughout his poetry, with their 'fear of fear and frenzy . . . / Of belonging to another' ('East Coker', II), might yet be seen as derivatives of a Laforguean detachment, and be distinguished from a Baudelairean company that Eliot came to respect more but could hardly imitate. And that respect remains qualified: Baudelaire's Satanism has to be 'dissociated from its less creditable paraphernalia'; many of his poems are 'insufficiently removed from their romantic origins' (*SE* 421, 426).

In the Baudelaire essay of 1927, Eliot again insists on the need to distinguish the serious spirituality of the French poet from its misappropriation by his English followers of the 1890s, whose theatricality and 'childish attitude' – 'the game of children dressing up and playing at being grown-ups' – resulted in a bogus religiosity: 'for Swinburne's disciples, the men of the 'nineties, Evil was very good fun' (*FLA* 72). Incriminated in Eliot's attack are writers like Symons, Wilde, Dowson and Lionel Johnson. We have noted how Eliot's turning to nineteenth-century France for poetic models and stimuli involves a corresponding denigration of the native English line of poetry of the same period – 'the kind of poetry that I needed, to teach me the use of my own voice, did not exist in English at all; it was only to be found in French' (*OP* 252). While the influence of the French Symbolists, and particularly Laforgue, was fundamental to Eliot's early development, his attitude towards English 'insularity' does lead him at times to obscure lesser debts owed to late-Victorian poets, to say nothing of figures like Browning and Tennyson. Thus James Thomson's poem *The City of Dreadful Night* (1874) has long been recognized as an influence on *The Waste Land* and Eliot himself belatedly noted the 'inspiration' he had found in the poetry of John Davidson.[36]

Eliot sees Baudelaire as engulfed by the 'romantic detritus' of his age (*SE* 423) but heroically struggling to clear a path through it to a genuine spiritual vision, though in this he remains 'a bungler compared with Dante' (*SE* 428). Returning to 'Prufrock', it seems fitting that the great 'opening poem' of Eliot's entire *oeuvre* should have an epigraph from Dante, and that indeed the dedication to the whole *Prufrock* volume includes lines from the same source (in this case *Purgatorio* 21. 133–6). In suggesting in these lines that human beings are shadows (*ombre*) and that existence is *vanitas* (*vanitate* in the Italian), the *Prufrock* poems align themselves with this tradition of disillusion in a novel and striking (and at times humorous) way. Once more we are led back to Eliot's insistence on poetry not as innovation but renewal, with established and familiar emotions and attitudes expressed in a challenging and unexpected manner.[37] In its verse-form too 'Prufrock', like many of the other early poems, melds continuity and departure in a novel way, and can be illuminated by Eliot's essay of 1917, 'Reflections on *vers libre*'. Here, Eliot argued for a free verse that should not be a rejection of established metre but, as it were, a constant skirmishing with it:

> the most interesting verse which has yet been written in our language has been done either by taking a very simple form, like the iambic pentameter, and constantly withdrawing from it, or taking no form at all, and constantly approximating to a very simple one. (*TC* 185)

Later in the essay the point is given metaphorical elaboration:

> the ghost of some simple metre should lurk behind the arras in even the 'freest' verse; to advance menacingly as we doze, and withdraw as we rouse. Or, freedom is only truly freedom when it appears against the background of an artificial limitation. (*TC* 187)

In works practically contemporary with these statements – some of the early poems of D. H. Lawrence, for instance – we do find a poetry that rejects traditional metre completely, but a poem like 'Prufrock' rather plays around with different patterns in an elaborate metrical choreography. Thus the opening line, 'Let us go then, you and I', is in regular trochees, as are lines 4 and 13, though with differing numbers of feet, while lines 6 and 7 are indeed regular iambic pentameters. Lines 15–16 are in regular iambics, though this time of 14 syllables (or 7 feet), and so on. It is this spectacular mix of metres that ensures the 'contrast between fixity and flux . . . which is the very life of verse' (*TC* 185), and the resulting metrical dialogue between 'freedom' and 'artificial limitation' is of course entirely relevant to the dramatic situation of 'Prufrock', with the protagonist's restless squirming under the weight of social restriction and communicative convention:

> It is impossible to say just what I mean!
> But as if a magic lantern threw the nerves in patterns
> on a screen . . .

Here the cry of protest and frustration breaks out of any regularity in these lines as far as the number of syllables is concerned, but it remains contained within an iambic stress pattern enforced by the rhyme.

I began this chapter by quoting Yeats's statement to the effect that though Eliot's arrival on the scene certainly indicated a new, shocking and even 'revolutionary' poetry, this operated within certain limits – 'his revolution was stylistic alone' – and I argued that this suggests it was the *manner* of Eliot's poetry that was challenging, rather than any intellectual or philosophical 'positions' it took up. These latter might, in fact, reflect traditional and even 'commonplace' attitudes. In particular it is the *mélange* of Eliot's poetry, its provocative mixing of discourses, metre, textual fragments, 'high' and 'low' experience, august tradition and modern detritus, that is spectacular, and that will reach its consummation in *The Waste Land*. In many ways 'the medium is the message', to adopt the famous phrase of Marshall McLuhan.[38] In this, there are obvious analogies with the visual arts of Eliot's time, particularly the collage procedures of Cubism, where everyday items like bus-tickets and newspaper/wallpaper are pressed into service in traditional genres like the portrait.

The lines from 'Prufrock' already quoted, where the protagonist's 'nerves' are exposed on a screen, remind us of Symons's comment on Laforgue's 'art of the nerves', which suggests that this sense of nervous exposure on the part of both the writer and his or her characters is a dominant feature of the early modernist period. Certainly, for Eliot, when modern poets are told the way to avoid artificiality is to 'look into our hearts and write', that is 'not looking deep enough; Racine or Donne looked into a good deal more than the heart. One must look into the cerebral cortex, the nervous system, and the digestive tracts' (*SE* 290). From the same essay I quote once more the statement that 'our civilization comprehends great variety and complexity, and this variety and complexity, playing upon a refined sensibility, must produce various and complex results' (*SE* 289). Eliot's acutely sensitive poetic antennae pick up all the manifold signals of the hectic modern world, as well as the voices and experience of the literary past, in a manner that parallels how contemporaries like Woolf and Joyce approach the situation of modernity. For the former, famously, 'the mind . . . receives upon its surface a myriad impressions – trivial, fantastic, evanescent, or engraved with the sharpness of steel. From all sides they come, an incessant shower of innumerable atoms',[39] while Joyce's *Ulysses* has an epic receptivity to the innumerable signs, discourses and trivia that make up contemporary urban living. Eliot expressed his admiration for the latter work on many occasions, both privately and publicly, especially in the *Dial* review of 1923 where Joyce's use of the Odysseus narrative is seen as 'a way of controlling, of ordering, of giving a shape and a significance to the immense panorama of futility and anarchy which is contemporary history' (*SP* 175–7).[40] Eliot made this comment conscious that his recently published *The Waste Land*, to which we now turn, had attempted a similar thing, a 'panoramic' poem shaped not by the journey of the *Odyssey* but by a religious narrative of quest and pilgrimage, and one that, in its earlier manuscript form, had opened with a 'nighttown' scene (*WLF* 4–5) that was a tribute to the 'Circe' episode in *Ulysses*.

CHAPTER 2

FROM *THE WASTE LAND* TO 'THE HOLLOW MEN'

For that thrill of excitement from our first reading of a work of creative literature which we do not understand is itself the beginning of understanding.
—'*A Note of Introduction*' to In Parenthesis, *by David Jones, p. viii*

THE WASTE LAND AND ITS NOTES

With *The Waste Land* we have the instance of Eliot's direct commentary on his own poetry in the form of the notes he added to the poem when it was first published in book form in 1922.[1] Although these notes have frequently been decried, not least by Eliot himself, who called them a 'remarkable exposition of bogus scholarship', and only there to pad out an 'inconveniently short' poem to the necessary length to constitute a book (*OP* 109), they do embody a particular reading of the poem which Eliot wants to promote, at least in the period immediately after the poem's publication. In an interview many years later Eliot seemed dismissive of the poem, calling it 'structureless' and declaring 'I wasn't even bothering whether I understood what I was saying' when writing it.[2] Many critics who have queried the notes as a guide to interpretation see them as a rather desperate act of retrospect, an attempt to take back into control a work whose power and value lie in its teeming disorder and anarchic energies, a control which Eliot had partly relinquished during composition in the collaboration with Ezra Pound.[3] The analogy with Mary Shelley's Victor Frankenstein springs to mind, the notes being seen as Eliot's attempt to contain the shocking and 'monstrous' creation he had unleashed upon the world, and perhaps this analogy is not so far-fetched, given that the poem is an extraordinary assemblage of different parts, many of them taken from the books, if not the graves, of the dead. But before we dismiss the notes completely, we should see whether there is any justification in the kind of reading of the poem they offer.

In this the individual notes are of vastly different significance: the entry on *Turdus aonalaschkae pallasii*, the hermit-thrush (V. 357), might well be gratuitous in the amount of information it gives and mainly there for padding-out purposes, while others (for example those to I. 60–64) show Eliot's consciousness of writing out of the heart of the European tradition, as discussed in the previous chapter. The 'key' note, however, is the celebrated commentary on the figure of Tiresias, at III. 218:

> Tiresias, although a mere spectator and not indeed a 'character', is yet the most important personage in the poem, uniting all the rest. Just as the one-eyed merchant, seller of currants, melts into the Phoenician Sailor, and the latter is not wholly distinct from Ferdinand Prince of Naples, so all the women are one woman, and the two sexes meet in Tiresias. What Tiresias *sees*, in fact, is the substance of the poem.

Here, Eliot offers a centre to the poem, so to speak, a 'uniting' of its multiple personae, and he also offers a 'substance', a predominant subject, which is what Tiresias 'sees'. Unity and substance are important considerations in relation to the baffling plurality of voices, settings and literary references that make up the poem, and remind us how Eliot saw in Joyce's *Ulysses* mechanisms of 'controlling', 'ordering' and giving shape to 'the immense panorama of futility and anarchy which is contemporary history' (*SP* 177).

In the previous chapter, I argued that for Eliot distinctions between past and present are more apparent than real, given that the same 'story', of disillusion, estrangement, *vanitas*, and so forth, is handed down through history, and kept alive by the cultural record and the literary tradition. Differences of place and person are subsumed within this underlying one-ness, and *The Waste Land* constantly relates such difference to an overall context of universality. Thus the final five lines of part III offer a 'collocation', according to Eliot's note, of 'two representatives of eastern and western asceticism', St Augustine and Buddha, whose *Confessions* and 'Fire Sermon' respectively, in their concerns with the 'burning' lust consuming humanity, re-iterate part III's emphasis on sexual degradation – rape, adultery, prostitution, betrayal, loveless lovemaking. The Orient and the West may be very far apart, but they meet here under the rubric of a perennial 'waste'. Similarly, the 'Unreal City' of I. 60 and V. 376 is all times and all places, ancient Athens and modern London; the very last line of the poem, with its repeated 'shantih', is an 'equivalent' to the Christian 'Peace which passeth understanding' (note to V. 433); and the concluding ritual of part V, with its examination of the individual conducted by the voice of the thunder ('Give, sympathise, control', note to V. 401), has obvious similarities with the Christian idea of the Last Judgement. Pagan fertility rituals, such as the drowning of the Phoenician sailor in part IV, enact like Christian baptism the death of the old and the birth of the new.

So the poem seems to feature an underlying synthesis that embraces different cultural and religious systems. Eliot's note on Tiresias sees this figure as the key representation of this unity embracing diversity and of the fact that the 'waste land' is all times and all places, a Tiresias who is all men and all women and who 'sees' the substance of the poem. And what Tiresias sees (and paradoxically, being blind, can be said to 'see' at a deeper level than with the vision alone) is the central and representative scene (beginning almost exactly halfway through the poem) of the sexual 'folly' between the typist and the 'young man carbuncular'. This again is an immemorial story, and Tiresias notes he has experienced it both in ancient Thebes and modern London (III. 243–6). Tiresias himself is a re-embodiment of the persona Gerontion (and the Cumaean Sibyl of the poem's epigraph) in his living and perennial decay ('Old man with wrinkled female breasts', III. 219), but he exceeds them in his hermaphroditic status, which emphasizes how the 'meeting' of the sexes, above all in sexual intercourse, is the very site of the waste and degradation that obsesses the poem. Tiresias is literally an embodiment of sterile sexual union: but all sexual union is sterile in the poem, even if it produces offspring, as the case of Lil shows in part II. In this, the state of marriage fares little better than the extramarital; Spenser's *Prothalamion*, or poem in celebration of marriage, is cited with intense irony in part III of the poem (ll. 175, 183–4), and the river Thames, referred to in these lines, carries none of the connotations of fertility often associated with water but is rather the setting for further tales of sexual distress. The three 'Thames-daughters' or river nymphs who briefly and indirectly tell their stories between lines 292–305 (in a manner

Eliot's note tells us he derived from Dante's portrayal of Pia dei Tolomei, *Purgatorio* 5. 130–6) suggest further betrayal and sexual 'undoing' (l. 294), all the way from Richmond in the west of London to the Margate estuary in the east. Indeed, the Thames becomes the axis round which the poem's central action is organized, in both a geographical sense, as it runs to the sea, and in a historical one, as it runs back into history with its accumulated story of sexual peccadillo (including the dalliance between Elizabeth and Leicester, ll. 279–289).

By positing a central scene, witnessed by Tiresias, as the 'substance' of the poem, Eliot endorses the statement in the poem's title that 'the waste land' is not only omnipresent but irremediable – that there is no way out of it nor journey through it. Eliot declares in his opening note that the title, 'plan' and 'a good deal of the incidental symbolism' were 'suggested' by Jessie Weston's *From Ritual to Romance* (1920), and he also acknowledges his debt to James Frazer's anthropological study *The Golden Bough* (1890–1915). Both works are concerned with myth and fertility rituals whereby the new year and season proceed out of the death of the old; thus the Fisher King, presiding over the waste land in a series of romance narratives discussed by Weston, must await the arrival of a stranger who will lift the curse of sterility his land and people lie under. Frazer too reports on a multitude of ancient vegetation ceremonies whereby fertility is brought back to the land; thus the drowning of the effigy of the sailor, which Eliot uses in part IV, ensures natural renewal through ritualizing the death and rebirth cycle. Yet if there was a 'plan' of the poem based on such narratives, Eliot stresses a Christian scheme of resurrection that changes their emphasis, given that here the waste land is not renewed, nor is there any passage through it to natural rebirth or fertility. The Fisher King features for the final time in the poem at lines 422–3, 'Fishing, with the arid plain behind me', and the hope of redressing this 'aridity' lies not in this world but with the transcendental 'Peace that passeth understanding' at the poem's very end – a post-apocalyptic glimpse ('London Bridge is falling down') of having finally left the waste 'behind', but only with the complete cessation of the temporal realm.[4]

Eliot's refusal to conflate natural with spiritual renewal is typical of what tends to be a negative response to the realm of 'nature' found throughout his work, and which might be regarded as a further facet of his anti-Romanticism, although in his later poetry, which tends to replace urban with natural settings, the dialogue between humanity's spiritual imperatives and a respect due to the realm of nature becomes more complicated, as we shall see. Right from the start, with its ironic rewriting of the opening of *The Canterbury Tales*, *The Waste Land* rejects any idea of felicity in seasonal renewal, and if the opening gesture to Chaucer suggests that Eliot's poem is too a pilgrimage of sorts, it has none of the humour or jollity or boisterous comic voices that make up Chaucer's ensemble. The mood embodied in Chaucer's Wife of Bath, who has had five husbands and continues to peddle her vigorous sexuality in search of the sixth, is precisely opposed by Lil in part II of the poem, who has had five draining childbirths and has forestalled the sixth with 'pills'; nor does the pub she drinks in have much in common with the hospitable Tabard Inn. In the extract from Ovid's *Metamorphoses* that Eliot gives in the Tiresias note, Tiresias is asked to adjudicate on which sex derives the greater pleasure ('voluptas') from the sexual act, but in Eliot's poem the very notion of sexual pleasure is an emphatic contradiction in terms. In *The Waste Land* the rain which finally arrives in part V (l. 394) is not the rain of natural renewal but rather the accompaniment of the thunderous 'black clouds' of divine judgement calling the individual to reckoning, just as the drowning ceremony of part IV concentrates on the insufficiency and vanity of the bodily state rather than its rebirth – 'Consider Phlebas, who was once handsome and tall as you' (l. 321). One repeated motif for the decay and senescence that is omnipresent in *The Waste Land* is that of 'bones', which is what Phlebas is reduced to in part IV, and which the narration is haunted by throughout: 'But at my back in a cold blast I hear / The rattle of the bones, and chuckle spread from ear to ear' (III. 185–6). Here the grinning death's-head infiltrates Eliot's use once more of Marvell's 'To his Coy Mistress' to urge, not the embracing of natural pleasures before life is consumed, but a mindfulness of a return to that 'handful of dust' which contaminates any possible idea of natural pleasure. The temporal is seen as in 'Gerontion' as a vindictive realm of death and abnegation – 'a dead sound on the final stroke of nine' (I. 68) – the unreality and absurdity of which is instanced by the chuckling skull, and which, as the bar-tender's call of part II proclaims – 'HURRY UP PLEASE ITS TIME' – is ever hounding us to a final good night.

The bar-tender's call, together with the upbraiding voice of the thunder in part V with its 'DA . . . DA . . . DA' ('Give, sympathize, control'), are the only lines in the poem bearing the authority of being printed in capital letters; the former is, like the thunder, an injunction directed at the poem's *dramatis personae*, though what is being enjoined on them is perhaps here open to doubt. Certainly not, as stated above, Marvell's insistence on pursuing our pleasures before life's closing time, but rather perhaps a call to repentance before it's too late. Nevertheless, Eliot would strongly resist any idea that *The Waste Land* is a sermon, in spite of moments like these and the warning voices of the Old Testament prophets featured in part I (ll. 20–3 – see Eliot's notes on these lines), and indeed in spite of the title – 'The Fire Sermon' – part III carries. Eliot would rather phrase it, as we have seen in the previous chapter, that the poet's function is to take an established philosophy or traditional way of thinking for the purpose of 'making poetry', just as the bee makes honey (*SE* 138), and that this attempt to 'express the emotional equivalent of thought' (*SE* 135) does not commit the poet to actually believing or even being 'interested in' the thought itself. Nevertheless, the theme of life as 'waste' and temporal existence as living death, which is played out in endless variations throughout Eliot's work both early and late, not only chimed with his own personal experience (he later remarks on 'the struggle – which alone constitutes life for a poet – to transmute his personal and private agonies into something rich and strange, something universal and impersonal' – note there is nothing here about transmuting personal joys or happiness – *SE* 137), but linked this experience with an immemorial collective wisdom that, he argued, stressed the same disillusioned conclusions. Here the demarcation between the personal and the universal, or the individual talent and 'tradition', melts away.

As we have seen, the poem does not make much use of the outcomes of renewal which are the end result of the fertility myths Eliot drew on, and the idea of an ineluctable waste land seems rather more congenial to him than that of progressing to any state beyond it. Although the baptismal rite of 'Death by Water' is staged in part IV as a prologue to references to Christ's resurrection, the arrival of rain, and the final reckoning of Judgement in part V, the sense of an end to the quest is hedged about with doubt and insecurity – 'Shall I at least set my lands in order?' (V. 424) – that suggest any hope of resolution or salvation at best remains uncertain or 'fragmentary' (l. 430) and only to be deferred to that realm of 'Peace which passeth understanding'. Eliot later made his well-known remark on Tennyson's *In Memoriam* that 'its faith is a poor thing, but its doubt is a very intense experience' (*SE* 336), and the waste of *The Waste Land* is far more clearly and emphatically realized than any 'exit strategy' (a judgement that could also be applied to 'Gerontion' as we have seen).[5]

REJECTING THE NOTES

Perhaps therefore *The Waste Land* as a whole can be seen to support the interpretative stance Eliot's notes suggest, in that, for all the poem's multiplicity, earthly existence continues to tell the one story it has always told, and Tiresias is there both to witness and embody it. Those who object to according Tiresias a central status in this way suggest that he simply cannot be seen as a 'ubiquitous narrator' or an 'inclusive consciousness' within the poem (Thormählen, *'The Waste Land'*, p. 78), nor as the poem's protagonist; for one thing, his appearance is delayed until part III, and it is difficult to argue for his retrospective 'presence' after first meeting him. This is, however, to give Tiresias a series of roles which Eliot does not, I believe, claim for him; he is more the key embodiment of the poem's abiding concern with sexuality, a representative scapegoat and victim ('And I Tiresias have foresuffered all'), and in this sense, as Thormählen recognizes, is 'sufficiently related to the Waste Landers and their existence to warrant the kind of status given him in the note' (p. 78). Other critics who see Tiresias as a 'failure' as a unifying figure similarly ask him to unify too much perhaps, to achieve a 'comprehensiveness of vision' or 'totalising intellectual framework' which is not his function (Habib, *The Early T. S. Eliot*, p. 227). By looking at Tiresias's role in ancient Greek drama Habib over-stresses his traditional status as mystical seer 'whose attempt [in Eliot's poem] toward a transcendent vision – and voice – was doomed to failure' (p. 231). But to undermine his unifying function in this way is again to undermine something Eliot never claims for him; his note on the source for his Tiresias refers exclusively to Ovid – 'The whole passage from Ovid is of great anthropological interest' – the very wording ('*The* whole passage') assuming that source as primary in its concentration on Tiresias's sexual experience.

Critical scepticism over the value or usefulness of the Tiresias note has doubtless been stimulated by the abuse to which the note has been put, in some readings, in the search for the poem's coherence. Thus the idea of Tiresias as the 'inclusive consciousness' of all the consciousnesses in the poem was the foundation of F. R. Leavis's reading in 1932, while seeing Tiresias as narrator/protagonist from the start of the poem is given classic expression in Grover Smith's influential study of 1956.[6] For example, Smith argues that Tiresias actually narrates the opening lines, which show him 'wrestl[ing] with buried emotions unwittingly revived'; a little later, 'at his meeting with the hyacinth girl . . . Tiresias as the quester has omitted to ask the indispensable question . . .' and so on.[7] And critics who argue that seeing the poem as practically the 'autobiography' of Tiresias in this way is 'to verge on absurdity' can still insist on Tiresias's 'consciousness' as 'inclusive of the other voices in the poem'.[8] Such procedures have not stopped more recent critics, however, from highlighting the potential of Tiresias's function in various ways when shorn of these excesses: for Michael Levenson, for example, 'the problem of Tiresias' is still paramount, and 'we may begin to see how Tiresias can serve the function of "uniting all the rest", without that obliging us to conclude that all speech and all consciousness are the speech and consciousness of Tiresias'. For Levenson, Tiresias is a 'moment of authoritative consciousness at the centre of the poem', a personification of Eliot's philosophy that truth has to encompass multiple viewpoints, his momentary or intermittent (rather than continuous) appearance reminding us of the struggle such unification constantly involves.[9] Versions of Tiresias as unifier or as central figure continue to be fairly common, though as with Levenson they tend to ignore the specifics of Eliot's commentary on him, which as I note above refers to his 'inclusiveness' in bodily and sexual terms, rather than in terms of consciousness or modes of knowledge.[10]

Resistance to a notes-inspired reading of *The Waste Land* remains much in evidence among critics, and is often based not on consideration of the specific role of Tiresias, but on the belief that any hypothesising of control and 'order' radically misrepresents the poem. Such a belief is found among the poem's earliest readers, like Eliot's friend Conrad Aiken: 'the poem succeeds—as it brilliantly does—by virtue of its incoherence, not of its plan; by virtue of its ambiguities, not of its explanations'. This observation is quoted by Lawrence Rainey in a recent endorsing and expansion of Aiken's position, in pursuit of what we might call the 'anti-Tiresias' approach to the poem.[11] Beginning with contemporary readers like Aiken, Rainey's study is, as its title proclaims, a 'revisiting' of the poem that goes back to a series of responses it evoked immediately after its publication; these are seen as somehow more authentic than much of the subsequent 'study' of the poem over the intervening decades, particularly that prompted by the notes. Rainey salutes early readers like Aiken and Burton Rascoe, who each found that 'the notes hinted at levels of narrative and/or structural coherence which jarred with his experience of the poem' (p. 111). Rainey ends his book with the following, emphatically 'Romantic' sounding, tribute:

> we can remain open to the pleasure of amazement and the sense of wonder that a reading of *The Waste Land* inevitably brings, attentive to the poem's vertiginous twists and turns of language, responsive to its richly varied ironic and climactic moments, receptive to its lacerating wildness and stubborn refusal to accommodate our expectations.

This exhortation concludes by quoting three adjectives another early reader, William Bishop, used to describe his own first reaction: '"IMMENSE. MAGNIFICENT. TERRIBLE." Yes, that will do as a starting point' (p. 128). Here is a reader enthusiastically reprising an earlier reader's sense of awe in the presence of the poem, and indeed complying with Eliot's own sense that 'some direct shock of poetic intensity' might well constitute our initial reading experience. Eliot expands on this point later in the same essay:

> the experience of a poem is the experience both of a moment and of a lifetime. It is very much like our intenser experiences of other human beings. There is a first, or an early moment which is unique, of shock and surprise, even of terror ... a moment which can never be forgotten, but which is never repeated integrally; and yet which would become destitute of significance if it did not survive in a larger whole of experience; which survives inside a deeper and a calmer feeling. ('Dante', *SE* 250–1)

Rainey's choice of words to describe his experience of *The Waste Land*, 'amazement', 'wonder', 'vertiginous', 'wildness', 'immense', 'magnificent', 'terrible', is in fact the stock vocabulary of Romantic responses to the 'sublime', notably in landscape, as for example in Wordsworth's poem 'Lines Written a Few Miles Above Tintern Abbey', whose subtitle, which begins 'On Revisiting the Banks of the Wye . . .', indicates a kinship with the 'revisiting' theme in Rainey's book. In the poem, Wordsworth talks of a younger self who experienced the dizzy delights of wild landscape who is now lost to the poet, and replaced by a maturer, more thoughtful self who yet brings 'abundant recompense' (l. 89) for that lost self with him; indeed, towards the end of the poem the sense that the younger self yet survives within the older, that 'wild ecstasies' have been matured into 'a sober pleasure', strikingly anticipates Eliot's discussion of the mature reading process above, where earlier intensity 'survives inside a deeper and a calmer feeling' (*William Wordsworth*, pp. 131–5). Rainey admits that the state of being overwhelmed by *The Waste Land* 'will do as a starting point', but it is not clear from his account of various readings of the text where, and indeed whether, he wishes to proceed anywhere at all from such a starting point, and that this reaction isn't in fact the desired end and furthest limit of reading the poem. Eliot, as we have seen, talks of 'the desire for fuller and fuller knowledge' supplementing that first 'direct shock of poetic intensity', but for Rainey 'knowledge', at least if it proceeds from Jessie Weston, or is based on the notes to the poem, can only impair its immense, magnificent and terrible nature. And it will impair it all the more, of course, if it is a knowledge that is deeply reactionary and unsympathetic to the modern liberal conscience.

The notes, by talking about an underlying identity to the dizzying array of voices and figures in the poem, threaten to constrain and put a fence round its momentous 'wildness'; the Grail legend as any kind of structural thread likewise threatens to instil 'easy expectations of narrative cohesion' (p. 126) which are at odds with the poem's 'stubborn refusal to accommodate' such expectations. It is no surprise that Rainey features Eliot's confession of 1956 that the notes were a 'remarkable exposition of bogus scholarship' (quoted above), and, from the same essay, 'The Frontiers of Criticism', the sentence 'it was just, no doubt, that I should pay my tribute to the work of Miss Jessie Weston; but I regret having sent so many enquirers off on a wild goose chase after Tarot cards and the Holy Grail' (*OP* 110, *Revisiting 'The Waste Land'*, p. 125). This statement, however, cuts both ways – it is hardly a wholesale repudiation of the importance of Weston's work for the poem (it is 'just' to acknowledge this) and in any case, if we cannot rely on what Eliot says in the notes, why should we rely on what Eliot says about the notes thirty years later? We also need to bear in mind the historical context in which the notes were produced, and that which informed this supposed recantation in 1956. In 'The Frontiers of Criticism' Eliot's doubts about the notes are occasioned by his worry about the emphasis on source-hunting they have helped promote in the practice of academic literary criticism (in the 1950s), whereas at the time the notes were produced his aim was to combat the then prevailing mode of what he calls 'impressionistic' criticism by supplying hard data about sources (*OP* 107–10, 117–8).

One might therefore see Rainey's reading, in its mystifying vocabulary of the sublime, as just as restricting as those obsessed with unity, plan and order; moreover, though it dismisses the notes it seems determined by them in the opposite extreme to which it runs. Rainey's neo-romanticizing nostalgia for the poem's original moment rejects any idea of Eliot's own classicist affiliation, at least in the earlier part of his career, suggesting that his 'conversion to Christianity, his growing allegiance to conservative political and social views, his concern with the aesthetic and ethical force of classicism—these constituted a profound change in his thought' (p. 117). This is in opposition to critics like Schuchard and Asher who regard these positions as in place, if not fully developed, from the beginning as we have seen. In the 1923 review of Joyce noted above, '*Ulysses*, Order, and Myth', Eliot salutes Joyce's novel for its structuring strategies, its pursuit of 'order and form' (*SP* 178), taking issue with critics who undervalue its controlling and shaping mechanisms, especially 'the parallel to the *Odyssey*', and who prefer to see Joyce as 'a prophet of chaos' or espouser of Dadaism (*SP* 175). In the same review he emphasizes that in this quest for order Joyce belongs to a contemporary movement which is 'classical in tendency', aiming for 'a goal toward which all good literature strives'. In many ways the modern world in its 'anarchy' is resistant to such a movement, but its adherents can only proceed 'by doing the best one can with the material at hand' (*SP* 176–7). It is entirely reasonable, of course, to reject a reading of *The Waste Land* informed by the notes, but it is another matter to argue that the principles on which such a reading is based were not actively present in Eliot's thought at the time.

Rainey's response certainly complies with Eliot's desire for poetry to provide a direct shock of engagement, but the question is how far this should be the entirety of the poem's relationship to the reader. One celebrated reaction to *The Waste Land* dating from shortly after its publication which Rainey doesn't mention is recorded in Evelyn Waugh's novel *Brideshead Revisited*, in the scene of Anthony Blanche intoning passages from the poem through a megaphone from a college window to passers-by outside, a scene based on a real-life incident.[12] This and other occurrences suggest that the bright young things of the 1920s were captivated by the sheer heady power of *The Waste Land*'s language and rhythm, the 'performance' opportunities it offered, seizing on it as a means for youthful self-expression. Here, something disruptive, shocking and new becomes a means of scandalizing one's traditionally minded elders, and it is the possibility the poem offers for this type of anarchical play that counts for far more than any 'thought' it might contain about *vanitas mundi* or final reckonings. Eliot would not have been unsympathetic to such a performance: as we have seen, 'poetry begins . . . with a savage beating a drum in a jungle, and it retains that essential of percussion and rhythm' (*UP* 155), and to realize that essential is in turn an essential experience in reading. We noted Eliot's insistence in the Dante essay of 1929, with its statement that 'genuine poetry can communicate before it is understood' (*SE* 238), that the *primary* experience of poetry is indeed one of 'shock and surprise, even of terror' (*SE* 250), but also that this remains only a starting-point, even if a crucial one: 'if from your first deciphering . . . there comes now and then some direct shock of poetic intensity, nothing but laziness can deaden the desire for fuller and fuller knowledge' (*SE* 238). That sensory, even visceral, reaction to poetry needs to be supplemented, but not superseded, by the effort of 'understanding' in order to arrive at a complete response.

Whether all readers will be able to achieve this completeness, however, that is, retain the primary excitement while deepening their 'knowledge' via Jessie Weston, James Frazer, Dante and so forth, is a question *The Waste Land* raises with particular insistence. While he was writing the poem, Eliot was also working out the notion of the 'dissociated sensibility' in his essay on 'The Metaphysical Poets' of 1921, a dissociation which 'set in' in the seventeenth century, and from which 'we have never recovered' (*SE* 288). Thought and feeling thereafter, Eliot argues, became opposed to each other in our poets and in our culture, whereas in poets of Donne's day and before 'there is a direct sensuous apprehension of thought, or a recreation of thought into feeling'. Later poets like Tennyson and Browning, unlike the Metaphysicals, 'do not feel their thought as immediately as the odour of a rose', whereas a thought to Donne 'was an experience; it modified his sensibility' (*SE* 286–7).[13] Eliot immediately goes on to talk of poetic 'wholes' that encompass, for example, the reading of Spinoza as well as 'the smell of cooking', a passage quoted in the previous chapter. It is clear that a full response to *The Waste Land* for Eliot should 'feel' its intellectual content and positions no less intensely than its jazzy rhythms, and feel them, so to speak, bodily, and see nothing at odds between these experiences, this attempt to establish the line of contact with the seventeenth century (via nineteenth-century France) being the quest to revive 'a mechanism of sensibility which could devour any kind of experience' (*SE* 287). In this sense an intellectual apprehension of the poem and a sensory response to it are false polarities, but polarities enforced by our 'dissociated' culture.[14]

A poem that is new, radical and outrageous in form and which yet harbours a series of extremely conservative attitudes might seem at first sight something of a paradox. Eliot's notes suggest that the plurality and multi-voicedness the poem records are subordinated to an overall unity, yet even if one ignores this authorial position and insists on the poem as an invitation to 'perform' fragmentation, disruption, discordance and so on, such a response is perfectly compatible with a politics of authority and discipline. Terry Eagleton sees *The Waste Land*'s 'conjuncture of "progressive form" and "reactionary content"' as 'united by a certain "élitism": the "*avant-garde*" experiments of a literary côterie match the conservative values of a ruling minority'.[15] The type of response to the poem in the privileged student circles mentioned above need find the reactionary values it embraces no obstacle to the performative pleasures it offers, however much or little it was aware of them. Such responses might be seen as preserving the integrity of poetry in according with Eliot's insistence that a poem is something over and above any 'beliefs' it may utilise: 'that which is to be communicated is the poem itself, and only incidentally the experience and the thought which have gone into it' (*UP* 30). Nevertheless poets and their poems do have 'thoughts', as we have just noted Eliot remark of Donne and others above; even if one accepts these are 'incidental' they can hardly be ignored, and Eliot will later, in the same set of lectures, ponder at length the difficult relation between poetry and 'belief', noting of Shelley, for example, that 'some of [his] views I positively dislike, and that hampers my enjoyment of the poems in which they occur' (*UP* 91).

Rainey's enjoyment, and that of others, seems not to have been 'hampered' by the presence of dislikeable 'views' in *The Waste Land*: in its glorying in the poem's 'magnificence' it resists any exploration of the despotic attitudes that the state of 'magnificence' can frequently embody. Other critics are less forgiving, if not of the universalizing stance of disillusion in the poem, then of, for example, its social class attitudes, its misogyny, the anti-Semitism of some of the earlier drafts. As several critics note, these are not separate categories in so far as a reactionary politics would conflate the lower social orders and women as both become gradually empowered in the growth of a liberal democracy.[16] With regard to class, although the poem's men and women who 'meet' in Tiresias come from a variety of social backgrounds and lie under an interdict that encompasses royalty and aristocracy (Elizabeth and Leicester, the figure of Marie, the arch-duke's cousin, in the poem's first section), what Eliot posits as the symptomatic scene does feature a protagonist viewed with particular disdain, the 'young man carbuncular', who is 'One of the low on whom assurance sits . . .', and so forth.[17] The manuscript versions of the poem amplify this disdain and revulsion with talk of his hair being 'thick with grease' and so forth (*WLF* 44). On the other hand, the manuscript version delivers its castigations forcibly right across the social scale, so that everyone is seen as in effect a species of 'low life': here the 'swarming life' of London encompasses not only the typist and clerk but also the society belle Fresca, whose morning toilet disguises her 'female stench' in an episode that was cut from the final poem (*WLF* 38–40). Both high and low merit a sardonic disgust, just as part II of the poem combines two scenes of sterility that run across the social spectrum, from Belladonna to Cockney Lil. Here, however, in spite of the class differences the subjects of these two scenes are united in gender, so that we witness what Maud Ellmann has called the poem's 'ferocious' misogyny, and further how it is in fact 'enthralled by the femininity that it reviles'.[18]

There has been much debate on the relation between Eliot's misogyny and the insecurity he purportedly felt about his own sexuality: in Christine Froula's interpretation, the former represents Eliot's aggressive repression of what she calls the poet's own 'forbidden female self', unleashed by the homosexual tenor of his relationship with Jean Verdenal.[19] Eliot had met Verdenal in Paris in 1910–11, and had dedicated the *Prufrock* volume to him after his death in the First World War. The argument for Eliot's possible homosexuality, and the impact on his poetry of the relationship with Verdenal, as developed by John Peter and James E. Miller, and more recently by Carole

Seymour-Jones, has been very fully and ably summarized by Suzanne Churchill, who investigates the frequent homophobia evident in both the 'accusations' of Eliot's homosexual status and in critics who refute such an idea. Churchill is more interested in stressing the 'limitations', both ethical and aesthetic, 'of the "homosexual reading" of the poet'; while this is essentially speculative, a reading which 'reorients criticism toward a homoerotic reading of his poetry' can find much evidence to support it, both in the bawdy poems and others like 'The Death of St Narcissus'.[20] And discussion of 'Homoeroticisms' in Eliot's poetry comprises a substantial chunk of a recent compilation of essays on Eliot which I return to in my Conclusion.[21] The idea that *The Waste Land* is, in whatever sense, a poem of repression is clearly abetted by the very factor of the existence of the notes, regarded as a would-be means of control and governance. The split between poem and commentary can be easily refigured as that between unconscious and conscious, id and ego, the forbidden and the censor, monstrous desire and repressive order.

Some of the most stimulating modern readings have taken a psychoanalytical approach, for example that of Maud Ellmann, who in resisting the directives proposed by the notes takes issue with critics who 'have overlooked [the poem's] broken images in search of the totality it might have been' (p. 92). For her *The Waste Land* cannot be unified but not because it is 'magnificent' in its wildness, but because it is too forcible a nightmare of disintegration, a 'sickening collapse of limits' (p. 94), or boundaries, where the dead invade the realms of the living, the identity of the individual 'I' dissolves in a welter of 'babbling' tongues (p. 107), and the urban waste and bodily decay which the poem 'teems with', cigarette ends, empty bottles, broken fingernails, rats, carious teeth and so forth, seep contagiously through every component of the text. The impotent Fisher King represents the loss of all authority and control within the poem, representing 'the fall of the father' in Ellmann's phrase, which unleashes 'infinite displacements, be they sexual, linguistic or territorial' (p. 107). Against the beleagured patriarchal principles of order, distinction and taxonomy, the text's 'sexology' (p. 106) represents woman as the embodiment of dislocation and loss of boundaries, with her drowning 'odours' and unguents (II. 86–9), and her troubling yet enticing *dis*order: 'On the divan are piled (at night her bed) / Stockings, slippers, camisoles, and stays' (III. 226–7). In this reading the relation between the poem and its notes is that of a momentous psycho-drama where the latter (and especially the note on Tiresias) are a feeble attempt to 'stabilise' (p. 97) the unruly pathologies of confusion and leakage that overwhelm the text: a belated bid indeed for mastery over the monstrous. But even the very note on Tiresias, Ellmann argues, while positing him as the site of *unification* of the sexes (and of everything else), draws attention, in its quotation from Ovid, that Tiresias's story is really one of *slippage* from one sex into the other, and back again, while the phrase in the poem itself, 'throbbing between two lives' (III. 218), shows that rather than embracing both sexes he is in danger of belonging to neither. Thus Tiresias can be seen as 'personifying all the poem's porous membranes' (p. 97), the very site of anarchy rather than containment.

In concentrating on the poem as 'nightmare' and on the notes as the ineffectual attempt to govern or repress trauma, particularly that occasioned by the death and destruction of World War I (p. 109), Ellmann insists on 'porosity' and slippage – between locations, languages, sexualities, personae – as the dominant state of the poem, and the fear thus provoked as the poem's dominant mood. Ultimately the very poem collapses in upon itself, or, as Ellmann puts it in a final rhetorical flourish, it 'stages the ritual of its own destruction' (p. 109). The psychological and linguistic discourses Ellmann provides as the context for the poem abet this postmodernist 'destruction', with their emphasis on the instability and self-division of the individual and on the conventional nature of all signifying systems as endlessly reconstituted from other texts. The contexts that Eliot's own prose writings bring to bear on the poem would of course read many of the details Ellmann focuses on differently. Thus the classicist/postlapsarian philosophy would see the 'babble of miscegenated tongues' (Ellmann, *The Poetics of Impersonality*, p. 107) as confirmation of divine punishment (following the city and tower of Babel story, Gen. 11. 1–9) and therefore of divine jurisdiction. Similarly, the fact that principal cities throughout time ('Jerusalem Athens Alexandria / Vienna London') are all 'Unreal' (V. 374–6) represents not so much a fear of 'contamination' and collapse of boundaries as confirmation that from a transcendental perspective all 'boundaries' are negligible: the 'one' city of 'Falling towers' (V. 373 – 'falling' being a key word in the poem, as also at V. 426) becomes the locus of temporal existence itself, with its 'dead sound on the final stroke of nine'. (This merging of cities reminds us that the attempt to 'unify' the poem does not occur simply in the notes, as retrospective gambit, but as we saw is a strategy frequently operative in the poem itself). Even the major anxiety Ellmann identifies in the poem, of the dead invading the realms of the living, suggests a distinction between the two (and hence a fear of the one infecting the other) which is forestalled several times in Eliot's early poetry and prose. We have noted the postlapsarian outlook that expresses itself in the trope of life itself as a living death, a procession of shadows, and in this sense World War I, and with it the death of Jean Verdenal, acts not as a recent exceptional trauma but as an enforcement of what was always already known. By the time Eliot published the first of the *Four Quartets*, 'Burnt Norton', in 1936, this perspective on existence had become explicit in the poetry, with those exiled from the rose-garden into time being shadows or mere reflections of the true self that occupies the transcendental dimension of 'reality', but this position can be seen to underlie the presentation of the 'Unreal City' of *The Waste Land* too. For Eliot there would be no necessity to establish whether he 'believed' such ideas as early as 1922; he might maintain, in his own words, that he merely made use of them, regarding them as a dominant outlook within the 'mind of Europe', and in voicing them allowing the 'tradition' to speak through him.

Ellmann's reading of *The Waste Land* has its roots in a Freudian model which Eliot himself saw emerging in the early twentieth century and which he rejects at several points in his writing: 'we take it for granted', he notes in the Dante essay, 'that our dreams spring from below: possibly the quality of our dreams suffers in consequence' (*SE* 243), and he might have said the same about our nightmares. Later in the Dante essay he will talk about the 'type of sexual experience' which the first meeting with Beatrice recorded in part II of the *Vita nuova* represented to Dante, noting that 'the same experience, described in Freudian terms, would be instantly accepted as fact by the modern public'.[22] Dante however, 'quite reasonably, drew other conclusions' and prolonged 'the experience in a different direction from that which we, with different mental habits and prejudices, are likely to take' (*SE* 273, 275), that direction eventually being understood as the spiritual quest instigated by God for renunciation of earthly and sexual attachments. In the Dante essay Eliot certainly fights Dante's corner in preferring Dante's interpretation to that occasioned by the 'different mental habits and prejudices' of the modern response, yet the insistence that 'his account is . . . just as reasonable as our own' implies that 'our' own, in its being a product of different cultural and historical circumstances, has its own reasonableness too – later in the essay he calls the *Vita nuova* among other (more important) things 'a very sound psychological treatise on something related to what is now called "sublimation"' (*SE* 275). Again it is worth stressing that Eliot was quite open to the idea that a work can elicit many different readings, given that 'there may be much more in a poem than the author was aware of' (*OP* 31), and of course much more in the self than the self can be aware of. It is not then a question of canvassing a reading that may be Eliot's own in preference to one like Ellmann's, which is an exhilarating reading for the 1980s as it pursues and gleefully enforces the poem's patriarchal anxieties until it auto-destructs.[23] But it may be worth emphasising that the contexts Eliot himself brings to the poem are 'just as reasonable as our own' and determined, just as much as our own contexts, by the reader's cultural and historical specificity.

In James Longenbach's words, 'Eliot recognized . . . that an interpretation potentially tells us more about the subjective or historical horizons of the reader than about the text itself.' At the same time,

> he was able to assert the validity of absolute values within a world of perpetual change. From the time he began as a student of philosophy until the time he became a sage of literary criticism, he believed that since all interpretation is relative to its own *system*, then the critic with the most *whole* and *ordered* system can assay interpretations that approach the absolute. (*Modernist Poetics of History*, pp. 164, 165–6)

Eliot's understanding of the literature of Europe as a whole in 'Tradition and the Individual Talent' and elsewhere, so that 'no poet, no artist of any art, has his complete meaning alone' (*SE* 15), embodies this belief in a systematic scheme of interpretation for finding what this 'meaning' is, rather than in a merely impressionistic response. According to Longenbach Eliot is indebted for this belief in systems to the work of F. H. Bradley. Certainly Eliot's enthusiasm for Dante, and Dante's own understanding of human emotion, is in part the result of Dante's systematic treatment in the *Divine Comedy*: 'Dante's is the most comprehensive, and the most *ordered* presentation of emotions that has ever been made . . . the significance of any single passage . . . is incomplete unless we ourselves apprehend the whole' ('Dante', *SW* 168, 170). The same emphasis runs through the later Dante essay of 1929.

THE WASTE LAND MANUSCRIPT AND NEW DIRECTIONS

The manuscript of *The Waste Land* was rediscovered in 1969 after having been lost for several decades, and it shows among other things how the final state of the poem was crucially determined by excising a good deal of surplus material, much of this being done at the instigation of Ezra Pound, the 'miglior fabbro' ('better craftsman') to whom Eliot dedicated the poem. We have already seen that Eliot's earlier thoughts for part III included an extended satire on Fresca, who alongside her other unsympathetic womanly qualities also 'scribbles verse' (*WLF* 27), and a fuller, and more caustic, dramatization of the typist and clerk episode. Pound commented on the latter that the verse was 'not interesting enough as verse to warrant so much of it' (*WLF* 45), while on the poem's hectoring apostrophe to 'London', with its 'swarming life', an apostrophe placed between the Fresca and the typist/clerk episodes, Pound commented bluntly 'Balls' (*WLF* 31). Pound's target was clearly a more laboured explicitness present in the drafts, whether this took the form of passages of extended narrative or overt didacticism; in editing such material the poem becomes more challengingly 'modernist' in its compression and its increasingly abrupt shifts from scene to scene, speaker to speaker.

The discovery of the drafts of course led critics to review their sense of the poem, and for many the (productive) confusions of the final version were confirmed in what seemed the even more inchoate state of the earlier version or versions (compare Eliot's comment from the *Paris Review* interview that the poem was 'just as structureless, only in a more futile way, in the longer version' (p. 54)). Hugh Kenner, however, felt that the original poem had in some ways a clearer and more focused agenda before Pound's interventions with part III and the suppression of some of the London episodes; thus 'the long poem was to be an urban poem, a London poem', perceiving London 'through various Augustan modes' deriving from Dryden and Pope.[24] While Eliot's more obvious didacticism seems unmistakably toned down in the final version, the sense that the original drafts were more localized, that is, London-centred, is questionable.

One could claim, in fact, that Eliot originally had an even more universalizing ambition for the poem, given that one of the most striking divergences between manuscripts and printed version is the complete absence in the latter of any scenes set in America, or featuring Americans. In the latter case, one might make an exception for the Stetson of part I, whose name is not only meant perhaps to suggest an American provenance but more specifically, in its resemblance to one of Eliot's own nicknames (Tsetse, based on his initials), suggests an identity as the poet's own double, in an anticipation of the famous encounter scene in 'Little Gidding'. The poem originally opened with a lengthy narrative scene set in an unspecified US city, the night-time escapade of a group of males doing the bar, club and brothel circuit in an episode that owes something to the Circe chapter of Joyce's *Ulysses*. A further cut in the progress towards the final poem was performed on another scene of extended narrative that opened part IV. Here American sailors on a fishing expedition in the North Atlantic hit an iceberg and are drowned, though not before a moment of fruition resumes the pleasures advertised in the poem's original opening, with the catch coming in and the sailors thinking fondly of 'Marm Brown's joint' with its 'girls and gin' (*WLF* 65). The episode ends with a clear reference to the final lines of canto 26 of Dante's *Inferno*, where Ulysses's ship is sunk in an act of divine castigation for his trespassing on forbidden knowledge and persuading others to follow him. The moral chastisement in Eliot's episode, however, in keeping with the poem as a whole, seems directed at a much less 'elevated' transgression of pursuing bodily, that is sexual, desires.

In the year following the poem's publication, Eliot's letter to Ford Madox Ford announces 'There are *I* think about 30 *good* lines in *The Waste Land* . . . The rest is ephemeral'; the italicized pronoun suggests that Eliot recognized that others might have different opinions. A follow-up letter indicates that these lines are 'the 29 lines of the water-dripping song in the last part', that is, from 'Here is no water but only rock' to 'But there is no water' (*WLF* 129). The judgement is striking, and will certainly not tally with many readers' experience of the poem, but it does anticipate that conspicuous 'turn' in Eliot's poetry which we witness in his next major poem, 'The Hollow Men' of 1925, 'a new form and style' that Eliot announced in correspondence immediately following the 'ephemeral' *Waste Land*'s publication (*WLF* xxv).[25] The 'water-dripping song', with its simple, insistent repetitions, and the bareness and restraint of its imagery, anticipates Eliot's movement towards an increasingly austere diction and disciplined range of poetic effects. In the Dante essay of 1929 Dante is saluted as the great mentor in the art of writing poetry, teaching the lesson that 'the greatest poetry can be written with the greatest economy of words, and with the greatest austerity in the use of metaphor, simile, verbal beauty, and elegance' (*SE* 252). Later for the verse-dramatist 'the gradual purging out of poetical ornament' will also be the desired trajectory:

> the course of improvement is towards a greater and greater starkness. The beautiful line for its own sake is a luxury . . . What is necessary is a beauty which shall not be in the line or the isolable passage, but woven into the dramatic texture itself. (*OP* 259–60)

Some readers have felt, as did George Orwell, that this movement towards a greater 'starkness' nullified much of the arresting power of Eliot's work, though there is a counter-school of thought which regards *Four Quartets* as the pinnacle of his achievement; the fact that the earlier and later poetry shows such a stylistic contrast – alongside the continuities – clearly abets this division of response.[26] In the previous chapter we discussed Eliot's awareness of the 'cosmetic' powers of poetic language, its ability to beautify states of moral or physical decay, thus acting in conspiracy with Belladonna's 'strange synthetic perfumes' to transform her into a Cleopatra figure. The key icon of this illicit metamorphosis in *The Waste Land* is the drowned body of Alonso, featured in the use of Ariel's song from *The Tempest* (1. 2. 397–405), whose bones are now coral and whose eyes are pearls, the whole experiencing a 'sea-change / Into something rich and strange'. The song mesmerises Belladonna's silent interlocutor (II. 125). In *The Waste Land* this transformation contrasts with that of Phlebas in part IV of the poem, whose 'sea-change' is to undo his 'once handsome and tall' beauty and reduce him to bones that do not figure as art-object but as reminders of mortality. In the earlier poem 'Whispers of Immortality' Eliot talks of Renaissance writers like Donne and Webster being 'possessed by death', but in the voluptuous and ornate manner that echoes Ariel's song:

> Daffodil bulbs instead of balls
> Stared from the sockets of the eyes!

He [Webster] knew that thought clings round dead limbs
Tightening its lusts and luxuries. (*CP* 52)

Eliot's poem guiltily throws in its own 'lot' in the final stanza with the necrophilia of the Elizabethan theatre, rather than with the living body, represented by the questionable attractions of Grishkin, but Eliot's later poetry, in moving from the 'luxury' of ostentatious poetic effects to a greater starkness and asceticism is following a trajectory that is at once religious and aesthetic. By 'Ash-Wednesday' (1930), the bones will have become divested of any 'gratuitous mystique', their function being to point beyond themselves to the realms of salvation and immortality (Ellis, *The English Eliot*, p. 35). 'The gradual purging out of poetical ornament' noted in the Yeats essay is thus a means of expressing ideas of moral purgation in which poetry itself, alongside the individual, aims at a kind of self-effacement in its dedication to a higher cause. In a 'great poet's . . . greatest moments', Eliot remarked in 1941, he is 'writing transparently, so that our attention is directed to the object and not to the medium' (*OP* 235), but the emphasis on this desired 'transparency' is already present in the Dante essay of 1929, where the lucidity, or rather 'translucency', of Dante's diction is compared with the 'opacity' that characterizes the much denser verbal medium of English poets, including Shakespeare (*SE* 239–40). Eliot's quest for a more ascetic poetry rejects, in short, the splendours and temptations of words (particularly tempting, as discussed below, for those writing in English) in its attempts to realise the Word, but this quest is already outlined in the movement in *The Waste Land* from the ornamentation of the Belladonna episode in part II to the spareness of the water-dripping song in part V. In an anticipation of *Four Quartets* Eliot noted in 1933 his ultimate ambition was to 'get *beyond poetry*, as Beethoven, in his later works, strove to get *beyond music*'.[27]

The Waste Land's first appearance was in the first issue of the *Criterion*, the periodical Eliot himself edited throughout its existence from 1922 to 1939. We shall return to this subject in discussing Eliot's later writing in Chapter 4, but his article on 'The Idea of a Literary Review', which appeared in the January 1926 issue, sets out an agenda for the magazine which both summarizes and anticipates many of his key concerns. Thus the editor's choice of content and contributors should not be merely miscellaneous but should aim to exhibit 'the keenest sensibility and the clearest thought' of its time, and also the cultural and intellectual 'tendencies' indicated by such sensibility and thought (pp. 2–4). 'I believe that the modern tendency is toward something which, for want of a better name, we may call classicism', Eliot continues, reprising his comment of ten years earlier (see above, p. 4), and while he then issues a series of caveats 'against measuring living art and mind by dead laws of order', it is clear what the term classicism, even if used 'with hesitation', continues to mean to Eliot. For example, it represents 'a more severe and serene control of the emotions by Reason'; in Eliot's discussion of recent works of an anti-classicist character by Bernard Shaw and others ('which represent to my mind that part of the present which is already dead') it is apparent that 'classicism' also upholds ideas of orthodoxy and authority against the 'curious amateur religions' such writers propagate. It stresses conformism to intellectual and religious tradition rather than the individualistic systems of Shaw, H. G. Wells and Bertrand Russell, which show 'intelligence at the mercy of emotion' (pp. 5–6). And it also continues to serve the notion of 'the mind of Europe', a cooperative legacy of thought which the *Criterion* will acknowledge by including in its pages 'work of continental writers of the same order of merit as our own' (p. 4). As well as such work, the *Criterion* did include in every issue digests of the contents of foreign periodicals, not only French, German and Italian but frequently, for example, Danish, Spanish, Swiss and Russian (as well as American). Regular 'Chronicles', or reports on literary and cultural events in Paris, Madrid and other Continental centres completed this European profile – one threatened, as we shall see, by the international crisis that led to the Second World War.

'THE HOLLOW MEN' AND AFTER

'The Hollow Men' of 1925 can be seen as a reworking of *The Waste Land*, but in Eliot's new, stripped down style.[28] Gone are the quotations in other languages and the multiple voices and personae of the earlier work, though the mingling of different discourses (nursery rhyme, prayer) remains in the final section of the poem. Here indeed we might discern the unified, centralized essence of the previous poem, but now revealed in the poem itself rather than in any authorial commentary. *The Waste Land*'s living dead, equated with the dwellers in the so-called 'vestibule' Dante describes just inside the gates of Hell – 'I had not thought death had undone so many', I. 63

(Eliot's note refers us to *Inferno* 3. 55–7) – reappear in a setting that again evokes this vestibule. They are 'Gathered on this beach of the tumid river', the river no longer individualised as the Thames, and comparable with Dante's river Acheron, but bordering a dead, rat-inhabited 'cactus-land' that duplicates *The Waste Land*'s arid locale. The hollow men protagonists inhabit both this life and life in the hereafter at one and the same time:

> Those who have crossed
> With direct eyes, to death's other Kingdom
> Remember us – if at all – not as lost
> Violent souls, but only
> As the hollow men
> The stuffed men. (p. 83)

Those who have 'crossed', Dante tells us in *Inferno* canto 3, are the damned proper, anxious to be ferried across the river Acheron into Hell because with damnation comes a kind of identity and a significant place in the scheme of divine justice. In thus crossing, they leave behind what Dante calls the wretched *ignavi*, those who never committed themselves to good or evil but retained through life a self-serving neutrality, to be equated with that of the angels who in Satan's rebellion against God took neither side (*Inferno* 3. 34–9). Such figures (and Dante makes it plain there are vast files of them, 'I had not thought death had undone so many' in Eliot's *Waste Land* translation) were never, in their spiritually null lives, truly alive, Dante claims (l. 64), so that in their case, as in Eliot's poetry, the difference between life and death, London and Hell-vestibule, is elided. Treated with disdain, and hardly remarked on (Virgil, Dante's guide, tells him merely to look and pass on, l. 51), they are condemned to spend eternity in a kind of waiting-room (though they have nothing to wait for) on the very outskirts of the hereafter.

Eliot's attitude to the hollow men is clarified by some extraordinary remarks on Baudelaire in the essay of 1930:

> so far as we are human, what we do must be either evil or good; so far as we do evil or good, we are human; and it is better, in a paradoxical way, to do evil than to do nothing: at least, we exist . . . Baudelaire was man enough for damnation. (*SE* 429)

Earlier in the essay Eliot had argued that

> the possibility of damnation is so immense a relief in a world of electoral reform, plebiscites, sex reform and dress reform, that damnation itself is an immediate form of salvation – of salvation from the ennui of modern life, because it at last gives some significance to living. It is this, I believe, that Baudelaire is trying to express. (*SE* 427)

The hollow men of Eliot's poem, without the courage or will to be damned, represent this state of 'ennui', a point emphasized by the poem's epigraph, 'Mistah Kurtz – he dead'. The Kurtz of Conrad's *Heart of Darkness*, 'man enough for damnation' in Eliot's phrase, gained a similar 'moral' stature in the narrator Marlow's eyes through the atrocious evil he practised; thus his cry of 'The horror!' becomes for Marlow 'a moral victory', even if paid for by 'abominable terrors, by abominable satisfactions'. Marlow contrasts Kurtz with the run-of-the-mill 'pilgrims', with their banal avarice and self-interest, 'their insignificant and silly dreams', representatives of a mediocre Western civilization more dead than living, based like Eliot's in a 'sepulchral' city.[29] 'Mistah Kurtz – he dead' might at first seem to signify for Eliot's poem a representative sinner whose moral state is a form of death; but what Eliot, like Conrad, really underlines is precisely that Kurtz is not one of the hollow men – his powers and capacities rather lie dead within us. 'We' are the hollow men: the poem incriminates a whole civilization in its mode of address.[30]

Eliot was originally planning to use a passage from Conrad, culminating in Kurtz's cry 'The horror! The horror!' (*Heart of Darkness*, p. 79) as epigraph for *The Waste Land* (*WLF* 2–3), but it is plain that the 'vision' that represents that horror is not Kurtz's own sense of the atavistic bestiality that underlies the veneer of civilization, but a 'civilisation' reduced to a mechanical, zombie-like routine where both good and evil have lost their significance. In Eliot's play *Murder in the Cathedral* (1935), the Chorus have a vision of the divine judgement lying 'behind the face of Death' that would condemn them to 'the Void, more horrid than active shapes of hell'. This horror is once more of an eternal 'vestibule' state, or 'empty land / Which is no land, only emptiness, absence, the Void' where the soul is 'foully united forever, nothing with nothing' (*CP* 272). The fear is not of damnation, but of a complete nullity that will eternalise the spiritual nullity of life, whether presented in 'The Hollow Men' or in the nightmare 'nothing again nothing' that echoes relentlessly in the conversation of the couple from 'A Game of Chess' in *The Waste Land*. The vision parallels that of the nightmare of ultimate nullity experienced in the Marabar Caves in Forster's near-contemporary novel *A Passage to India*.[31]

Nevertheless, the hollow men have some faint sense remaining of spiritual matters, just as Stetson in *The Waste Land*, the commuter singled out from the crowd, is still in touch with primal fertility rituals in however furtive and suburban a manner ('That corpse you planted last year in your garden . . .', I. 71). They may never enter the true 'Kingdom' that alone 'gives some significance to living', but in the second part of 'The Hollow Men' they can dream of another 'kingdom' where the terrifying 'Eyes' of judgement are absent, and, in a similar vein, where there is no 'final meeting'; a dream in fact of a kind of diluted salvation represented by sunlight and (distant) singing, but one that involves no spiritual commitment or responsibility and is all of vision that the enfeebled energies of the hollow men can muster.[32] Parts III and IV continue to play out variations on the theme of the vestibule-dwellers and their hopes and questions about this other 'kingdom' of pseudo-salvation:

> Gathered on this beach of the tumid river
>
> Sightless, unless
> The eyes reappear
> As the perpetual star
> Multifoliate rose
> Of death's twilight kingdom
> The hope only
> Of empty men. (p. 85)

The 'multifoliate rose' is a common symbol of Heaven, but one cannot get to Heaven by bypassing the interrogating 'eyes' of judgement, and the idea that these eyes can simply be substituted by the comforting icons of star or rose is undercut by the confession that this is no true 'Kingdom' of God but again a (lower case) kingdom of 'twilight' rather than radiance.[33] This kingdom has various identities as it migrates through the poem, both the void of an unspiritual life on earth and the void this will lead to in the hereafter, as also the dream-kingdom that in its dilutions and evasions is represented as merely a more benign kind of void, and the limit of the hope available to 'empty men'. In the last part of the poem, the line from the Lord's Prayer, *For Thine is the Kingdom*, is repeated in a faltering and truncated manner by the congregation of the hollow men, and represents the poem's final 'whimper'. Here the inability of the straw men to carry actions to fruition is emphasized, be these of worship or, in a final reference to Guy Fawkes, involving the violence or evil necessary to at least secure the status of damnation. That they should end with a whimper rather than a bang is suggested in this final part as a consequence of the falling 'Shadow' that comes between the commencing and culmination of all enterprises, and that indicates once more the ineluctable conditions of alienation proceeding from the Fall.

In some ways the obverse situation to that of 'The Hollow Men' is presented in that curious fragment which Eliot published in two parts in the *Criterion* in 1926–7, *Sweeney Agonistes*, in which he revives some of the cast of the earlier poem 'Sweeney Erect'.[34] Here Sweeney reminisces about having once met one of the 'lost / Violent souls', 'I knew a man once did a girl in' (*CP* 124), whose damnable action has released him from the bleakly comic vision that life is, once more, essentially 'Nothing . . . but three things': 'Birth, and copulation and death' (*CP* 121–2). Sweeney's characteristically Eliotic summing up that thus 'Life is death' (*CP* 124) implies that the murder is a form of protest at the banality of this situation, in line with the formulation from the Baudelaire essay, 'it is better, in a paradoxical way, to do evil than to do nothing: at least, we exist' (*SE* 429). The paradoxes of the situation are exploited in a tone of black humour in *Sweeney Agonistes* – 'He didn't know if he was alive / and the girl was dead . . . If he was alive then the milkman wasn't / and the rent-collector wasn't / And if they were alive then he was dead' (*CP* 125), but certainly the sense that the murderer has crossed to another dimension that is the opposite of daily routine is indicated here. The murderer has entered a profound state of being 'alone', is singled out from the crowd; the confounding of habitual categories he has effected – 'Death is life and life is death' (*CP* 125) – suggests that through the action he has committed and the punishment that awaits him he has indeed achieved a kind of authentic 'life'. As early as 1917, in fact, in the dialogue 'Eeldrop and Appleplex', Eliot had presented the similar case of a man who had murdered his mistress: 'the important fact is that for the man the act is eternal, and that for the brief space he has to live, he is already dead. He is already in a different world from ours. He has crossed the frontier'.[35]

Lyndall Gordon discusses an earlier draft of *Sweeney Agonistes* in which the murderer appears to be Sweeney himself. She also suggests that Doris, the prostitute of the first part of the published version, impersonates Sweeney's victim in the coffin symbol she draws in cutting the pack of playing cards. Her argument that the piece shows Eliot's moral condemnation of the murderer, in giving us a Sweeney 'trapped in the toils of remorse', a figure 'cut . . . off from all humanity', and one 'inwardly . . . dead, more truly dead than his victim since he is damned for all eternity' gives us however a conventional moral verdict far removed from Eliot's curious approval of evil and damnation as a superior form of spiritual existence to that of 'all humanity'.[36] In 'Eeldrop and Appleplex', the description of the murderer having 'crossed the frontier', and leaving behind a world where 'many are not quite real at any moment' (p. 105) anticipates the enviable 'crossing' in Eliot's poem to a reality where the 'hollow men' are left behind. This also anticipates the case of another murderer in *The Family Reunion*, where 'Harry has crossed the frontier', in Agatha's words (*CP* 342; see below, pp. 96–9). Compare Eliot's remark from 1920: 'in Dante's Hell souls are not deadened, as they mostly are in life . . .' (*SW* 166).

'The Hollow Men' preceded Eliot's formal conversion to Christianity, in 1927, by two years, and in using some of the post-conversion work like the essays on Baudelaire and Dante as commentary for it and other works, it may seem as if I am 'reading back' into the poem positions that Eliot only confirmed later. But 'The Hollow Men' itself looks back as well as forwards, to ideas of original sin that have always been present in Eliot's work (as in 'Gerontion') and to a Dantesque topography and moral classification that is drawn on as early as the epigraph to 'The Love Song of J. Alfred Prufrock' and is apparent in *The Waste Land*. By the time of 'The Hollow Men' and its ascetic pruning of discourse, such presences in Eliot's poetry have come to the fore, to the detriment and exclusion of many other voices that previously existed alongside them. The Clark Lectures on 'metaphysical' poetry that Eliot gave at Cambridge in 1926 involve a sustained comparison between the poetry of Dante and that of Donne, and in Eliot's constant elevation of the former above the latter signal, in fact, the turning-point between Eliot's own early and late poetic manner:

> I want now to show, if I can, how the acceptance of one orderly system of thought and feeling results, in Dante and his friends, in a simple, direct and even austere manner of speech, while the maintenance in suspension of a number of philosophies, attitudes and partial theories which are enjoyed rather than believed, results, in Donne and in some of our contemporaries, in an affected, tortuous, and often over-elaborate and ingenious manner of speech. (*VMP* 120)

Order and unity in one's thoughts lead to direct expression, multiplicity and disorder to a reprehensible elaboration of style; later in the lectures he will talk of the 'chaos' of the mind of Donne, 'a mind of the trecento [that is, fourteenth century] in disorder' (*VMP* 133), and later still suggest that, again in comparison with Dante, 'the peculiarity [in Donne] is the absence of order, the fraction of *thought* into innumerable *thoughts*. Donne is a poet, a true poet, perhaps even a very great poet, of chaos' (*VMP* 154–5). A year later, Eliot reports that he finds it

> quite impossible to come to the conclusion that Donne believed anything . . . at that time, the world was filled with broken fragments of systems, and . . . a man like Donne merely picked up, like a magpie, various shining fragments of ideas as they struck his eye, and stuck them about here and there in his verse. (*SE* 138–9)

Eliot's second book of criticism, *For Lancelot Andrewes*, published in 1928, with its significant subtitle *Essays on Style and Order*, continues the comparison of 'ordered' and disordered writers, and of the good or bad stylistic consequences, and however much the Clark Lectures continue to show a qualified admiration for Donne's 'greatness', Eliot's later poetry now seeks to leave the chaotic waste land of 'innumerable thoughts' behind as it enters the territory of 'belief'.

CHAPTER 3

'ASH-WEDNESDAY' AND THE WRITING
OF THE 1930S

The World is trying the experiment of attempting to form a civilized but non-Christian mentality. The experiment will fail; but we must be very patient in awaiting its collapse.
— '*Thoughts After Lambeth*', SE 387

THE ARIEL POEMS

'I thought my poetry was over after "The Hollow Men" . . . writing the Ariel poems released the stream and led directly to "Ash-Wednesday"' (quoted in Southam, *Student's Guide*, p. 235). Between 1927 and 1930 Eliot published four 'Ariel' poems in successive years (*CP* 103–10), together with the separate publication of parts I–III of 'Ash-Wednesday', with the latter poem appearing in its entirety in 1930; these are Eliot's first poems of declared Christian belief. The Ariel poems were produced as illustrated Christmas greetings by Eliot's publishers and employers Faber and Gwyer (afterwards Faber and Faber), and many other poets were to contribute to the series, though not all of them felt the significance of Christmas, perhaps, as much as Eliot, for whom the temporal moment of Incarnation will feature centrally in *Four Quartets* and in Becket's Christmas sermon in *Murder in the Cathedral*. Eliot's Ariel poems are severe and rigorous examinations of the significance of Christmas, and hardly 'festive' in the accepted sense (though a final Ariel poem, 'The Cultivation of Christmas Trees', produced in 1954, relents a little in this respect, *CP* 111). Indeed, the later two poems, 'Animula' (1929) and 'Marina'

(1930), have no obvious relevance to Christmas at all, while the first two, 'Journey of the Magi' (1927) and 'A Song for Simeon' (1928), concentrate not on the Nativity as a joyous event but on the 'bitter agony' of death that is inextricably entwined with it.

Thus the speaker of the first poem is one of the Magi for whom Christ's birth represents his own death, not only ending the 'old dispensation' to which he belongs but also undermining the power and status of his earthly kingdom with the arrival of the heavenly king. The speaker thus finds himself in a kind of limbo state, 'no longer at ease', ousted from old securities but uncertain of the significance of what he has witnessed, with the last line of the poem, 'I should be glad of another death', testifying to his need for release. 'A Song for Simeon' is also spoken by an old man longing for death, a narrative based on Luke 2. 25–35, where Simeon has been told that 'he should not see death, before he had seen the Lord's Christ' (v. 26). Unlike the Magi, he has seen and understood the 'salvation' the birth represents, and Eliot's poem is couched in the form of a prayer, 'Grant me thy peace', not only the peace of death itself but of spiritual 'consolation'. In many ways these two poems of 1927 and 1928 seem to look backwards and forwards respectively at this pivotal point of Eliot's life, given his formal entry into the Anglican Church at this time. The earlier poem suggests the 'agony' of being stranded between the old dispensation and the new, a situation evoking that of a previous 'old man', Gerontion, dissatisfied with the former but guarded and uncertain about the latter. Simeon, however, fully realizes and embraces the significance of the birth, but regrets he lives and dies before the heroic days of ministry and apostleship – 'Not for me the martyrdom, the ecstasy of thought and prayer, / Not for me the ultimate vision'. In this he gives voice to the sense of spiritual limitation several of Eliot's future speakers will also declare, from the Chorus in *Murder in the Cathedral* to the poet of 'The Dry Salvages', who speaks explicitly not on behalf of the 'saint', but for 'most of us' who occupy humbler stations. Becket, in preaching his Christmas sermon in Eliot's play, stresses like Simeon the death, sorrow and turmoil that the divine birth brings into the world – 'Is it an accident, do you think, that the day of the first martyr follows immediately the day of the Birth of Christ? By no means', and he explains that the 'peace to men of good will' the angels announced at the Nativity was 'not peace as the world gives', but, to the disciples, 'torture, imprisonment, disappointment . . . [and] death by martyrdom' (*CP* 261).

If the first two Ariel poems are Christmas 'greetings' that counter modern institutions of festive jollity, 'Animula' of 1929 is in many ways the bleakest of the set, a tracing of the human life from birth to death (taking in the child's delight 'In the fragrant brilliance of the Christmas tree') which is seen as a progressive crippling and process of degradation. The opening line, 'Issues from the hand of God, the simple soul', derives from Dante's *Purgatorio* (16. 85), where Dante too talks about the primal joy the infant derives from its 'happy maker' (1. 89) being lost as existence continues (ll. 85–114). Not only, however, is there a far more emphatic sense of this initial joy in Dante, but the reason it is jeopardized is laid at the door of Church and State misgovernment. In Eliot however, the reason the soul issues 'from the hand of time . . . / Irresolute and selfish, misshapen, lame' is not because of any remediable institutional practice but is an inevitable consequence of merely existing in time, the simple 'pain of living'. Once more, to be born is in fact to die; one only first lives 'in the silence after the viaticum', that is, after the final communion administered to the dying, which is 'the hour of our [true] birth' in the poem's final line. The picture of the shrivelled soul in old age, or at the point of death, 'Unable to fare forward or retreat', will be expanded upon in *Four Quartets*, though here the relationship with time will be far less passive and the injunction to the living to 'fare forward' insisted upon.

'Marina' of 1930 seems the most hopeful of the Ariel poems, with 'hope' itself being saluted four lines from the end. The Marina of the title derives from Shakespeare's play *Pericles*, Eliot's poem being voiced, so to speak, by the play's eponymous hero, Marina's father, who had believed his daughter lost to him as a baby. The restoration of Marina to her father after an interval of many years is used by Eliot as a representation of a new spiritual life, and is associated with the returning images of the landscapes, or rather seascapes, of Eliot's childhood, the 'scent of pine and the woodthrush singing through the fog'. Marina, who in Shakespeare's play is born at sea (the name derives from the Latin for sea, *mare*), is a means whereby Eliot introduces into the poem the basic metaphor of life as a voyage, envisaging a 'new ship' that will replace the 'rotten' and leaking fabric of the old. The poem presents the hope of reaching a promised new land, rather than anticipating a secure arrival there; at times it is couched in the form of a prayer, 'let me / Resign my life for this life', and the 'fog' through which the alluring destination calls still has to be negotiated at the end of the poem. Eliot will return to using this voyage motif in 'The Dry Salvages', as he will the 'Whispers and small laughter between leaves' in 'Burnt Norton', where states of childhood and spiritual restoration are associated. In its hopes for renewal, 'Marina' is very much akin to 'Ash-Wednesday', published in the same year, as it is in the use of a female figure to represent such renewal.

'ASH-WEDNESDAY'

All the essays collected in *For Lancelot Andrewes* of 1928 date from around the time of Eliot's conversion the previous year, the opening essay, on Andrewes himself, including a comparison between its titular subject and Donne, with regard to the two speakers' sermons. The 'emotion' expressed by the former is 'not personal, it is wholly evoked by the object of contemplation, to which it is adequate; his emotion is wholly contained in and explained by its object', a situation that contrasts with Donne's sermons which, 'one feels, are a "means of self-expression"' (*FLA* 24–5). But preaching, to borrow from 'Tradition and the Individual Talent', is 'not the expression of personality, but an escape from personality', and admirers of Donne are in danger of being 'fascinated by "personality" in the romantic sense of the word' (*FLA* 26). Stylistically, Eliot presents a contrast between the exactitude and precision of Andrewes's language and what is often 'vague and unformed' in Donne (p. 16); the former's repetitions, eschewing of 'decoration' (p. 17) and 'dwelling on a single word . . . squeezing and squeezing the word until it yields a full juice of meaning' (pp. 19–20) parallel the verbal discipline Eliot signals in his own poetry in 'The Hollow Men' and which becomes even more apparent in 'Ash-Wednesday'.

The classicist, royalist and anglo-catholic 'point of view' described in the Preface to *For Lancelot Andrewes* (*FLA* 7) had been broadly defined in similar terms by Eliot in his 1916 characterization of the ideals of classicism as '*form* and *restraint* in art, *discipline* and *authority* in religion, *centralization* in government (either as socialism or monarchy)' (above, p. 4). The restraint, verbal economy and self-effacement represented by Andrewes combine with Catholic emphases (for example, the Virgin Mary and Purgatory) as the basis of 'Ash-Wednesday'. If Andrewes 'takes a word and derives the world from it' (*FLA* 20), then one word that is squeezed in 'Ash-Wednesday' for its 'full juice of meaning' is announced in the opening line: 'Because I do not hope to turn again'. The simple word 'turn' becomes a key site of the poem's complex dramatization of spiritual struggle, representing the movement towards God, the corresponding turning away from 'the world', the ever-present danger of turning back to temptation and taking another 'turn' with it, and even the constant turning over in the mind of such issues, 'These matters that with myself I too much discuss / Too much explain' (I, *CP* 89). This verbal deployment climaxes at the beginning of part III:

> At the first turning of the second stair
> I turned and saw below
> The same shape twisted on the banister
> Under the vapour in the fetid air
> Struggling with the devil of the stairs who wears
> The deceitful face of hope and of despair
>
> At the second turning of the second stair
> I left them twisting, turning below . . .

Here the ascent of the purgatorial staircase represents the turning towards God and away from the sins and 'distraction' of the world (including the sensory pleasures of the 'maytime' and the pagan music that await on the third stair), yet at the same time there can be no final overcoming of such temptations, and the 'same shape', the protagonist himself, remains locked in an endless twisting and turning with 'the devil of the stairs'. The Dante persona who in climbing Purgatory proper becomes completely purged of his sins is told at one point not to look back now that he is on the road to salvation (*Purgatorio* 9. 131–2; compare Lk. 9.62). The protagonist of 'Ash-Wednesday', however, exists in this world, not the hereafter, where there is no assurance of victory and where the action 'I turned and saw below' recognizes that part of the self that will continue to grapple with sin at all stages of the spiritual journey. Christ's remonstrance to the devil in the wilderness therefore, 'Get thee behind me, Satan' (Lk. 4. 8), cannot be duplicated here with any confidence that the devil will ever be fully left 'behind'.

The temptations that the 'devil of the stairs' offers in part III seem not to be those of earthly pleasure or success, but the twin snares 'of hope and of despair', that is, spiritual rather than worldly states that could occasion the protagonist's going astray in other ways. In part I of the poem, the renunciation of secular achievement at the outset – 'this man's gift and that man's scope' – as well as any fulfilment the world can offer – 'The one veritable transitory power' – seems merely a preface to the more difficult sacrifice of spiritual ambition represented by the renunciation of the 'blessèd face'. Ash Wednesday, as the first day of Lent, inaugurates a period commemorating Christ's entry into the wilderness and his 'being forty days tempted of the devil' (Lk. 4.2), a period of self-denial and spiritual introspection for the Christian, and just as Christ's temptations included the offer of worldly status and the displaying of his own spiritual power (Lk. 4. 5–6, 9–11) so Eliot's poem too turns away from both 'attainments'. When Eliot powerfully returns to the temptation theme in his first complete verse drama, *Murder in the Cathedral* (1935), his hero Becket finds it far easier to reject the first three tempters and their offers of temporal power and pleasure than he does the fourth tempter with the visions of heavenly glory he holds out to entice Becket's spiritual vanity (*CP* 252–6).[1] Part I of 'Ash-Wednesday' withdraws into its own Lenten wilderness where hope itself is a temptation to be relinquished, for as 'East Coker' will later put it, even hope 'would be hope for the wrong thing' (*CP* 180). As in this later poem, the search is for a minimalist state of spiritual agency that recognizes in all humility the self's helplessness and necessary passivity. In 'East Coker' this is expressed in lines like 'I said to my soul, be still, and let the dark come upon you / Which shall be the darkness of God', together with the recognition that 'the hope [is] all in the waiting' (*CP* 180). Part I of 'Ash-Wednesday' also finishes at a point of 'stillness' where all ambition and self-vaunting has shrivelled and the individual's only possibility is prayer (in this case the conclusion of the 'Hail Mary'):

> Because these wings are no longer wings to fly
> But merely vans to beat the air
> The air which is now thoroughly small and dry
> Smaller and dryer than the will
> Teach us to care and not to care
> Teach us to sit still.
>
> Pray for us sinners now and at the hour of our death
> Pray for us now and at the hour of our death.

Towards the end of 'East Coker' we are told 'We must be still and still moving' (*CP* 183), and the paradox of being taught 'to care and not to care' reflects a similar idea that the desired spiritual state is one of self-abnegation indeed, but one that avoids the complacency that could attach even to this recognition of our nothingness. Recognizing that only God and the divine intercessors can deliver the protagonist, and that he cannot deliver himself, is itself a stage in a spiritual 'journey' that he remains committed and attentive to; in this sense he must be mindful of going somewhere even while he has to remain 'still'. Later, in 'Burnt Norton', Eliot plays with the image of a 'descent' in a lift to suggest a mode of spiritual movement that is in fact 'abstention from movement' (*CP* 174). The paradox is paralleled by the idea already traced in part III of 'Ash-Wednesday' that in terms of the battle with sin and the devil we are going somewhere and nowhere at the same time. And although, as discussed below, there is an idea of a progressive 'journey' through the poem as a whole, there is also the sense that by the time we reach the last part, part VI, with its opening line 'Although I do not hope to turn again', which picks up the near-identical line that opens part I, we are being invited to turn back to the beginning and go round the never-ending circle again. Spiritual growth is a matter of slow uncertain increments.

By the end of part I of 'Ash-Wednesday', therefore, we have arrived at a kind of zero point of self-esteem and agency, but this is a necessary prologue for the next stage of spiritual growth, and as 'Burnt Norton' will also testify at the end of its third part, descent into the depths is in fact a mode of ascent towards God. 'East Coker' will then take up the theme of how thus 'the darkness shall be the light, and the stillness the dancing' (*CP* 180). The line from 'Ash-Wednesday' quoted above on the wings being now 'merely vans to beat the air' evokes Dante's depiction of Satan, trapped in the ice at the very bottom of Hell and still flapping wings that once were used for flight (*Inferno* 34. 46–52). Dante, who has to climb along Satan's body to begin the climb out of Hell up to Purgatory, thus also signals via a ritual of self-abasement and acknowledgement of his status as sinner that any 'ascent' must begin here, at the very bottom.

The thinking behind 'Ash-Wednesday' is also greatly indebted to Eliot's reading of the work of the sixteenth-century Spanish mystic St John of the Cross (1542–91), already quoted by Eliot in the second epigraph to *Sweeney Agonistes* (*CP* 115). St John's *The Dark Night*, a commentary on one of his own poems, describes how 'the dark night with its aridities and voids is the means to the knowledge of God and self', a process of sensory and spiritual deprivation that God himself inaugurates in order to purify the individual.[2] The imagery of the desert and of aridity that St John frequently draws on figures this situation whereby 'the soul departs from all created things, in its affection and operation' (compare the *Sweeney* epigraph, *CP* 115), and in this 'quenching' of earthly satisfactions begins that process of 'emptying' the soul 'which is the requirement for [God's] divine inflow' (1. 11. 4, 1. 12. 4). But St John insists that the dark night divests the soul of its former 'spiritual delights and gratifications' also (1. 12. 6), delights that often induce in the soul feelings of spiritual pride, or frustration and anger that such gratification is short-lived. To truly progress towards the divine, the soul must go beyond any sense of 'satisfaction derived from one's spiritual exercises' to arrive at a conception of its own complete 'wretchedness' and lack of worth:

> it considers itself to be nothing and finds no satisfaction in self because it is aware that of itself it neither does nor can do anything.
>
> God esteems this lack of self-satisfaction and the dejection individuals have about not serving Him more than all former deeds and gratifications, however notable these may have been. (1.12. 2)

This descent into the dryness of the dark night, renouncing both the world and the previous motions of the spirit, is staged in part I of 'Ash-Wednesday'; part II will trace the beginnings of the next stage, whereby 'the longings for God become so intense that it will seem to individuals that their bones are drying up in this thirst' (1. 11. 1).

This 'dark night and its terrible traits' in St John's words (2. 10. 10) is a formidably arduous and painful process, whatever final delights it leads to, described at one point in the analogy of a log of wood being consumed by fire (2. 10. 1–8), and the later parts of 'Ash-Wednesday' continue to be staged within it. Thus part II of the poem maintains the theme of self-abasement (indeed, here self-dismantling) and the need for intercessory prayer. The sins that Dante meets in the form of three beasts in the opening canto of the *Inferno* are here the 'three white leopards' that have dismembered the protagonist: the recognition of a self utterly destroyed by sin and symbolically reduced to a heap of bones becomes a paradoxical source of rejoicing, in a scheme that sees any suggestion of worth in the individual as an obstacle to communion with the divine:

the bones sang, scattered and shining
We are glad to be scattered, we did little good to each other.

The penultimate line of 'Ash-Wednesday', 'Suffer me not to be sepa-
rated', plays with the contrast between the appalling separation
from God and this needful undoing of the self, as in the rite of self-
scattering described in part II. The lines from the 'Hail Mary' quoted
above are followed in part II with an extended address to the Virgin
herself, ending in the lines 'Grace to the Mother / For the Garden /
Where all love ends'. The protagonist cannot enter the paradisal
garden – he must remain, so to speak, in the Lenten wilderness – but
the acknowledgement of it as the 'end' of the journey occasions the
rejoicing at the conclusion of part II, so that even the desert becomes
more hospitable, with its 'blessing of sand' – the desert is thus where
the garden is found, if not literally. There is, of course, a further
intercessory figure in part II, the mysterious 'Lady' it is addressed to,
the Lady robed in a white gown who 'honours the Virgin in meditation' and whom we return to below.
    Once the poem has probed the depths of the self, and established
the self's nullity, it can begin the ascent, staged, as discussed previously, in part III. This ascent to a vision of a 'higher' reality – which
will be portrayed in part IV – is shadowed by the ongoing struggle
with sin, which as stated can never be left behind. The final lines of
this part again stress that any access to the divine relies upon God's
grace rather than the individual's value or volition: 'Lord, I am not
worthy / but speak the word only'. These lines are a direct quotation
from Matthew 8. 8, and feature in the priest's office during the rite of
communion, and remind us that though Eliot has made extensive
use of the pronoun 'I' throughout 'Ash-Wednesday' the poem is to be
distinguished from any 'Romantic' tradition of self-expression and
related rather to those experiences that have some 'impersonal value',
such as Dante records (*SE* 273). Even the opening line, 'Because I do
not hope to turn again', is a translation of the first line of a poem by
Guido Cavalcanti, one of Dante's contemporaries (see Southam,
Student's Guide, p. 223), though Eliot has invested the theme of political exile in the Italian poem with the more far-reaching (in his eyes)
longing for a spiritual return. In this sense the protagonist of the
poem is an Everyman figure, and the context within which he works
comprises fundamental Christian themes of the Fall, Redemption and
ministering of the Church. In part IV of the poem the first-person

pronoun does not in fact feature at all; here we arrive at a garden, which replicates the Edenic garden Dante situates at the top of Mount Purgatory, where the figure of Beatrice is restored to him. In Eliot's garden we meet a 'silent sister veiled in white and blue', and also witness a rite of restoration akin to Dante's:

> Here are the years that walk between, bearing
> Away the fiddles and the flutes, restoring
> One who moves in the time between sleep and waking, wearing
>
> White light folded, sheathed about her, folded.

As the years move by in ceremonial procession, taking with them the transient pleasures of life (the 'flute' of the previous part recurs here), this original contact with some numinous figure, since lost, is re-established. I take it that this figure is the same Lady, 'in a white gown', featured in part II, only now restored to her original, Edenic splendour, as Dante's Beatrice was when Dante met her after her death in the earthly paradise. In Dante's poem, the protagonist moves from the earthly paradise to Paradise proper in Beatrice's company, but Eliot's offers only a glimpse of this transcendent realm: part IV ends with 'our exile' back into the temporal world where the rest of the poem, in parts V and VI, is played out.

Again, first-person experience is not paramount in part V; the repeated line 'O my people, what have I done unto thee' is taken from the Good Friday Reproaches in which, in the Roman Catholic Mass, Christ speaks from the cross, a Christ who, though denied and 'unheard', is still in Eliot's view at the centre of our modern life and culture:

> And the light shone in darkness and
> Against the Word the unstilled world still whirled
> About the centre of the silent Word.

In this section Eliot returns to examine the limbo-land of a civilization that seems unable either to fully accept or reject Christianity, characterized as 'children at the gate / Who will not go away and cannot pray', and who later both 'affirm' and 'deny'. The denial significantly takes place

> In the last desert between the last blue rocks

> The desert in the garden the garden in the desert
> Of drouth, spitting from the mouth the withered apple-seed.

Here the spiritual self-scrutiny signified by the Lenten withdrawal to the desert, a locus interchangeable with the 'garden' if put to fruitful use, is rejected as too much of an ordeal for those who 'are terrified and cannot surrender' (and perhaps this is hardly surprising given the self-recognition it involves, as traced in parts I and II). The rejection of the idea of original sin is signified by the spitting out of the apple-seed, which though withered is the only source of nutriment and pro-creation in the desert. Part V also asks, in keeping with one of Eliot's major concerns in the 1930s, what the role of the Church is in this culture of acceptance/rejection, with regard more specifically to the office of prayer performed by this 'veiled sister between the slender/Yew trees' who reappears from part IV now in her earthly mission.

The final section returns to the mode of self-examination, the 'Although I do not hope to turn again' of the opening line being followed by two sections presenting the ever-present 'tension' between spiritual and natural desires, the latter represented by the sea with its sails, smells and seabirds (their wings still 'Unbroken' in contrast to the disused wings of part I), as well as by lilac, golden-rod and so forth, stimuli whereby 'the weak spirit quickens to rebel'. Eliot will again use the sea in 'The Dry Salvages' to represent a series of forces antagonistic to Christian desire and belief. 'Though I do not wish to wish these things', and 'Although I do not hope to turn' back to them, their potency in this 'time of tension between dying and birth' (that is, dying to the world and being born into the spirit) is never eradicated, and the power to resist them comes in the final lines through prayer for the support of the 'Blessèd sister' and 'holy mother', the Church and the Virgin Mary. At the conclusion of the poem we are emphatically back in the Lenten wilderness, 'among these rocks' of the desert, a scene of 'terrifying' exposure and isolation, as at the end of part V, and although the final line forms a rhythmically satisfying conclusion to the poem the tone remains one of imploring a salvation that cannot be guaranteed:

> Suffer me not to be separated
>
> And let my cry come unto Thee.

The fact that the penultimate line is addressed to the 'spirit of the river, spirit of the sea', as well as to the divine powers, suggests that 'separation' between incompatible but equally real affiliations is an unstilled danger.

In the Dante essay of 1929 Eliot spoke about Dante's poetry being 'in one sense, extremely easy to read . . . The thought may be obscure, but the word is lucid, or rather translucent' (*SE* 238–9). The 'austerity' it shows 'in the use of metaphor, simile, verbal beauty, and elegance' (*SE* 252) helps toward a 'universality' and a translatability into other languages (*SE* 238, 241) which Shakespeare, for example, with his richer and more 'opaque' language, has not. Moreover, Dante's use of allegory and exploitation of a '*visual* imagination' (Eliot's emphasis) – 'Speech varies, but our eyes are all the same' (*SE* 243) – also contributes to this greater accessibility. Whether the simplified diction of 'Ash-Wednesday' (compared say to *The Waste Land*) or its 'allegorical moments' (the beginning of part II, the procession of the years in part IV, which is an instance of the 'higher dream' and clearly indebted to what Eliot calls the 'high dream' of the pageant of Beatrice, 'Dante', *SE* 262) make this poem more accessible than some of his earlier poetry is debateable. We may be dealing, as again he says of Dante, with 'a *poetic* as distinguished from an *intellectual* lucidity' (Eliot's emphasis), but the admission remains that 'the thought may be obscure' (*SE* 239). What is perfectly apparent, however, is the fact that 'Ash-Wednesday' is veritably saturated in Dante. The paralleling of a movement from Hell up through Purgatory in the first four parts of the poem makes use, as we have seen, of a Beatrice-type intercessor, the 'Lady' introduced at the beginning of part II, and this section originally bore the Dantesque title 'Salutation' when first published separately in 1927.[3] The obvious reference here is to part III of the *Vita nuova*, where Dante records the 'dolcissimo salutare' ('sweet greeting') he received from Beatrice.[4] But it raises the issue of who, or what, *is* Eliot's Beatrice, just as the debate is still active about whether the young girl (at the beginning of her ninth year) Dante describes meeting in the *Vita nuova* was someone who really existed or was an allegory (as she later becomes in the *Purgatorio*) of Theology or the institution of the Church. In Eliot's case, these two options are supplemented by a third, that she is an element simply borrowed from Dante to make the Dantesque correspondences more complete, and has no autobiographical significance. Intriguingly, Eliot originally dedicated 'Ash-Wednesday' 'To my Wife', though the troubled and disintegrating relationship with Vivienne Eliot presumably led to the fact that the dedication does not survive into later reprintings. It is possible of course that a sense of guilt relating to Vivienne (the 'Lady' is introduced in 'Ash-Wednesday' in close proximity to the white leopards who have devoured the protagonist's body, in the tableau of the confession of sin discussed above) means that she might still function as a means to salvation. Someone who prompted essentially a consciousness of personal sin would be a rather different type of Beatrice than the one in Dante who dispenses a heavenly radiance – the way up would really be the way down here – but this would tie in with Eliot's unusual emphasis in the *Dante* essay on Dante's child-hood meeting with Beatrice constituting a 'type of sexual experience' (*SE* 273). In the reunion in Purgatory, moreover, Eliot argues that these feelings are still troubling Dante, that they 'persist beyond the grave' and must be 'explained and made reasonable by the higher love' (*SE* 263, 274), which again suggests a 'Lady' whose spiritual efficacy resides in the sense of sin she evokes. In one of the French poems of *Poems* (1920), 'Dans le Restaurant', a 'lecherous' old waiter ('vieux lubrique') confesses to an erotic experience in boyhood with a girl less than seven years old, the protagonist being scandalized by the recognition of an experience and emotion he shares with this unsavoury figure, and it is possible that Eliot's response to Vivienne reactivated such an emotion.[5] 'Som de l'escalina', the original title of part III of 'Ash-Wednesday', is a phrase taken from words spoken to the Dante pilgrim by Arnaut Daniel, whose designation 'miglior fabbro' ('better craftsman', *Purgatorio* 26. 117) was used in Eliot's dedi-cation of *The Waste Land* to Ezra Pound, and is a tribute bestowed on Arnaut in the *Purgatorio* by another poet, Guido Guinizelli. This spectacle of poets purging the sin of lust in the flames of Dante's topmost terrace held a special resonance for Eliot; he had already used the final line of Dante's canto (26. 148) as one of the talismanic 'fragments' at the end of *The Waste Land,* '*Poi s'ascose nel foco che gli affina*' ('Then he hid himself in the fire that refines them'). And he would make a final reference to the need for that 'refining fire' in the famous encounter scene between two poets in 'Little Gidding'.

AN EXPANSION OF INTERESTS

'Ash-Wednesday' is very much a poem of withdrawal from the world, of a deep spiritual introspection, and clearly harbours private experiences and a sense of self-reckoning that can only remain a matter of speculation, however much it casts its protagonist as a representative figure and wishes to separate itself from the genre of personal 'confession'. In the late 1920s and 30s, however, Eliot's writing conspicuously enters areas of public debate, and Eliot himself becomes much more of a public figure, repeatedly pronouncing on issues like government (both ecclesiastical and secular), education and the nation's cultural health (or impoverishment).[6] When *The Sacred Wood* appeared in a new edition in 1928, Eliot added a Preface in which he explained how his concerns had altered in the years following the writing of the essays between 1917 and 1920: 'what had happened in my own mind, in eight years, was not so much a change or reversal of opinions, as an expansion or development of interests' (*SW* vii). Looking back on his first critical book, he notes its insistence on proclaiming what he calls 'the integrity of poetry'; that is, the need to 'consider it primarily as poetry and not another thing', and he continues to stress in the Preface how 'poetry is not the inculcation of morals, or the direction of politics; and no more is it religion or an equivalent of religion' (*SW* viii–ix). Certainly we have seen Eliot repeatedly declare that poetry, while 'making use of' various ideas, or philosophical positions, is not to be read as endorsing such positions, nor even displaying the author's 'belief' in them; systems of ethics, philosophy and so forth are at the service of poetry (and may be, as it were, the gel that holds the poem together) rather than the other way around. Eliot also notes, however, that his 'development of interests' has now led to a concern with 'the relation of poetry to the spiritual and social life of its time and of other times', and that, in fact, poetry 'certainly has something to do with morals, and with religion, and even with politics perhaps, though we cannot say what' (*SW* viii, x). The nearest he gets to expressing what this 'what' might involve, at the end of the Preface, is to declare his preference for 'the poetry of Dante to that of Shakespeare . . . because it seems to me to illustrate a saner attitude towards the mystery of life' (*SW* x).

These were difficult issues, however, and Eliot never achieved certitude on this matter, that is, on how the 'integrity of poetry' can be preserved while acknowledging that the writer's and the reader's own 'beliefs' must be of some significance in its production and reception. The 'expansion or development' of Eliot's interests announced at the outset of the second edition of *The Sacred Wood* is shown by the fact

that *For Lancelot Andrewes* of the same year contains essays on political theorists and theologians, like Machiavelli and John Bramhall,
whereas the earlier volume confined its attention to 'poetry and criticism', to quote from its subtitle. By 1931 Eliot is producing works
like 'Thoughts after Lambeth', a substantial report on the 1930
Lambeth Conference of the Church of England (*SE* 363–87). Indeed
by now, for Eliot, poetry clearly 'has something to do with morals,
and with religion, and even with politics perhaps', though the difficulties of saying what this is are illustrated in the Dante essay of 1929,
notably in the extended footnote to section 2 of the essay, where Eliot
admits that what he calls his 'theory of poetic belief' is 'still embry-
onic'. He now goes back on earlier positions in accepting that 'we are
forced to believe' that poets do not solely 'make use of' ideas in their
work but, in the case of Dante and Lucretius, for example, actively
believe the ideas their work promotes, and 'mean what they say'. But
he continues to insist that there is no call upon the reader to believe
such ideas, maintaining that 'full poetic appreciation is possible without belief in what the poet believed' (*SE* 269). A few paragraphs later
he flatly, if somewhat off-handedly, contradicts this: 'Actually, one
probably has more pleasure in the poetry when one shares the beliefs
of the poet' (*SE* 271), while earlier in the essay, in the comparison
between Dante and Shakespeare that is a conspicuous feature of it,
he argues for a poetic 'equality' between them that does not imply
Dante should be awarded the preference because of a 'saner attitude'
towards life, as the Preface to *The Sacred Wood* had maintained (*SE* 252).

The contorted state of the argument is a little smoothed out with
the publication of *The Use of Poetry and the Use of Criticism* in 1933,
a series of lectures Eliot had recently delivered at Harvard, where the
refocusing of his attention on poetry and criticism signals a desire to
maintain the integrity, and even limitation, of literary discourse.
Poetry may have something to 'do with' religion, but Eliot emphatically rejects Matthew Arnold's belief that it can 'supersede' or act as
a 'substitute' for it in the modern world, just as he attacks I. A. Richards's doctrine that 'poetry is capable of saving us' (*UP* 113, 130);
'the current tendency', Eliot adds, 'is to expect too much, rather than
too little, of poetry' (*UP* 148–9). The proposition that poetry 'is
capable of saving us' comes at the end of Richards's *Science and
Poetry*, but only, Richards adds, if man is able to 'loosen in time the
entanglement with belief which now takes from poetry half its power'
(pp. 82–3). Richards salutes *The Waste Land*, as we have seen, for

ridding itself of this entanglement; for him, science is the right means to deal with belief, whereas poetry's ability to contribute to the emotional and sensitive enrichment of humanity will be enhanced if irrelevant issues of belief don't get in the way, hence his enthusiasm for what he held *The Waste Land* had achieved. Eliot discusses Richards's position of using poetry as a 'ritual for heightening sincerity' in *The Use of Poetry* (pp. 131–5), but it is clear he rejects his quest to 'preserve emotions without the beliefs with which their history has been involved' (*UP* 135). In his review of *Science and Poetry,* Eliot had already questioned the idea that poetry 'is capable of saving us': 'it is like saying that the wall-paper will save us when the walls have crumbled. It is a revised version of [Arnold's] Literature and Dogma.'[7]

In quoting from Jacques Maritain, Eliot upholds a hierarchy in which poetry occupies a humbler place: 'by showing us where moral truth and the genuine supernatural are situate, religion saves poetry from the absurdity of believing itself destined to transform ethics and life: saves it from overweening arrogance' (*UP* 137).[8] In wishing to keep poetry and religion separate, Eliot gives a rather one-sided summary of his previous views: 'I have maintained elsewhere, and still maintain, that it is not essential to share Dante's beliefs [nor those of Lucretius] in order to enjoy his poetry' (*UP* 95). But this is not the end of the matter, given that a poet's beliefs cannot simply be ignored when, as with Shelley, those beliefs strike one as absurd or unjustifiable. Eliot finally formulates his position thus:

> when the doctrine, theory, belief, or 'view of life' presented in a poem is one which the mind of the reader can accept as coherent, mature, and founded on the facts of experience, it interposes no obstacle to the reader's enjoyment, whether it be one that he accept or deny, approve or deprecate. (*UP* 96)

We cannot get 'some illusory *pure* enjoyment' by 'separating poetry from everything else in the world' (*UP* 98), but active disbelief on the reader's part need by no 'obstacle' to enjoyment.

This readerly liberality seems however put to the test the following year when Eliot published *After Strange Gods*, subtitled *A Primer of Modern Heresy*, also a series of lectures given this time at the University of Virginia. Here Eliot's Preface declares that he was not lecturing as a literary critic but 'ascended the platform of these lectures only in the role of moralist' (*ASG* 12). Although with a writer like Milton 'we can certainly enjoy the poetry and yet be fully aware of the intellectual and moral aberrations of the author' (*ASG* 33), the whole prospect of modern literature seems to fill Eliot with dismay, and its 'intellectual and moral aberrations' are impossible to disregard. This is because we live in a society 'worm-eaten with Liberalism' (*ASG* 13), where 'extreme individualism in views' is a besetting vice: it is 'disastrous' that the modern writer should 'deliberately give rein to his "individuality"' and that his readers should 'cherish' him for so doing (*ASG* 32–3). This position of course had long informed Eliot's outlook, as 'Tradition and the Individual Talent' shows; what is different in *After Strange Gods* is the offence, as a 'moralist', Eliot takes from a vast range of modern writers, from the 'narrow post-Protestant prejudice' of Ezra Pound (*ASG* 41) to Yeats's work ('not a world of real Good and Evil', *ASG* 46), George Eliot ('we must . . . deplore her individualistic morals', *ASG* 54), Hardy (the acme of 'self-expression', *ASG* 54), and Lawrence ('the man's vision is spiritual, but spiritually sick', *ASG* 60). Here Eliot is, as a reader, the possessor of a set of beliefs which not only lead him to 'deprecate' the positions of others but which certainly impair his enjoyment: with the 'disappearance of the idea of Original Sin, with the disappearance of the idea of intense moral struggle, the human beings presented to us both in poetry and in prose fiction today . . . tend to become less and less real' (*ASG* 42). Eliot's feeling that the 'moralist' had impinged excessively on the proper function of the reader was one reason, I think, why he never allowed *After Strange Gods* to be reprinted, confessing later to a state of personal unhappiness when writing the book that 'distorted his judgement' (Spender, *Eliot*, p. 131).[9] By contrast, in the Preface to the 1964 edition of *The Use of Poetry and the Use of Criticism*, which treats the relation between readerly belief and enjoyment more cautiously, Eliot is 'still prepared' to accept the work 'as a statement of my critical position' (*UP* 10). Even so, the 'position' of *After Strange Gods* has a lot in common with a play like *The Family Reunion*, as we shall see, and other essays of the time, while less trenchant and acerbic, still insist that it is 'necessary for Christian readers to scrutinize their reading, especially of works of imagination, with explicit ethical and theological standards. The "greatness" of literature cannot be determined solely by literary standards' ('Religion and Literature' (1935), *SE* 388).

ELIOT'S DRAMA

Eliot's greater public role is also signalled by his ambitions to write for the theatre in the 1930s, and indeed by producing dramatic work for fund-raising activities, as with *The Rock* of 1934, which is, to quote its full sub-title, *A Pageant Play Written for Performance at Sadler's Wells Theatre 28 May–9 June 1934 on Behalf of the Forty-Five Churches Fund of the Diocese of London*. *The Rock* takes its title from Christ's words to St Peter, 'upon this rock I will build my church' (Mt. 16.18), and dramatizes and affirms the church-building enterprise (and raises funds for it) at a time when the need for churches seems in decline in an increasingly secular age. 'We have too many churches, / And too few chop-houses,' the Chorus reports people as saying, and notes 'the Church does not seem to be wanted / In country or in suburb; and in the town / Only for important weddings' (*CP* 147–8). Only the Choruses from *The Rock* are collected in Eliot's *Complete Poems and Plays*, the dialogue between the builders and other parts of the original text being the work of several hands.[10] These Choruses (as well as some of the omitted material) are an important supplement to Eliot's later work, anticipating several of the positions in *Four Quartets* – see, for example, the meditation on God's creation of time in Chorus VII (*CP* 160–1). They also contain some withering satire on the prevailing culture of religious neglect: 'the wind shall say: "Here were decent godless people: / Their only monument the asphalt road / And a thousand lost golf balls"' (*CP* 155), as well as the indictment, already familiar in Eliot, of our living in a morally tepid age: 'Our age is an age of moderate virtue / And of moderate vice' (*CP* 163).

After Strange Gods had suggested that this climate of moderation was in effect the result of diabolic strategy, developing the theme from the Baudelaire essay that 'it is better, in a paradoxical way, to do evil than to do nothing: at least, we exist' (above, p. 65). Similarly, blasphemy, which in former times 'might once have been a sign of spiritual corruption', might now be seen 'rather as a symptom that the soul is still alive, or even that it is recovering animation: for the perception of Good and Evil – whatever choice we may make – is the first requisite of spiritual life'. And blasphemy's power to endanger others spiritually would now be seen as an indication of the spiritual life of these others too, given that 'the modern environment is so unfavourable to faith that it produces fewer and fewer individuals capable of being injured by blasphemy.' Eliot therefore sees what he calls the 'Forces of Evil' or the 'Evil Spirit' instigating not to blasphemy or evil in the modern world, but to what he has consistently regarded as more alarming, that is a spiritual listlessness or apathy. He is 'not defending blasphemy; I am reproaching a world in which blasphemy is impossible' (*ASG* 52–3). It is along these lines that he later argues in *The Idea of a Christian Society* that 'in the modern world, it may turn out that the most intolerable thing for Christians is to be tolerated'; at least a persecuting society is taking Christian belief seriously as a threat, whereas a modern liberal democracy conspires in the idea that 'belief' is a matter of public and even private indifference (*ICS* 23). As Chorus VII from *The Rock* puts is, 'it seems that something has happened that has never happened before: though we know not just when, or why, or how, or where. / Men have left GOD not for other gods, they say, but for no god; and this has never happened before' (*CP* 161).

It is within the context of this prevailing spiritual tepidness that we should understand Eliot's aims in his first and, some would say, finest drama, *Murder in the Cathedral*, which was written for the Canterbury Festival of 1935 and staged in the cathedral Chapter House, before transferring to London's Mercury Theatre and afterwards elsewhere. Although the play is concerned with a specific event, the martyrdom of Thomas Becket in 1170, and although Eliot himself recognized that 'the essential action of the play . . . was somewhat limited. A man comes home, foreseeing that he will be killed, and he is killed' (*OP* 80), the play raises issues that are central to Eliot's later work and it also intervenes in the highly charged political debates of the 1930s. As he further noted in the discussion of his plays in the 1951 essay 'Poetry and Drama', 'I wanted to bring home to the audience the contemporary relevance of the situation' (*OP* 80). The play's very title, not in fact Eliot's own, evokes the contemporary crime novel (compare Agatha Christie's *The Murder at the Vicarage* of 1930), an evocation further realized when the Knights in part II suddenly 'step into' modern time, with one of them putting the question *Who killed the Archbishop?* to the audience (*CP* 279), in the manner of the detective in the crime novel's customary post-murder explication.[11]

Eliot also noted the polemical aspect of the play, how he wanted 'to shock the audience out of their complacency' (*OP* 81). Here in Canterbury, right at the centre of the English Church establishment, we have a play that seems to question the very nature of an established Church, which in matters of appointment, revenue and ultimate governance, is answerable to Parliament, with the monarch as its Head. Thus in the words of the second knight as he addresses the audience in 'defence' of Thomas's murder:

> if you have now arrived at a just subordination of the pretensions of the Church to the welfare of the State, remember that it is we who took the first step. We have been instrumental in bringing about the state of affairs that you approve. We have served your interests; we merit your applause; and if there is any guilt whatever in the matter, you must share it with us. (*CP* 278–9)

The play naturally loses some of this topical and controversial edge in being transferred from the Canterbury Festival setting of 1935 into the theatre at large, or in its modern revivals, given that Eliot was highly conscious of the original audience of 'regular churchgoers' with whom he wanted to communicate (*OP* 81).[12] And he wanted to raise some problematic issues with them, including the claim made by the knight that participation and acquiescence in a modern Church which is moderate, liberal and established is tantamount to supporting, consciously or not, Becket's assassins. In losing its original occasion the play also loses some of its satirical bite and humour, given Eliot's tempting and teasing of a specifically English (or Anglican) audience: as the first knight reiterates, 'you are Englishmen, and therefore you believe in fair play . . . You are Englishmen, and therefore will not judge anybody without hearing both sides of the case' (*CP* 276). The question therefore of how successfully the play can transfer from its original Chapter House setting to the theatre proper is not only raised by the fact that it was first staged a mere fifty yards or so from the spot in the cathedral transept where the actual killing of Becket took place, but must also be asked at the level of the intended audience too. Indeed, the inclusion of a sermon in the play points up the fact that the 'audience' themselves have a multiple role as congregation and also as jury.

Eliot enlarges on the nature of the specific audience he wished to 'shock' in 'Poetry and Drama':

> my play was to be produced for a rather special kind of audience – an audience of those serious people who go to 'festivals' and expect to have to put up with poetry – though perhaps on this

occasion some of them were not quite prepared for what they got . . . it was a religious play, and people who go deliberately to a religious play at a religious festival expect to be patiently bored and to satisfy themselves with the feeling that they have done something meritorious. (*OP* 79)

We can understand why, in 1935, Eliot insisted on writing this commissioned play on the Becket theme, even though the festival organizers were 'somewhat dismayed' with the prospect of yet another play on this theme after the staging of Tennyson's play *Becket* in 1932 and 1933 and Laurence Binyon's *The Young King* in 1934, which centred on Henry II (though dealing with his relationship with his eldest son, not with Becket).[13] Clearly, if the organizers wanted a change from the twelfth century, Eliot wanted to increase the shock-value of his play by addressing an audience who had got used to the picturesque-romance treatment of medieval history and were therefore settled into a state of 'complacency'. In 'Poetry and Drama' he notes how, in choosing his theme, he 'did not want to write a chronicle of twelfth-century politics, nor . . . tamper unscrupulously with the meagre records as Tennyson did (in introducing Fair Rosamund, and in suggesting that Becket had been crossed in love in early youth)'; quite bluntly, instead, 'I wanted to concentrate on death and martyrdom' (*OP* 80–1).

This uncompromising stance reflects Becket's own within the play, his refusal of any accommodation between his Christian belief and State concerns:

> I give my life
> To the Law of God above the Law of Man. (*CP* 274)

This determination is offered to an audience of churchgoers who now live in the different dispensation of Church subordination to the State, thus raising questions about the continuing validity of Thomas's martyrdom. These questions are given tremendously added point not only by the setting in Canterbury – the headquarters, so to speak, of Anglicanism – but by the fact that the splendour and prestige of the cathedral itself is heavily indebted to the martyrdom, and the tradition of pilgrimage that arose from it. If Thomas Becket could not get a sympathetic audience in Canterbury Cathedral, he was unlikely to get one anywhere, and yet the Thomas of Eliot's play

is by no means counting on such an audience, as he announces
directly at the end of part I:

> I know
> What yet remains to show you of my history
> Will seem to most of you at best futility,
> Senseless self-slaughter of a lunatic,
> Arrogant passion of a fanatic. (*CP* 258)

And this, of course, is what the fourth knight in part II (who in his
doubling as the fourth tempter in part I has already shown his insight
into Thomas's mind) can play upon in taking Thomas's own judgement here to parodic excess, answering thus his own question '*Who
killed the Archbishop?*': 'I think, with these facts before you, you will
unhesitatingly render a verdict of Suicide while of Unsound Mind'
(*CP* 279).

In raising that prospect of a gulf between Thomas and his audience, and suggesting that even Christian believers may well find
Thomas's behaviour extreme and alien, or only comprehensible in
terms of modern secular explanations, we might ask what state it was
Eliot wanted to shock his audience into, after shocking them out of
their 'complacency'. I don't think Eliot is offering Thomas as a kind
of 'model' of Christian behaviour, or promoting an Anglican spiritual renewal where dying for one's beliefs becomes standard practice;
in any case, as the play insists, 'a martyrdom is always the design of
God . . . It is never the design of man' (*CP* 261). Nor on an institutional level is Eliot calling for the disestablishment of the Church of
England; this is a 'difficult question' on which he has 'not made up
my own mind' ('Thoughts after Lambeth', *SE* 381–2), though later
he did come to a firm conclusion. Thus by the time of *The Idea of a
Christian Society* (1939), Eliot argues that an Established Church is
desirable (*ICS* 48–9), and that 'the national faith must have an offi-
cial recognition by the State' (*ICS* 50–1). The danger of the Church
becoming a mere organ of the State and subordinate in all things to
it (Erastianism) is however very real to him (*ICS* 51) – the Church
should have 'final authority within the nation' in matters of 'dogma . . .
faith and morals'; at times 'it can and should be in conflict with the
State' (*ICS* 47), a position dramatized in *Murder in the Cathedral*.
However, an Established Church clearly unites Eliot's declared positions as 'royalist in politics, and anglo-catholic in religion' (*FLA* 7).

But what really questions any reconciliation between what Thomas calls the 'Law of God' and the 'Law of Man' is ultimately Eliot's fundamental sense of opposition between the eternal and temporal realms, between the 'reality' of the former and the essential unreality of time and history. Any programme of Church reform, or governance, or membership will be limited in its results by the inherent defectiveness of the temporal dimension, as announced in *The Idea of a Christian Society*:

> it is very easy for speculation on a possible Christian order in the future to tend to come to rest in a kind of apocalyptic vision of a golden age of virtue. But we have to remember that the Kingdom of Christ on earth will never be realised, and also that it is always being realised; we must remember that whatever reform or revolution we carry out, the result will always be a sordid travesty of what human society should be – though the world is never left wholly without glory. (*ICS* 59)

We might contrast the impossibility of finally realizing the true 'Kingdom' here on earth (*For Thine is the Kingdom*, 'The Hollow Men') with the utopianism of King Henry in Eliot's play, who, according to the second knight,

> intended that Becket . . . should unite the offices of Chancellor and Archbishop. Had Becket concurred with the King's wishes, we should have had an almost ideal State: a union of spiritual and temporal administration, under the central government.

But the knight adds, in sheer puzzlement, that this vision foundered on Becket's affirmation 'that – God knows why – the two orders were incompatible' (*CP* 278). The relation between Becket and the audience is rather like that between the 'saint' and 'most of us' at the end of 'The Dry Salvages', and the audience is called on, not to aspire themselves to such exceptional spirituality, but to 'bear witness' to it. This is the role of the Chorus within the play, who 'acknowledge ourselves as type of the common man' (*CP* 282), and the opening verse paragraph of whose first speech ends with the words 'We are forced to bear witness' (*CP* 239). They do not want to do this, of course, and would prefer like all Eliot's 'hollow men' to continue leading a quiet, insignificant and evasive life, feeding that life 'with dried tubers' in the state of hibernation that opens *The Waste Land*: 'O Thomas, return, Archbishop; return, return to France. / Return. Quickly. Quietly. Leave us to perish in quiet' (*CP* 243). But Thomas's return to England and his death force them to acknowledge spiritual realities, and the 'eternal design' that at any moment may 'appear' in the world (*CP* 265); this is, as Thomas tells them, 'your share of the eternal burden, / The perpetual glory' (*CP* 271). Even if at the end of the play they are still confessing that they 'fear the injustice of men less than the justice of God', they finally embrace their participation in the event they have witnessed: 'Therefore, O God, we thank Thee / Who hast given such blessing to Canterbury' (*CP* 282)

The sense of the world of humans being governed by a divine 'pattern' is evoked by much of the imagery in the play – the turning wheel, the seasonal cycle – as by the symmetry of the four tempters appearing in part I and the four knights in part II; here, the structural pattern of the artwork itself is a representation of the divine order, an idea developed in *Four Quartets*. E. Martin Browne argues that when the four tempters and four knights are played by the same actors, this symmetry emphasizes the parallel between the temptation of Becket in part I and the 'temptation of the audience' in part II held out by the knights' apology. Eliot himself, however, came to have doubts about this, as he noted in a letter to Browne: 'one question which is left for [the audience] if the knights and tempters are different actors, is whether the fourth tempter is an evil angel or possibly a good angel' (Browne, *The Making of T. S. Eliot's Plays*, pp. 57–8).

The urging of the acknowledgement rather than the evasion of the divine 'design', the renewal of commitment to something beyond the secular, is in a sense the 'message' of *Murder in the Cathedral*. Eliot was very conscious of the rise of what he saw as the new 'State-religions' in the 1930s, fascism, communism, and if the Church was to compete with such systems it could only do so not by diluting or compromising its teaching and dogma but by reaffirming its key doctrines of sin and atonement, its rejection, as in the more private discourse of 'Ash-Wednesday', of the promises and allure of 'the world', and its insistence on being founded in the blood-sacrifice of Christ and his martyrs. This fundamentalism risks being imperilled by the forces of modernisation and liberalism within the Church; in 'Thoughts After Lambeth', Eliot had rejected the idea of 'a religion that is watered down or robbed of the severity of its demands', and warned that 'there is no good in making Christianity easy and pleasant' (*SE* 372–3).[14] One of the key terms in the play, as in *Four Quartets*, is the verb/participle 'wait'/ 'waiting', as in the opening Chorus, indeed the opening line: 'Here let us wait / . . . What shall we do in the heat of summer / But wait in barren orchards for another October?' The same Chorus ends with the lines 'For us, the poor, there is no action, / But only to wait and to witness' (*CP* 239–40). But waiting can be the hardest kind of activity, as Thomas himself declares in relation to his coming death ('Heavier the interval than the consummation' (*CP* 246)), especially if 'consummation' is the eventual outcome: 'We wait, we wait, / And the saints and martyrs wait, for those who shall be martyrs and saints' (*CP* 240). As opposed to secularism and the State-religions that offer their consummation in the here and now, there is a strong sense in *Murder in the Cathedral* of the life of the Christian being that of an agonized passivity, a displacement of eternal longings through the unsatisfactory medium of time, a note evident in Eliot's earlier work and in *Four Quartets*, with its series of variations on the related themes of stillness and motion. 'All my life / I have waited', says Thomas (*CP* 271).

As well as the emphasis on 'waiting', two other terms have a particular prominence in the play. The first is 'Peace', the first word Thomas himself speaks in the play (*CP* 245), and one explored in his sermon where its Christian significance is analysed rather than its secular meaning – 'So then, He gave to His disciples peace, but not peace as the world gives' (*CP* 261). The incompatibility of the two 'orders' of Christianity and politics is again manifest here. The other key term is 'blood', which summarizes the play's insistence on the uncompromising first principles of religion:

> This is the sign of the Church always,
> The sign of blood. Blood for blood.
> His blood given to buy my life,
> My blood given to pay for His death,
> My death for His death. (*CP* 274–5)

While these lines evoke the central Christian rite of the eucharist, and although *Murder in the Cathedral* can be seen as the most specifically Christian of all Eliot's works (the absence of reference to other religions signalling not only its being set in the Christian Middle Ages but also its original occasion and audience, as discussed above), the emphasis on blood also carries a pagan charge in the play. The offering of blood is seen as a kind of libation, renewing the natural order: in the final Chorus, not only are we told that 'wherever a martyr has given his blood for the blood of Christ, / There is holy ground', but the Chorus, in the wake of the murder, also offers a hymn to the natural creation – 'We praise Thee, O God, for Thy glory displayed in all the creatures of the earth' (*CP* 281). Earlier, in their despair and mis-recognition of the import of Thomas's death, the Chorus voice that extraordinary passage on the hideousness and corruption of the natural order, cataloguing all that is putrid, slimy, and scaly from the 'rat tails twining' to the 'horror of the ape' (*CP* 269–70). *Four Quartets* will powerfully revisit the relationship between natural and spiritual renewal.

Eliot's next play, *The Family Reunion* (1939), sums up many of his key concerns in the 1930s, and has a good deal in common not only with *Murder in the Cathedral* but also with the first of the *Four Quartets*, 'Burnt Norton', published in 1936. Once more, as in *Murder*, we have the contrast between a principal figure leading his life on an exceptional spiritual level and a baffled Chorus of an everyday understanding, who just begin to feel, by the end of the play, 'there is something I *could* understand' about the remarkable events they have witnessed (*CP* 345). There is the notable addition, however, of a comedic element in this play which is occasioned by this contrast. Harry, the main protagonist, complains about his aunts and uncles who form the Chorus that 'They don't understand what it is to be awake', continuing his complaint that others of the family, like his brother John, are permanently 'unconscious' (*CP* 324, 330). Another of his aunts, Agatha, reflects on being the agent of Harry's final awakening:

> Harry has crossed the frontier
> Beyond which safety and danger have a different meaning.
> And he cannot return. That is his privilege.
> For those who live in this world, this world only,
> Do you think that I would take the responsibility
> Of tempting them over the border? No one could,
> no one who knows. (*CP* 342)

The situation echoes Eliot's comment in *After Strange Gods* that

> most people are only very little alive; and to awaken them to the spiritual is a very great responsibility: it is only when they are so

awakened that they are capable of real Good, but that at the same
time they become first capable of Evil. (*ASG* 60)

In order to cross this 'frontier' into a world of reality and wakeful-
ness from one of shadow and sleep, Harry obtains from Agatha a
final piece of information that completes his spiritual understanding
of how the sins of the fathers are passed on to the children.

In *After Strange Gods* Eliot noted 'I doubt whether what I am
saying can convey very much to anyone for whom the doctrine of
Original Sin is not a very real and tremendous thing' (*ASG* 57), and
this doubt is also relevant to *The Family Reunion*. Harry, like
Sweeney before him, has felt and possibly succumbed to the temptation to 'do a girl in' (*CP* 124); in this case his wife, who has
drowned on an ocean voyage while in Harry's company. This action
(which Harry confesses to several times in the play) is now however
only the beginning of a process rather than a means of achieving a
kind of 'moral' superiority per se, the 'salvation from the ennui of
modern life' that Eliot had saluted in the earlier phase of his career.
Unlike in the 1917 'Eeldrop and Appleplex' and associated pieces
(above, p. 69), Eliot is now not so much interested in the individual
act of sin as a means of 'crossing the frontier', but in the broader
context of Original Sin as an ineluctable inheritance from generation to generation, an understanding of which is now the passport
to the world of 'reality'. Harry returns to the home of his childhood
hoping for a return to a world of innocence and happiness that
predates his unhappy marriage and its consequent events, only to
find that the Eumenides, the pursuing agents of justice Eliot rede-
ploys from the *Oresteia* of Aeschylus, are more present in that
home than ever: 'They are very close here. I had not expected that'
(*CP* 295). He discovers from Agatha that murdering his wife is a
playing out, one generation along, of his own father's desire to kill
his mother while she was pregnant with him, an 'origin of wretchedness' (*CP* 331), and that far from simply committing a sin in his
adulthood he was born into a state of sin in which 'the future was
long since settled' (*CP* 315). Thus the expiation that Harry learns
he has to undertake in the course of the play is not for his own
wrongdoings only, but for the accumulated weight of generations;
as Agatha tells him, 'It is possible / You are the consciousness of
your unhappy family, / Its bird sent flying through the purgatorial
flame' (*CP* 333). In the course of this expiation the 'curse' that

afflicts the family will be resolved, and 'The crooked be made straight' (*CP* 350).

The 'house' into which Harry is born has a wider significance than representing a single family, and the occasional associations of Harry with Christ as expiator (as in the promise of his second coming, *CP* 343) underline the universality of the situation presented in the play. There are also associations between Harry and Shakespeare's Hamlet, particularly in that sense of his tormented apartness from those around him being occasioned by 'deeper' levels of experience. Thus his interview with Mary in part I scene II, in the presence of ghosts seen by him but not by her, resembles Hamlet's encounter with Gertrude in her bedchamber in Act III of Shakspeare's play. The idea of existence as exclusion from the rose-garden, an exclusion imaged as 'walking / Away, down a concrete corridor / In a dead air' emphasizes the Fall and original sin themes of the play in a manner that evokes 'Burnt Norton', just as the further image of life as transiting 'the stone passages / Of an immense and empty hospital' anticipates 'East Coker' IV (*CP* 335). The hope of a return to the garden voiced by Harry is expanded upon by Agatha, who notes there is no return 'to the door through which we did not pass' but a 'long journey' of suffering and expiation that will lead there by a different route, in a remarkable anticipation of the overall trajectory of *Four Quartets* (*CP* 335–6). In this life, there is no state of innocence to go back to; *The Family Reunion*, set in a house called Wishwood, and in the season of Spring, presents glimpses of past happiness and present sunshine that initially tempt Harry with the possibility of 'a door that opens at the end of a corridor, / Sunlight and singing; when I had felt sure / That every corridor only led to another, / Or to a blank wall'; but it is precisely at this moment of intuition that the Eumenides reveal themselves barring the way (*CP* 310–1). Once more we might say for Eliot that 'April is the cruellest month' in the moral and spiritual demands, rather than easy returns, rebirth asks of us.

One such demand, in Harry's case, is the sacrifice of his closest familial ties, and it is difficult not to feel with *The Family Reunion*, the first of Eliot's plays with a contemporary setting, some autobiographical import: not in the desire to murder an importunate wife, but rather in Harry's abandoning of his mother, whose death is the final episode in the play, in order to pursue his vocation.[15] Eliot's own later reaction suggests some inhuman quality in what is being presented, as well perhaps as the workings of personal conscience:

my sympathies now have come to be all with the mother, who seems to me, except perhaps for the chauffeur, the only complete human being in the play; and my hero now strikes me as an insufferable prig. ('Poetry and Drama', *OP* 84)

By the 1950s, as we shall see in the Conclusion, Eliot was making a habit of apologizing.

CHAPTER 4

FOUR QUARTETS

*Perhaps [Matthew Arnold] cared too much for civilisation, forget-
ting that Heaven and Earth shall pass away, and Mr. Arnold with
them, and there is only one stay.*
— The Use of Poetry and the Use of Criticism, *p. 119*

'BURNT NORTON'

Murder in the Cathedral was staged in the same year as the first of the
Four Quartets, 'Burnt Norton', was written, 1935, and there is much
in common between the two works, including the duplicated statement 'Human kind cannot bear very much reality' (*CP* 271, 172).
'Burnt Norton' originally was to be a stand-alone poem, since it was
only in writing the second Quartet, 'East Coker' (published in 1940),
that Eliot 'began to see the *Quartets* as a set of four'.[1] Although all
four of the set have common themes and a closely interlinked relationship, there remains some sense of the separate character and
individual identity of 'Burnt Norton'; for one thing, it was not written during a time of war, as the later Quartets were, and it shows a
finality in some of its positions which are complicated and questioned by the subsequent poems.

The concluding verse-sentence of 'Burnt Norton' –

> Sudden in a shaft of sunlight
> Even while the dust moves
> There rises the hidden laughter
> Of children in the foliage
> Quick now, here, now, always –

Ridiculous the waste sad time
Stretching before and after

– incorporates another phrase from *Murder in the Cathedral*: 'I have
seen these things in a shaft of sunlight' (*CP* 240). The first section of
the poem describes an entry into a garden, where again sunlight mystically transforms a 'dry concrete' pool into one filled with water, in
the glittering surface of which, as out of a 'heart of light', some mysterious figures are reflected, behind the 'we' of the poem who have
entered the garden.[2] The expression 'human kind / Cannot bear very
much reality' is used at the end of this first section to accompany the
injunction of the bird (who in an act of 'deception' originally invited
the human protagonists into the garden) to now leave it, and as with
the end of 'Ash-Wednesday' IV the opening of 'Burnt Norton' dramatizes the theme of human existence as exile – as exile from 'our
first world', that Edenic setting into which humanity was originally
born, imaged here as a place of childhood felicity. This 'first world' is
presented as the 'reality', a paradise state of light and laughter, in
opposition to Eliot's continued insistence, in the *Quartets* and elsewhere, on the 'Unreal City' in which we live our temporal and historical lives. Although the mystical 'they' of this first section are referred
to as invisible and 'unseen', and only glimpsed as reflections, it is in
fact the 'we' who move in a counterpoint pattern with them who are
ghostly and 'unreal', shadows more than substance, the genuine
'reflections', just as the eternal rose-garden is offset by the 'dust on a
bowl of rose-leaves' as an image of this life as death and desiccation.
The final lines of 'Burnt Norton', quoted above, return to this contrast between light and dust, laughter and sadness, as a representation of the two orders.

The final lines also return specifically to the presentation of 'time',
the word with which 'Burnt Norton' opens. The eternal world is
'always present' alongside our actual world of present time; at any
moment we might have access to a sense of this presence, might suddenly pierce through the temporal barrier and experience such a
dimension of being, either in a rose-garden or 'draughty church at
smokefall' or the other 'moments' recorded at the end of part II.
Conversely, our human life within the illusory medium of time is
seen as an absurdity, a 'ridiculous' situation meriting the laughter of
the children, or the teasing deception of the thrush who leads us into
a world of true being only to usher us back again into the earthly

dimension of paradox and contradiction, the labyrinth of history with its passages and corridors already anticipated in 'Gerontion' (above, p. 26). The most fundamental paradox of all is presented at the end of 'East Coker' III: 'where you are is where you are not': not only is temporal existence non-existence, but true existence is where at present, being in life, you do not exist. In 'Ash-Wednesday' VI, human life is seen as a 'time of tension between dying and birth', where the customary meanings of 'birth' and 'death' have been reversed, a motif repeated in the final section of 'Burnt Norton' where the span of earthly life is a form of 'limitation / Between un-being and being'. 'East Coker' will be framed by similar declarations that the beginning of earthly life is an 'end', just as the death that ends life is a 'beginning'. As the last three Quartets will insist, the only way back to the rose-garden, 'to arrive where we started' as the finale to 'Little Gidding' puts it, is via the 'detour', as it were, of history. No more than Harry in Eliot's play can we simply reverse our steps down the corridor and open the closed door, but have to use the dimension of time as a means of 'exploration', a gruelling journey of 'prayer, observance, discipline, thought and action' ('The Dry Salvages' V) that brings us back round to our starting-point and fits us to re-enter the garden. The medium of time, however absurd, is where we are, for better or worse – and rather than essentially decrying it, as 'Burnt Norton' does, the later Quartets salvage in more assiduous ways the lessons and experience it teaches.

The second part of 'Burnt Norton' approaches the 'reality' presented in part I in a different way, describing it among other things as 'a grace of sense, a white light still and moving', where human longings and tensions are resolved and everything is finally 'understood'. If this sounds a rather vague formulation, this part introduces a theme that resounds through the *Quartets*, that is, the inadequacy of language itself, as an earthly and temporal medium, to express experiences that lie 'out of time' – as the text here repeats, 'I cannot say'.[3] The divine 'still point' that exists at the centre of everything that is can only be expressed using a series of 'neither'/ 'nor' formulations; moreover, to describe one's experience of it using categories of location and duration, that is, 'where' one has been and for how long, is to falsify it by defining the timeless in terms of the temporal. Any experience of timeless reality reveals our earthly coordinates of time and place to be provisional and insubstantial; the *Quartets* insists throughout that the division into past, present and future is itself merely conventional, and in the first section of 'Little Gidding' 'the intersection of the timeless moment' will take place simultaneously in 'England and nowhere', its very occurrence 'in England' revealing the contingency of national frontiers. We do however have to bring back such experience to the worldly dimension we inhabit in order to hold onto it, just as the poet has to use the inherently inadequate medium of language to communicate it (the 'shabby equipment always deteriorating' of 'East Coker' V). Thus the memory at the end of 'Burnt Norton' II plots the various moments of intersection on the axes of time/place which frame our lives, emphasizing that time is undone here as the very act of utilizing it to 'place' the timeless reveals its provisionality: 'Only through time time is conquered'. Each of the *Quartets* is indeed set in a specific place: Burnt Norton is a manorhouse in Gloucestershire which Eliot visited in the company of his childhood sweetheart Emily Hale in 1934 – the immediate occasion for the poem – and 'the door we never opened / Into the rose-garden' contains allusions to roads not taken and fruition not achieved in relation to human as well as spiritual states, the laughing children being perhaps part of the 'What might have been' if Eliot had married Emily Hale (see Gordon, *T. S. Eliot*, pp. 265–9).[4] But in 'Burnt Norton' this localized, autobiographical narrative becomes the universal story of time's denials and contradictions as a symptom of our exclusion from reality, of our existing where we are 'not'.

It is worth reintroducing here the issues raised in the Dante essay as to whether 'the reader must share the beliefs of the poet in order to enjoy the poetry fully' (*SE* 269). In fact, 'Burnt Norton' contains very little explicitly Christian or doctrinal material, unlike the contemporary *Murder in the Cathedral*.[5] Among other references, there is that to 'The Word in the desert' in part V, which we shall come onto, and the idea of expulsion from a rose-garden has unmistakable suggestions of the Fall, though even here the featuring of the lotus-flower indicates the poem's availability for readings drawing on a variety of religions and spiritual systems.[6] Eliot seems deliberately to have provided a more 'open' context for the poem, and indeed as we go forwards through the set of *Quartets* the Christian teaching becomes more prominent, with, for example, the intersections of the timeless and time being presented in 'The Dry Salvages' V as all derivative from the prototype intersection, that of the Incarnation. 'Burnt Norton' is arguably concerned to address all those who have experienced 'moments' of wholeness or transcendence, a sudden, unaccountable sense of 'release' from the confines of life, and by concentrating on presenting these in terms of a philosophical debate over time and being, rather than a persistently religious one, Eliot extends the terrain of shared belief.

Nevertheless, 'Burnt Norton' does talk of 'heaven and damnation' in its second part, and just as traditional images like the rose are used to signify the former, so in part III we return to the familiar territory of Dante's Hell-vestibule in the vision of 'the gloomy hills of London' and the 'torpid' souls driven about them. As with the 'twilight kingdom' of death in 'The Hollow Men', here we have the 'dim light' of spiritual nullity imaged as an underground station, with 'Men and bits of paper' who are 'whirled by the cold wind' living their lives solely on the horizontal axis, so to speak, of secular time. Life plotted along this illusory axis of temporal sequence is represented in the image of the tube-train, moving 'In appetency, on its metalled ways / Of time past and time future', a hectic, shuttered and 'driven' existence that is the antithesis of spiritually significant journeying, or 'exploration'. This latter is represented here, conversely, by the intersecting 'vertical' axis, which either leads upwards into the light or downwards into a 'purifying' darkness (one of the Greek epigraphs to 'Burnt Norton', taken from Heraclitus, translates as 'The way up and the way down are the same'). This part now concentrates on the downwards direction, the 'descent' into an abnegation where, as in the opening of 'Ash-Wednesday', all the pretensions of the self and attractions of the world are cast aside, and where even 'Inoperancy of the world of spirit' must precede spiritual progress itself, in the manner of St John of the Cross's *Dark Night*. This descent is not so much movement in the busy, worldly sense but 'abstention from movement', an entry into a vacancy and stillness which is a mode of communing with the previously declared 'still point', and which will be specified later in 'East Coker' III: 'I said to my soul, be still, and let the dark come upon you / Which shall be the darkness of God'.

Eliot's use in this section of terms like 'appetency' (desire for, longing towards) or 'eructation' (belching) is symptomatic of a linguistic programme throughout the *Quartets* that conspicuously invests in formal, Latinate terms, a type of 'classic' English mindful as ever with Eliot of its roots in Europe, and one which is explicitly featured in the final Quartet, 'Little Gidding', where we shall consider it in more detail.[7] But even a glance at 'Burnt Norton' will show how the poem has conducted that 'sacrifice' of the 'opulence and variety of . . .

tongues' which Eliot identified in Virgil's *Aeneid* (*OP* 70) and which started to be apparent in Eliot's own poetry with 'The Hollow Men'. Compared with *The Waste Land*, we find no amalgam of different dialects, registers, discourses, quotations and languages in *Four Quartets*: one German word is used in 'Burnt Norton', one French term in 'East Coker' and one Italian phrase in 'The Dry Salvages'. These no doubt deliberate deployments, signalling cultural linkage with Europe, preface the absence of any foreign terms at all in 'Little Gidding', which, as we have noted, comes home to 'England' though only to pass much beyond it. Eliot's consciousness of 'the mind of Europe' works in a different way in the *Quartets*, drawing for instance on a common stock of religious and biblical images and reminding us that 'we are all, so far as we inherit the civilization of Europe, still citizens of the Roman Empire' (*OP* 130) through the medium of its classicizing English, its philological testimony. These gestures towards unity and uniformity are of course tremendously significant given the context of European war within which the *Quartets* was largely written, but 'Little Gidding', heavily conscious of various 'tongues' (a key word in the Quartet), looks beyond such difference to a linguistic homogeneity that images, as we shall see, a final (transcendental) unity between the nations.

Part IV of 'Burnt Norton', a lyric interlude, reminds us that though the natural world of roses and sunlight is used as an analogy for the supernatural realm, that world per se remains under the dispensation of time and is, like all things temporal, limited, finite and provisional. In other words, Eliot is no 'nature poet' who regards the divine as a permanent force *within* nature: the actual sun disappears along with the day, and the 'kingfisher's wing' records a brief flash of light, but this contrasts with a light that does not fail and remains 'still' (in the sense, among other meanings, of 'permanent') at the divine centre. In part III of 'Burnt Norton' Eliot castigates the urban as 'a place of disaffection', and although his later writing does advocate a policy of ruralism in various ways this is not to be seen as any kind of link with the 'sublime' Wordsworthian notion of a 'presence' or 'spirit', 'Whose dwelling is the light of setting suns', and which 'rolls through all things' ('Tintern Abbey', *William Wordsworth*, p. 134).

The final part of 'Burnt Norton' suggests indeed that it is 'art' rather than nature that approximates to the divine, returning to a meditation on language itself. Words and music, the latter analogous in some ways to the quartet form of Eliot's poem (above, p. 63), move 'in time', are sequential, build up their effects of meaning or melody by a succession of elements; words moreover lose original meanings, become fluid and changeable over time, 'Decay with imprecision'. This temporal medium, where words themselves will not 'stay still', can only convey a sense of the 'still point' where 'past and future are gathered' (part II) and 'all is always now' (part V) by being organized into a patterned poetico-musical 'form' that confounds the notion of sequence, and undoes the distinction between beginnings and ends. Thus the circle, which has no point where it stops or starts, is a traditional symbol of God, and Eliot's model of eternity is here the Chinese jar, a simple circular form that communicates a sense of stillness even as its circularity suggests motion around a central axis, or invites a spectator to walk around it.[8] Poetry is not an instantaneous form like the jar, but remains of course sequential; nevertheless, by crafting words into rhythmic patterns it sets up emphatic harmonies between different parts of the sequence, achieving a layered effect whereby, for example, ends and beginnings are enacted simultaneously. Thus at the very end of 'Burnt Norton' key terms like 'dust', 'sunlight', 'Quick', 'always' are informed in their meaning by a weight of accumulation that begins with their appearance in the opening part, and when the poem is read again our understanding of the 'beginning' will be informed by what we already know of the end. Staying with the finale of the poem, one could indeed take each of even the most basic words – 'now', 'here', 'before', 'after' – and show how it is in a dialogue with its occurrences elsewhere, in a 'pattern' that counters simple arrangements of before and after, a 'vertical' axis of layering rather than a merely 'horizontal' one of sequence. Of course, this type of linguistic complexity might pertain to all literature, but 'Burnt Norton' is conspicuous in the way it takes a relatively limited set of terms and re-deploys them in a large number of variations, prime instances being the multiple occurrences of, for example, 'still' and 'end'.

In doing this, Eliot is still following mentors like Lancelot Andrewes, who 'takes a word and derives the world from it; squeezing and squeezing the word until it yields a full juice of meaning' (*FLA* 20), but as 'Burnt Norton' notes, language is reluctant to subject itself to this sort of capture, or 'stay still' long enough to permit the operation to take place. When in part V Eliot talks of 'The Word in the desert' being 'attacked by voices of temptation', he is simultaneously referring to the temptations of Christ and the temptations faced by the poet who is striving for the disciplined and ascetic style of his own later work, its 'purging out of poetical ornament' as he put it in the Yeats essay of 1940 (*OP* 259). The shrieks, cries and laments that assail words at this point in the poem all signify temptations towards a more dramatically expressive or imagistically charged or multi-voiced treatment, things that Eliot had bid farewell to after *The Waste Land*. 'Burnt Norton' is, it is true, the tautest and most 'disciplined' of the *Quartets* in the sense of being the most homogeneous – the later three, for example, have more variation in their verse-forms, such as the sestina of 'The Dry Salvages' or the emulation of *terza rima* in 'Little Gidding'. It is also the Quartet that seems to express its frustrations most emphatically at any challenge to the 'stillness' it aspires to, either the stillness of language or that of transcendence itself, the exclusion from which is categorized as 'ridiculous' in the poem's penultimate line.

In short, 'Burnt Norton' has yearnings for finality, and when it was first published in 1936 as the final poem in Eliot's *Collected Poems 1909–1935* it did not know that it would later be joined by three further poems in the sequence and would in fact be a beginning rather than an end. The later three Quartets, as I noted above, embrace the historical context in which they find themselves, the turbulence of war, rather than seeking to dispense with it, even if that context confirms the essential 'unreality' and vanity of the secular. This kind of journey *through* history results in a 'deeper communion', a greater intensity of spiritual commitment, as the ending of 'East Coker' specifies. Whereas 'movement' in 'Burnt Norton' tends to be stigmatized as symptomatic of the dimension of time (as opposed to the stillness of eternity), the need to be 'explorers' who are 'still and still moving' at the end of 'East Coker' suggests that time's very lack of stasis – the decay of language, the destruction of houses, the ageing of the body, the multiple deaths (of individuals, political factions, the elements themselves) – can bear spiritual fruit and should not be evaded. At the beginning of 'Burnt Norton' II a short rhymed stanza talks of a pattern of oppositions on earth being 'reconciled' among the stars; the equivalent stanza in 'East Coker' II has a far more disturbed vision of war among the constellations that accosts this previous statement of concord. More than this, 'East Coker' then goes on to immediately challenge its own vision in this stanza as 'not very satisfactory' from a poetical point of view. The whole Quartet is indeed rather more 'moving' and restless than

'Burnt Norton', even as it begins to build up the pattern of the *Quartets* as a whole.

'EAST COKER'

In 'East Coker' III we are referred back to 'The laughter in the garden' of 'Burnt Norton', an 'echoed ecstasy / Not lost, but requiring, pointing to the agony / Of death and birth', the agony not merely of physical death but, as the concluding section of part III goes on to describe, that of spiritual renewal involving the sacrifice of pride, pleasure, knowledge and the entire worldly sense of the self and its status. The poet at this stage admits 'I am repeating / Something I have said before', but although this position is implied in the equivalent part of 'Burnt Norton' (the conclusion to part III) it is now expressed more forcefully, even didactically, as a preface to the allegory of the Christian atonement presented in 'East Coker' IV. The whole mood of 'East Coker' is as noted above more urgent, sombre and turbulent than 'Burnt Norton': 'death' is one of its key terms, as is 'dark', which while it develops the darkness theme of 'Burnt Norton' III contrasts with the overall emphasis on light in the first Quartet. The village of East Coker in Somerset is where Eliot's ancestors set out from in the seventeenth century to settle in America: this journey through the 'vast waters' of the Atlantic is seen at the end of the Quartet as an analogue, in its venturesome embracing of the New World, for the life of spiritual exploration the end of the poem enjoins (the following poem, 'The Dry Salvages', continues the narrative by being set off the Massachusetts coast). The protagonist of 'East Coker' is reversing this journey by coming back to the English village whence his family line derives – in a sense here is his 'beginning' as an individual, the poem having by now established that the past, however remote, survives into the present culturally, genetically, politically and so on and is never 'finished' (as the next Quartet specifies). If the past is always present in a way that questions the sequential plotting of time on the merely 'horizontal' axis, so the future is always already in the past, in that we are born into a cycle of living and dying whose end is determined. Thus 'In my beginning is my end' as the opening has it, and the first section of part I broods on the end-phase of that cycle, the ultimate absorption into the earth of whatever is born or built. The final line of this section talks of 'the tattered arras woven with a silent motto', an image of time's ravages which returns us to the opening sentence, 'In my beginning is my end', given that this was the motto of Mary Queen of Scots, and a reminder that Eliot is here talking not merely on the level of personal history.

There is a time for all things, or, the book of Ecclesiastes tells us, 'to every thing there is a season, and a time to every purpose under the heaven' (3. 1); that is, for all the things that, being transient and offering no stay, constitute the world's vanity. 'East Coker' continues its lugubrious theme by now presenting the village itself on a summer's day, though this is hardly a picturesque, rural invocation: the light is 'sultry', the approaching lane is 'dark in the afternoon', all is empty, somnolent and like all things (metaphorically) waiting for the evening, presided over by the bird of death, the owl. At this point Eliot insists again on the confounding of temporal categories by staging a kind of resurrection, a vision in the 'open field' of peasants dancing, who are in fact 'long since' dead, 'under earth / Nourishing the corn'. Eliot inserts into this vision some words from a work by one of his ancestors, the *Boke Named the Governour* by Sir Thomas Elyot (1531), in which dancing is seen as a representation of the 'concorde' of matrimony, but these 'clumsy' dancers with their 'Earth feet, loam feet' are hardly part of the 'dignified and commodious' ritual that Sir Thomas presents. This vanished rural community does indeed contrast with the modern urban crowd of 'Burnt Norton' III: whereas the latter have 'strained time-ridden faces', the former are 'Keeping time' in their dancing, the dance here representing the organic cycle (picking up on 'The dance along the artery' in 'Burnt Norton' II). The dancers are in harmony with the seasons and constellations, but such harmony is not presented as an end in itself: the dancers, like all things, end in 'Dung and death', their natural lifestyle being an acknowledgement of the finite and limited cycle of life, rather than an attempted evasion of it as with the 'distracted' tube-commuters, hurrying on their 'metalled ways'.

It is important to realize that although Eliot adopted a ruralist outlook in the 1930s – 'real and spontaneous country life ... is the right life for the great majority in any nation'; 'it is necessary that the greater part of the population ... should be settled in the country and dependent upon it'[9] – he is always insistent that this programme has nothing to do with becoming 'a worshipper of Nature', in Wordsworth's phrase ('Tintern Abbey', p. 135). In *The Idea of a Christian Society*, published the year before 'East Coker' in 1939, Eliot plainly wishes such a society to be settled on the soil, and suggests the rural parish, threatened by 'urbanisation' ('in which I am including also *sub*-urbanisation') as the principal 'religious-social' unit of society, its constituent cell (*ICS* 29). He also insists with a notable ecological prescience on 'a life in conformity with nature', that is, one where 'unregulated industrialism' will not lead to 'the exhaustion of natural resources':

> for a long enough time we have believed in nothing but the values arising in a mechanised, commercialised, urbanised way of life: it would be as well for us to face the permanent conditions upon which God allows us to live upon this planet.

Thus 'a wrong attitude towards nature implies, somewhere, a wrong attitude towards God' (*ICS* 61–2). However, he does not wish in any way to idealize rural life in calling for a return to it ('I am not presenting any idyllic picture of the rural parish, either present or past . . .', *ICS* 31), just as we saw, in our discussion of *Murder in the Cathedral*, that he has no illusions of a 'possible Christian order in the future' leading to 'a golden age of virtue'. The 'right' attitude towards 'nature' is to realize its limitations, its finiteness, both in terms of its resources and in its subordination to the divine. To live in conformity with it, as the vision of 'East Coker' I suggests, is to inhabit a natural cycle which is ever mindful of the universal rhythms of living and dying; indeed a kind of 'humility', to anticipate an important term from part III of the poem, which recognizes our finite state, and the need once again to think beyond time and nature altogether to our ultimate 'end'. In 'The Dry Salvages' Eliot will present the natural world as a more forceful, frightening place than the sleepy silence of the English village, and the rituals of milking and harvest that are connected with it. 'East Coker' is not so much an exercise in pastoral charm as a satire on that powerful discourse of rural nostalgia that flourished in English culture in the 1930s and 40s, the coarse 'rustic laughter' of the ghost-dancers being as far removed from the myth of 'Merrie England' as it is from the children's laughter in 'Burnt Norton', the index of true felicity.

The end of part I of 'East Coker' has a short passage on dawn, corresponding with that on dusk in 'Burnt Norton' IV, a dawn that ushers in simply 'another day'. 'The Dry Salvages' will talk of 'the trailing / Consequence of further days and hours' in continuing the theme of 'waste sad time' from 'Burnt Norton'. One aspect of this 'waste' is next explored in 'East Coker' II at the level of the individual life, the point being stressed that growing old brings no benefits with it in terms of greater 'wisdom', maturity or 'autumnal serenity', the reference to the season in this last phrase reinforcing the limitation to any idea of a positive cyclical kinship between humanity and nature. We face fresh problems at every turn for which our previous experience only doubtfully fits us; we are 'In the middle, not only in the middle of the way / But all the way', the reference to the opening line of Dante's *Inferno* indicating that the symbolic 'dark wood' is always present, whether in the past, present or future. This part's insistence that time's 'deceit' consists in refusing to synchronize our abilities and opportunities with the dangers and problems we face, but is always providing us with the former when it is too late, is restated in part V with regard to the act of writing poetry itself: 'one has only learnt to get the better of words / For the thing one no longer has to say'. It also strikingly parallels the passage on the deceit of 'History' in 'Gerontion', published 20 years earlier. Ageing, it seems, rather than bringing ripeness, brings disillusion and desiccation, a cautious, self-serving drawing-in of the self, the fear 'old men' have of 'fear and frenzy, their fear of possession, / Of belonging to another, or to others, or to God'. In the contemporary essay on Yeats, Eliot saluted the Irish poet for his work's embrace of an old age that was the reverse of this, passionate, angry, 'not very pleasant', describing him as 'a poet who in his work remained in the best sense always young, who even in one sense became young as he aged'. Yeats's 'revelation' in his poetry 'of what a man really is and remains' deflates in Eliot's eyes any pretensions to 'progress' in the individual life, and is given a Christian gloss in 'East Coker' where the 'only wisdom' the old can hope to acquire is that of humility. Better to recognize and declare the self's inherent and insuperable corruption than aspire to the careerist 'temptation . . . of becoming dignified, of becoming public figures with only a public existence – coat-racks hung with decorations and distinctions' (*OP* 257 – Eliot is here taking his cue from Yeats's poem 'Among School Children'[10]). In 'Little Gidding' Eliot will continue to pour scorn on 'the gifts reserved for age', this time from the mouth of a visiting ghost-figure who many commentators have seen as a representation of Yeats himself.

Part II of 'East Coker' ends with two separate single lines reminding us of the earthly fate of all things whether material or human; part III continues the theme of questioning secular versions of eminence in the picture of distinguished public figures all heading into the 'dark'. It is now clear that this is not only a metaphor for death but also for the nullity of an old age that may bring honours but is empty of the true knowledge discussed above, without which the world's 'successes' are truly nobodies – 'Nobody's funeral, for there is no one to bury'. The poem contrasts this vacant darkness with what it calls 'the darkness of God', which is precisely the acknowledgement of 'vanity'(both of the self and of the 'bold imposing façade' the world sets up), including the vanity of spiritual self-regard discussed above in connection with 'Ash-Wednesday'. Even the Christian virtues of faith, hope and love cannot bring the self nearer to God; that nearness can only be effected by the divine will itself, so that 'the faith and the love and the hope are all in the waiting'. Part III ends, as we noted in beginning our discussion of 'East Coker', with a climactic insistence that the worldly self must be totally unlearned, so to speak, through 'ignorance' and 'dispossession' before the true self can be found, and that what we truly 'are' is all that we 'are not'.[11] To live in time, to grow old temporally, as the sequence thus far has insisted, is no progress but only a distancing from the state that images true happiness: 'except ye . . . become as little children, ye shall not enter into the kingdom of heaven' (Mt. 18. 3); the next verse in the gospel talks of a return to this state as a process of 'humbling' oneself. One cannot literally reverse time and head back towards such a state, but ageing should ideally be a journey of exploration and self-undoing that takes us back where we started (in all senses) – 'In my end is my beginning', as 'East Coker' concludes.

As we pointed out, 'Burnt Norton' largely avoids an explicitly Christian, and even religious, terminology, and this avoidance continues into 'East Coker', though to a lesser extent: by the end of part III, for example, we have met the word 'God' on two occasions. But part IV of the poem is the first sustained reference to Christian doctrine, the Fall and the Atonement being presented in an extended allegory of the world as a 'hospital', our fallen state as a 'disease' and Christ as the intervening 'wounded surgeon' assisted by his 'dying nurse', the Church on earth. It ends with a reference to Good Friday, the day of Christ's sacrifice, and to the blood and 'bloody flesh' of his body, instituted in the sacrament of Holy Communion as our 'only' food and drink. The grim allegory, in its insistence that our 'health' lies in recognizing our diseased state, and in rejecting the idea that 'we are sound, substantial flesh and blood', is plainly in keeping with the overall tone of 'East Coker'.[12]

The final part of 'East Coker' introduces a rare note of explicit autobiography into the poem, a brief review of the poet's career *entre deux guerres*, between the two World Wars, a career of inevitable 'failure' given the conditions of temporality discussed above, and the deteriorations the *Quartets* commemorates – of body and mind, of culture, of language, now intensified by the 'unpropitious' circumstances of wartime. It is at this point, however, that 'East Coker' begins to assert itself in the face of the adverse 'conditions' it has been piling up, insisting, to begin with, that the (wartime) 'fight' must be continued, the fight of 'trying' to write poetry against all the odds, including linguistic odds, so to speak ('a language is always changing; its developments . . . even, in the long run, its deterioration – must be accepted by the poet and made the best of', 'The Music of Poetry', *OP* 37). And as a more general context for this fight, 'time' itself, essentially demonized as exclusion and limitation throughout the sequence, is now investigated as something to be worked with productively in the 'Old men ought to be explorers' passage. 'East Coker' at this point gestures back to the conclusion of the first Quartet, but in order to make distinctions: it is now not talking of 'the intense moment / Isolated, with no before and after', that is, the transcendental rose-garden 'moment' which makes all time lying outside it 'ridiculous' and 'sad'. Rather it is talking of time itself as having its own potentially valuable plenitude, the fact that our own lives resume those of past generations, and our own lifetimes are not 'of one man only'. If the future is always present in the past, suggesting in the despairing emphasis of the poem hitherto that we are merely born to die, the past is always here in the present in what can be an exemplary sense, as in the cases of former poets who refused to give up on the quest to find again and again what was 'lost' (and 'Little Gidding' will inform us of other reasons for 'celebrating' the dead). This exemplary sense can indeed be present *within* us, in Eliot's case in the form of voyager-ancestors and the courageous precedent of exploration they provide. At the end of 'East Coker', 'here and now cease to matter', not because the mystical moment makes a nonsense of all time, as in 'Burnt Norton', but because we are, as individuals, constituted by a much more productive range of time than we may realize.

It may seem strange to talk of 'East Coker' as a poem of 'assertion' when such a note is only introduced near the very end. However, as I noted at the start of this chapter, it was in writing this poem that Eliot 'began to see the *Quartets* as a set of four', and 'East Coker', in introducing the question of what can be 'done' with time (rather than solely lamenting it), is plainly looking ahead to the remainder of the sequence to continue the theme and provide an answer. This answer essentially centres on the idea that time and 'history' can be used to deepen and intensify faith in the face of an omnipresent destruction, not only that occasioned by war but by natural catastrophe – 'History may be servitude, / History may be freedom' ('Little Gidding'). Thus rather than our merely 'waiting' with faith intact, the demons that challenge that faith can be actively confronted and faith strengthened by the trial. This, among other things, is what the final two Quartets have to divulge. However, Eliot does not want to obscure the fact that this more active pursuit is of little avail given that salvation is God's offering rather than anything to be achieved by human effort – we are still essentially 'waiting', though we can wait in a more active sense: 'We must be still and still moving'.

'THE DRY SALVAGES'

'The Dry Salvages' takes us to the American coastal waters off Cape Ann, Massachusetts, a vastly different setting from the English country-house garden or Somerset village. This Quartet can be seen among other things as an exploration of religious doubt, here a process whereby faith is ultimately strengthened; thus the world of natural forces is presented in all its fury and destructiveness as a means of testing yet affirming the existence of a higher beneficent power. At the outset the river is seen as a 'sullen', 'implacable' god, a pagan force seemingly domesticated by modern technology and thus, in effect, 'almost forgotten', but the cost of that forgetfulness is to vitiate our religious and cultural sensibilities, as Eliot argued in *The Idea of a Christian Society*:

> the struggle to recover the sense of relation to nature and to God, the recognition that even the most primitive feelings should be part of our heritage, seems to me to be the explanation and justification of the life of D. H. Lawrence . . . But we need not only to learn how to look at the world with the eyes of a Mexican

Indian . . . We need to know how to see the world as the Christian Fathers saw it; and the purpose of reascending to origins is that we should be able to return, with greater spiritual knowledge, to our own situation. We need to recover the sense of religious fear, so that it may be overcome by religious hope. (*ICS* 62)

Moving out of the urban opening of 'The Dry Salvages' to the American seaboard, we are under no illusion that the 'anxious worried women' who dwell within earshot of the howls, yelps and groans of the sea will be in danger of not developing this 'fear': they are the mothers and wives of the fishermen of part IV of the poem, 'who have seen their sons or husbands / Setting forth, and not returning'. The sea and its 'ground swell' introduce another measure of time into the *Quartets*, one that dwarfs human mechanisms, 'Older than the time of chronometers'; indeed the sea, 'that is and was from the beginning', is seen as a powerful rival to God, and presents the prospect of a universe governed solely by awe-inspiring natural, rather than supernatural, forces. Thus the sea is not only the destroyer of individual lives but of entire species, tossing onto the beach 'Its hints of earlier and other creation', and 'The Dry Salvages' in some ways re-enacts the debate of Victorian poems like *In Memoriam* or Arnold's 'Dover Beach', which question the idea of divine governance in the face of powerful evidence that suggests existence is a purely material affair. This threat to belief is summed up in the phrase 'The salt is on the briar rose'.[13] In Eliot's poem, however, the recovery of this fear in the face of the elements is seen as a stimulus to a strengthened sense of the 'hope' that will overcome it.

Part II of 'The Dry Salvages' initially takes the form of a sestina, that is, a sequence of six six-line stanzas, with the corresponding line of each stanza rhyming throughout. The conspicuous regularity of this part enforces the vision of a life that is cyclical and purely governed by the rhythms of nature, a cycle that goes round and round with no 'end' other than the inevitable 'annunciation' of death. In this sense, the 'voyage of life' (the poem uses the activity of the fishermen, 'forever bailing, / Setting and hauling', as a metaphor for what would be the futile regularities of existence) would have 'no destination': the poem returns to the lamentable theme of ageing in 'East Coker', with the individual's 'failing powers' imaged as being 'In a drifting boat with a slow leakage', and inevitably going under rather than safely reaching port. In this picture of a Godless universe the only constant is 'the drift of the sea and the drifting wreckage', evident throughout time. Indeed it seems folly in the face of the natural evidence to think otherwise – 'We have to think' this, 'We cannot think' anything else. The poem stresses here the difficulties of holding onto faith, the fact that the 'only' rescue from the cycle of death is 'hardly, barely prayable', that being the 'Prayer of the one Annunciation' which puts an end to the sestina and also of course to the futility of getting nowhere. As with 'The Hollow Men', Eliot contrasts the initial upper case letter of 'Annunciation' with the 'annunciation' that is merely death, thus signalling the haven of a spiritual reality beyond the natural realm.

The rest of part II of 'The Dry Salvages' reiterates the insistence on not 'disowning' the past which 'superficial notions of evolution' or progress might involve. Here Eliot picks up the idea from 'East Coker' that our present experience – this time, our receptivity to 'moments of happiness' or 'sudden illumination' – is constituted by the 'many generations' that have preceded us; it is indeed a recurrence of such moments experienced by others in the past, and results in a recognition of the common nature of their true 'meaning'. Going back in time beyond 'recorded history' we then return to the proposition from *The Idea of a Christian Society* that the 'primitive terror' should also form part of present experience as a necessary spiritual endowment. However, time 'preserves' not only these positives for the present generation, but the 'moments of agony' also, moments which are more disturbing and durable when they affect the lives of others, for 'our own past is covered by the currents of action', which presumably helps us to repress such moments. Here Eliot returns to the dominant metaphor of this Quartet, the idea of life as a voyage, and the dangers of the 'ragged rock' against which that voyage could founder, suggesting it is precisely others' agony – 'unworn by subsequent attrition' – which constitutes the threat of shipwreck. Here it seems we have a kind of allegory of the dangers of despair, not the loss of faith constituted by the extermination of species, but that occasioned by witnessing the cruelty of others' suffering, which is harder to bear than our own. This rock of agony is bearable in 'halcyon' or 'navigable weather', can always be steered round, so to speak, in such times, but there are 'sombre' moods or a 'sudden fury' when its dangers to belief are always liable to assert themselves.

Part III of the poem returns to the idea of horizontal and vertical axes of movement, now applied to the metaphor of voyaging. Although the voyagers are repeatedly told, as in the concluding line, to 'fare forward', this forward direction is described as 'the way back' earlier in the section, just as 'the way up is the way down', echoing 'Burnt Norton'. The poem again questions the idea of a sequential progress, where past, present and future can be divided from each other, as in the idea of the sea-voyage as entry into a 'different' future, via emigration for example. Our 'real destination' is not to another country, or port, or different 'terminus', but to a death that shall bear 'fruit'. The voyage is not geographical, so to speak, but spiritual, and the opportunity to re-route it to the correct track occurs in that interval of suspension 'between the hither and the farther shore / While time is withdrawn', where the 'vertical' axis might be said to intersect with the horizontal. Such moments of possibility occur throughout the *Quartets*, where the ordinary activities of action and the 'distractions' of the world are suspended; in 'East Coker' III the tube 'stops too long between stations', but the opportunity to embrace the resulting 'emptiness' – to descend deeper into the darkness and thus go 'up' by going down – is something the passengers cannot respond to. Once again, all the disappointments of merely sequential time are rehearsed in part III of 'The Dry Salvages': that the future is in a sense already determined in its inevitable decay ('In my beginning is my end'), and that 'time is no healer' because 'the patient' (remembering we are all 'hospital' patients, 'East Coker' IV) 'is no longer here'. This last position is a reiteration of time's tricks, along the lines previously discussed, namely that we only acquire the necessary experience or language or healing to deal with our situation after these would be of use to us, when our situation has changed and demands new responses in a never-ending game of catch-up. The really significant moments of our lives are those when we are mindful of eternal realities, not of temporal attachment, a lesson imparted here by the Hindu god Krishna.[14] Our 'real destination' is embraced through death, a death that can happen at any moment and which should thus be always present to us.

Part IV, as with the other three poems, is a short stanzaic interlude, explicitly Christian in doctrine as with the corresponding sections of 'East Coker' and 'Little Gidding', here a prayer to the Virgin asking for her prayers and intercession for both the living and the dead, for those who 'are in ships' and who 'were in ships'. Given that the sea-journey has metaphorical status throughout the Quartet, this encompasses everybody, so that the request is for universal intercession, but there is particular reference to those 'Whose business has to do with fish' which maintains the specific location of the poem. But the local relates to universal themes: the women who 'have seen their sons or husbands / Setting forth, and not returning' include all those left at home in a time of war, while those whose 'business has to do with fish' are not only the Massachusetts fishermen but the clergy everywhere in their pastoral role, the 'fishers of men' in Christ's words to his apostles (Mk 1.17). The whole foundation of this Quartet, the narrative of faith aided by intercessors undergoing the trial of the sea, could be said to derive from the gospel story of St Peter's similar trial told in Matthew 15. 24–32. The phrase Eliot quotes from the opening line of the final canto of the *Paradiso* (33.1) that Dante uses to address the Virgin – 'Figlia del tuo figlio' ('Daughter of your son') – not only anticipates the introduction of Christ into part V of the poem, but in its 'impossible' temporal paradox shows once again how the divine realm lies outside and confounds our fixed sequences of time.[15]

Part V begins with a dismissal of the outlook that 'clings to' the dimension of past and future, evidenced now not by commuters on their 'metalled ways' or emigrants hoping for a new life, but those with a misdirected 'curiosity': spiritualists of various kinds, fortune tellers and their clients, Freudians (see p. 58), all those who try to see into the future or the pre-conscious past of the 'womb'. This is still to investigate along the 'horizontal' axis, but the 'moment' that reveals the insufficiency of this axis, 'The point of intersection of the timeless / With time', is now revealed as the Incarnation, a true grasp or apprehension of which is an 'occupation' for the saint alone. The poem now presents itself in the voice which is familiar to Eliot's readers of those who are on the margins of this true apprehension, whether the 'hollow men' or the Chorus from *Murder in the Cathedral*: for 'most of us' spiritual reality will take a more diluted form, the various 'moments' of half-grasped significance when we feel eternity is upon us, 'lost in a shaft of sunlight'. The Incarnation is seen as 'conquering' and 'reconciling' past and future, in effect undoing time and our categorizations of it by revealing the existence of the 'timeless'. 'Action' is also thereby redefined as not merely physical movement, whether the secular movement of men or the 'chthonic' movement of the ocean, but spiritual, 'right action', which enables us to escape from the temporal into the timeless (this type of action being in large measure, as we have seen, a 'stillness', and as with

Murder in the Cathedral, 'all in the waiting').[16] 'For most of us' spiritual life will be limited in its achievements, but once again, as with the writing of poetry in 'East Coker' V, the necessity is to go on 'trying', and the Quartet ends on the safe return to land, the voyage completed and the trials of the sea withstood. We end up as part of 'significant soil', and 'Not too far from the yew-tree', that is, gathered within the church-yard and within the Christian communion. This end is another beginning for the sequence, in its anticipation of the chapel setting for the final Quartet, back on English *terra firma* at 'Little Gidding'. The *'significant* soil' (my emphasis) also acts as a retrospective commentary on the limitations of the purely natural cycle of 'East Coker', where the 'Earth feet' of the dancers have returned to the earth from which they came.

'LITTLE GIDDING'

'Little Gidding' is a poem of pilgrimage, a deliberate journey to the 'world's end' where the protagonist experiences another 'intersection of the timeless moment' in the sense of communion with the dead. The dead are those of the seventeenth century, participants in the English Civil War: Nicholas Ferrar established the Anglican religious community of Little Gidding in rural Huntingdonshire in the 1620s, and it provided among other things a brief refuge in 1646 for Charles I, who 'came at night like a broken king'.[17] The poem suggests that the motive for visiting Little Gidding can only be known in the process of fulfilment, but that ultimately this is an act of piety, 'kneel[ing] / Where prayer has been valid' – not simply praying per se, but putting oneself in the very position of those who have previously prayed there to enable 'communication' with them to be effected. What this communication is will be expanded upon in part III of the poem, but it obviously relates to the common condition of seeking 'answers' or assurance in a time of war; this can only proceed from those who have passed to the realm of the 'timeless' reality, whose speech is now 'tongued with fire'. This key theme of 'pentecostal fire' is introduced in the opening section of 'Little Gidding', and refers to the beginning of the disciples' ministry after Christ's death:

> And when the day of Pentecost was fully come,
> they were all with one accord in one place.

> And suddenly there came a sound from heaven
> as of a rushing mighty wind, and it filled all
> the house where they were sitting.
> And there appeared unto them cloven tongues
> like as of fire, and it sat upon each of them.
> And they were all filled with the Holy Ghost, and
> began to speak with other tongues, as the Spirit
> gave them utterance. (Acts 2.1–4)

The supernatural visitation that enabled the disciples to speak in multiple languages, and thus disseminate the Christian teaching, is reproduced in 'Little Gidding' in a series of messages from beyond, both from the departed and from the *revenant* ghost of part II. The tongues of fire theme also doubles however as a representation of the multiplicity of, and hostility between, the nations, a feature underlining how this final Quartet is much more conspicuously a 'war poem' than the previous ones.

Before the arrival at Little Gidding itself in part I, the poem stages an appropriate setting for the moment of 'communication': a visionary experience of 'Midwinter spring', when in the coldest and darkest time of the year (spiritual) heat and a dazzling light are experienced, while the snow that mimics the may-blossom 'blanches' the hedges. This representation of spring arriving in the middle of winter is 'Not in the scheme of generation', nor in 'time's covenant'; it confounds the seasonal cycle in gesturing to the appearance of the timeless within time once again. On this occasion the Nativity is signified, the Son appearing, in the words of Lancelot Andrewes (quoted by Eliot in his essay on Andrewes, *FLA* 23), precisely when 'the days [were] short, the sun farthest off, *in solstitio brumali*, "the very dead of winter"', this last phrase having already been used by Eliot in 'Journey of the Magi'. Although the beauty of the natural scene – 'The brief sun flames the ice', and so forth – is the prompt for this epiphany at the start of 'Little Gidding', the scenic is valued not as an end in itself but only in so far as it gestures to the true 'spring time': the actual 'brief sun' contrasts, as the setting sun does in 'Burnt Norton' IV, with a light that is permanent. Indeed, the first part of 'Little Gidding' ends with a dismissal of the climax of the natural light cycle in representing the summer as 'Zero', as (comparatively) nothing, just as it is careful to set the holy place of Little Gidding itself in a landscape of 'rough road', 'pig-sty' and 'dull façade'. From the start of the *Quartets*, as with the vision of a light-filled pool in a drained pool that is actually one of 'dry concrete' and is 'brown edged' in 'Burnt Norton', the poem has been careful to avoid lulling its spiritual imperatives with any emphasis on the beauties of England.

Of all the *Quartets*, 'Little Gidding' is the most embedded in time and place, explicitly addressing the ongoing war (the London blitz figures later in the poem) and being staged in an England that is seriously threatened (in the early 1940s) by that war. But this makes the desire for a reality beyond time and place more acute, and in the tensions between opposing forces 'Little Gidding' acts as a dramatic and fitting climax to the entire sequence. The visit to Little Gidding itself occurs 'in place and time, / Now and in England', but the access to the timeless it provides reveals, as we noted above, the provisionality of nationhood, taking us to a 'location' that is both 'England and nowhere'. In part II the rituals of destruction and decay inherent in the temporal cycle are revisited, given added urgency by the destruction of wartime, and the idea of the elements resuming their control over human habitation and civilization is outlined in a series of rhyming stanzas. This may take us back to the primal powers of the ocean we should acknowledge and respect in 'The Dry Salvages', but in fact 'the death of air', 'the death of earth' and 'the death of water and fire' are all ambiguous expressions. Thus water and fire may obliterate towns and pasture, but this is a preface to the death of the very elements themselves in the apocalyptic vision underlying 'Little Gidding' of an end to all things temporal and the entry to the eternal, when 'the first heaven and the first earth were passed away; and there was no more sea' (Rev. 21.1). Before this vision can be realized, however, at the end of the poem, there is more to do in affirming the vanity of the world and of the 'bitter tastelessness' of the 'shadow fruit' it has to offer. These temporal vanities include, in a sense, poetry itself; the fact that each of the *Quartets* is identified with an element – in sequence air, earth, water and fire – indicates the passing away of poetry too at that final reckoning. This is the substance of the famous passage describing the meeting with the 'familiar compound ghost' that occupies the rest of part II.

Here we have Eliot's last major tribute in his poetry to the poetry of Dante: as he explained several years later in 'What Dante Means to Me', the intention was 'to present to the mind of the reader a parallel, by means of contrast, between the *Inferno* and the *Purgatorio*, which Dante visited and a hallucinated scene after an air-raid'. Eliot also attempted to give the sense of Dante's *terza rima* form not by reproducing it exactly but by adopting 'a simple alternation of unrhymed masculine and feminine terminations' (*TC* 128).[18] The scene takes as its starting point the episode in *Inferno* 15 where Dante meets the spirit of his former poetic and philosophical mentor Brunetto Latini, damned for the sin of sodomy and, like Eliot's ghost, exhibiting 'brown baked features' as a consequence of the punitive fire that rains down on him in hell. But whereas the interview takes place in the hereafter in Dante's poem, in Eliot's the ghost comes back to this life, providing another instance of an 'intersection' occasion; like Brunetto, he is a poetic mentor of some kind, but markedly does not wish to 'rehearse' his 'thought and theory' with the protagonist of 'Little Gidding'. Where Brunetto is keen to discuss Dante's political and poetic future and ends by imploring that his own work be remembered, Eliot's ghost, in keeping with the entire tenor of the *Quartets*, is no longer concerned with earthly attainments or poetic achievements. The gist of his 'message' is the worthlessness of such things compared with the 'refining fire' of spiritual purification, and his 'disclosure' of this begins with a list of 'the gifts reserved for age', even in the case of a distinguished poet – the breakdown of the body, the embittering of the spirit, the realization and regret occasioned by the harm one has done in life. This is a more extensive and devastating account of the disillusions of old age than the scepticism about 'autumnal serenity' in 'East Coker' II, but it clearly continues in the same vein. What is proffered in the equivalent section of 'Little Gidding' is in fact the 'wisdom' of age that was earlier sought for, and a scorching wisdom it is, 'tongued with fire' from the ghost's state of posthumous enlightenment. Although the identity of the ghost has been the subject of much debate, Yeats is one very likely candidate, a poet much in Eliot's mind as he was writing the later Quartets, as we have seen, and recently (1939) dying abroad, thus leaving his body 'on a distant shore'. In *After Strange Gods* Eliot had quoted with approval the lines from Yeats's poem 'Vacillation' that are so consonant with the theme of 'Little Gidding':

> Things said or done long years ago,
> Or things I did not do or say
> But thought that I might say or do,
> Weigh me down, and not a day

But something is recalled,
My conscience or my vanity appalled.
(Yeats, *Variorum Poems*, p. 501, *ASG* 46)

But the ghost is explicitly described as 'familiar' and 'compound',
and the 'hallucinated' sense of the protagonist being split off from
himself, assuming a 'double part', suggests that the ghost and his
interlocutor can also be seen as one and the same figure. Certainly,
much of what the ghost has to say has already, in effect, been said
throughout the *Quartets*.

The ghost talks of the griefs of age as including 'the rending pain
of re-enactment / Of all that you have done, and been', this pain
being contrasted at the very end of his speech with the only means of
escape from it, 'that refining fire / Where you must move in measure,
like a dancer'. We saw how Eliot was seeking a parallel in this passage
with both the *Inferno* and the *Purgatorio*, and the purgatorial fire of
'restoration' is here introduced as antidote to the hellish fire of
destruction, or the bitter self-recrimination that age brings with it.
Eliot had already referred to the purgatorial fire in including the final
line from *Purgatorio* 26 among the 'fragments' at the end of *The
Waste Land*, 'Poi s'ascose nel foco che gli affina' ('Then he hid himself in the fire that refines them'). As noted previously, the reference
is to the poet Arnaut Daniel, whom Dante meets purging the sin of
lust on the topmost terrace of Mount Purgatory, the process requiring meditation on and contrition for one's earthly sins or 'passada
folor' ('past folly', 26. 143) stimulated by the purging mechanism of
fire itself, at once a cleansing agent and an embodiment of the heat
of physical passion that is being repented of. This spiritual 're-enactment' removes one from the fires of hell, and from a world that, with
its present air-raids, resembles hell, a theme continued in the short
part IV, where the stark choice – 'To be redeemed from fire by fire' –
is given lyrical expression. Here the 'dove descending' (a traditional
image of the Holy Ghost), with its pentecostal 'tongues', doubles as
a bomb falling 'With flame of incandescent terror'; 'the choice of
pyre or pyre' that part IV presents is that between divine Love or
earthly conflagration.

Between the present war that is referred to in parts II and IV, Eliot
inserts in part III a return to meditating upon Little Gidding and a
previous war ('If I think, again, of this place') and of the lessons
imparted by 'History': 1942, when 'Little Gidding' was published,

was the tercentenary of the beginning of the English Civil War. The focus here is on the need for 'detachment', a detachment from the party politics and partisanship that the historical record both illustrates and promotes (as a second-best, however, 'attachment' is to be preferred to the 'indifference' of the vestibule-dwellers whom Eliot is always castigating). As a self-declared 'royalist in politics', a stance that is part of his wider commitment to Anglican authority, we might expect Eliot to take the side of the figure he had previously referred to as 'Charles, King and Martyr',[19] especially given his declaration that 'the Civil War is not ended: I question whether any serious civil war ever does end' ('Milton II', *OP* 148). But in 'Little Gidding' the historical retrospect now, like the re-evaluation in age of the individual life, is to provide 'freedom' from, rather than 'servitude' to, a political cause. The lesson that the protagonists on both sides of the Civil War teach (Charles I is 'opposed' here by, among others, 'one who died blind and quiet', namely the republican Milton) is one of unity rather than opposition: from our modern perspective they are 'United in the strife which divided them', and reconciled in death:

> These men, and those who opposed them
> And those whom they opposed
> Accept the constitution of silence
> And are folded in a single party.

They have bequeathed to us a 'symbol', which is far more important than the oppositional party causes they served, a symbol of a final conciliation not only in death but in the hereafter, where hostility and division, an inevitable part of the 'exile' of temporal history, will be resolved.

The word 'folded' here will be picked up at the end of the *Quartets* in the line 'When the tongues of flame are in-folded', referring to the final return to a state beyond time and its destructions and beyond the expiations of purgatory. The last part of 'Little Gidding' begins with the poem's last act of auto-criticism, but now not stressing the difficulties of mastering language, as in the first two Quartets, but celebrating the (inevitably relative) success the poem has achieved, in the cases of 'every phrase / And sentence that is right'. The 'rightness' of language occurs when that language avoids extremes, being 'neither diffident nor ostentatious', 'common' but not vulgar, and so forth, this attempt to maintain a linguistic *via media* between oppositions taking us back to the 'still point' of 'Burnt Norton' II, which is mystically sited in that intervening space between linguistic antitheses, 'Neither flesh nor fleshless', and so forth. Moreover, this mediate language of *Four Quartets* is one where individual words and phrases are less significant than the total design: words are only 'at home' in this poem where their primary function is not to parade themselves 'ostentatiously' but 'to support the others'; again as 'Burnt Norton' has already told us, it is only the overall 'form' or 'pattern' that can communicate a sense of the 'stillness'. The extreme formal consciousness of *Four Quartets*, its insistence on music and dance as providing an appropriate 'pattern' for its own procedures, the formal replication of the five-part structure in each Quartet, the recurrence, with variations, of key themes and diction, are stressed here once more in the analogy between the achieved poem and the 'complete consort dancing together'. Everything, we might say, is 'in step'; a formally constrained motion that, revolving on itself, signals a stillness that takes the form of dancing.

The poem thus 'ends', though only on a qualified note of self-congratulation, for ends are only important in so far as they lead to beginnings. 'Any action' leads to death, another end whose true value lies in its beginning the transit from the temporal to the eternal, while 'History' is here defined not as a record of temporal events but precisely of those 'moments' that signal that which lies beyond the temporal. The *Quartets* thus reminds us that in doing the best it can to communicate with a perishable medium, language, it perforce occupies a particular time and place ('now and England'). For all its formal exertions, the poem is inevitably provisional: 'next year's words await another voice', and our perceptions of the timeless change according to our historical situation – it cannot be 'fixed' forever. Moreover, Eliot was well aware, as we have seen, that the reading process itself is dynamic and mobile, and that it changes over time, just as language itself does, so that the *Quartets*, whatever its aspiration towards 'stillness', can never escape an endless process of cultural renegotiation, or be preserved in a kind of interpretative aspic. Nor indeed would Eliot want it to. Every poem is 'an epitaph', that is, it is inscribed with its own place and date; we might want to embody or finalize our meaning as best we can, and we might be promoting death as the key to a new beginning, but we do not want the poem itself to become a dead thing. In the *Quartets* this linguistic tussle between stillness and motion is kept in play throughout the sequence. Such tensions are symptomatic of our historico-linguistic state, but the poem ends on our destiny beyond language, 'the end of all our exploring', and our return to the rose-garden, now in its paradisal glory:

> When the tongues of flame are in-folded
> Into the crowned knot of fire
> And the fire and the rose are one.

The last word is 'one': earthly divisions, signified by the different 'tongues', are knotted together into a 'crowned' unity, and the divine chastisement, whether of the fires of destruction or purgatorial renewal, is seen as part of the same scheme of joy and childish laughter as that represented by the original rose-garden.

SPEAKING TO EUROPE

In a key essay that brings together many of Eliot's perennial interests, 'What is a Classic?', originally delivered as a lecture in 1944, a year after the *Quartets* was published in its entirety, he talks at some length about a 'common style' in writing poetry which has clear links with the poem he had recently finished: 'a common style is one which makes us exclaim, not "this is a man of genius using the language" but "this realizes the genius of the language"' (*OP* 63). One of the qualities of a 'classic' work of literature for Eliot is that it should display not the poet's personal skill or style or idiosyncrasy but suppress these in the interests of this common 'genius'; he argues in fact that English has never produced a 'classic' work, because in the case of our greatest writers, like Shakespeare and Milton, 'we are always conscious of the greatness of the man, and of the miracles that *he* is performing with the language' (*OP* 63). In presenting the 'common word' in 'Little Gidding' and in avoiding ostentation or extremes of language it would seem Eliot is trying to write in this non-individualistic, 'classic' style. His rejection of precisely those things that featured in *The Waste Land*, dialect, colloquialisms, multiple voices, suggests that the setting of this Quartet in 'England' requires an English that does not belong to this locality or that, or this social class or that, but is representative of a linguistic norm, one that approaches the 'genius of the language'. As we have noted, this is an English often highly conscious of its Latin roots; in 'What is a Classic?' Eliot argues under a variety of heads for Virgil's *Aeneid* as the absolute classic, a work that brought the Latin language to perfection at a time when, as far as Europe was concerned, that language had a universal status. Virgil is 'our classic, the classic of all Europe', and Latin, and through Latin Greek, remains the 'blood-stream of European literature' (*OP* 70). In 'What is a Classic?' Eliot reminds a war-torn Europe of its common cultural inheritance, and *Four Quartets* nourishes itself at that 'blood-stream'.

Thus the poem's English displays an essential unity, rather than diversity, not only embodying linguistically the need for national unity in wartime but, as importantly, exhibiting that bringing together of one tongue as a figure, in little, of the final unification of the separate languages. The 'common style' with its Latinity and avoidance of individualistic extremes also makes the poem available for translation into other European languages – just as Dante's common style made him far more translatable than Shakespeare (*OP* 63, *SE* 241) – in a manner indicating Eliot's poetic contribution to the 'war effort' as simultaneously a speaking on behalf of 'England' and a reminder that the relation between England and Europe is indissoluble. In *Notes Towards the Definition of Culture*, published in 1948 but made up of work 'begun four or five years' previously, Eliot outlines in an appendix his understanding of 'The Unity of European Culture', an account previously given in 'three broadcast talks to Germany' at the end of the war (*NDC* 9). Here he resumes the argument from 'What is a Classic?' on the importance of Europe's unifying heritage 'in Christianity and in the ancient civilisations of Greece, Rome and Israel, from which, owing to two thousand years of Christianity, we trace our descent' (*NDC* 123).[20] He also argues that

> for the health of the culture of Europe two conditions are required: that the culture of each country should be unique, and that the different cultures should recognise their relationship to each other, so that each should be susceptible of influence from the others. (*NDC* 119)

Both national isolation and the reducing of the different countries to one identity are to be rejected; in short, 'we need variety in unity: not the unity of organisation, but the unity of nature' (*NDC* 120).

Eliot also spoke in these broadcasts of his editorship of the *Criterion* between 1922 and 1939 (see above, pp. 63–4), and of the magazine's 'international scope', its publishing European writers alongside native ones, linking with other reviews in 'every capital of Europe', and cementing a 'fraternity of men of letters' which 'did not replace, but was perfectly compatible with, national loyalties' (*NDC* 115–8). As national separatism and international enmity grew during the 1930s, this network of communication became increasingly difficult to maintain; in Eliot's sombre 'Last Words', the editorial to the final issue of January 1939, he notes how gradually 'the "European mind", which one had mistakenly thought might be renewed and fortified, disappeared from view'. The editorial is a valediction to this ideal:

> in the present state of public affairs – which has induced in myself a depression of spirits so different from any other experience of fifty years as to be a new emotion – I no longer feel the enthusiasm necessary to make a literary review what it should be.[21]

His contribution to 'the unity of European culture' continues in other forms during his wartime writing, and expands in scope after the war.[22] *Notes Towards the Definition of Culture*, for example, talks not only about the relation of England to Europe, but about the relation of the former to internal regionalism and the latter to ideals of 'world culture'. In arguing against the assumption 'that the unity of wartime should be preserved in time of peace' (*NDC* 51), Eliot insists on the need for what he calls 'satellite' cultures to flourish, with Scotland, Wales and Ireland in a relation of mutual enrichment with England rather than comprising a state whereby 'we should all become indistinguishable featureless "Britons"' (*NDC* 55). The relation between Europe and its national parts should be mirrored in that between a nation and its constituent localities: 'a national culture, if it is to flourish, should be a constellation of cultures, the constituents of which, benefiting each other, benefit the whole'. Indeed, Eliot elaborates on 'the vital importance for a society of *friction* between its parts' (italics in original); not only is this a source of creative energy, but it helps redress that centralization that, in the recent cases of Germany and Italy, led to belligerence: 'a country which is too well united . . . is a menace to others' (*NDC* 58–9). If *Four Quartets* emphasizes aspirations towards unity, integration and 'oneness', this is part of its character as a wartime poem; it may be Eliot's 'last word', poetically speaking, but as *Notes Towards the Definition of Culture* shows, Eliot's thought continues to develop beyond it.

CONCLUSION: NEW ELIOTS FOR OLD?

So I assumed a double part . . .

—*'Little Gidding' II*

It is the case, I think, that at the moment Eliot is not a popular writer on university courses. His poetry is often felt to be tiresomely 'difficult' and expressive of alienating prejudices like anti-feminism and anti-Semitism. The simple fact of his being a poet rather than novelist, together with his Christian belief, identifies him with minority interests that fewer and fewer readers are likely to feel comfortable with, or knowledgeable about, and this further contributes to his lack of popularity. And besides factors that relate to Eliot personally, he has suffered a representative unfashionableness, that of being a great white male, or more correctly *the* great white male, whose poetry and criticism was so revered in the academy in the third quarter of the last century in particular. Even without the elements of his work now regarded as unsympathetic, and without the opposition to the 'canon' that has been a feature of recent literary study, he would have been affected by the generational pendulum.

As we saw above, Eliot came to regret the extremist thinking of a book like *After Strange Gods*, but we can find plentiful examples elsewhere in his work not only of his anti-liberal viewpoint, but of its being expressed with a categorical assurance that can also be exasperating: the epigraph to the third chapter of this book can stand as an example. On the other hand, Eliot frequently apologized, in retrospect, for the tone of his earlier writing. He does this as early as 1928, in the Preface to the reprinted *The Sacred Wood* of 1920, where he detects in the essays 'frequently a stiffness and an assumption of pontifical solemnity which may be tiresome to many readers' (*SW* vii). He continues in this vein in an essay written near the end of his life which is the fullest review he made of his own critical work, 'To Criticize the Critic (1961): 'there are errors of tone: the occasional note of arrogance, of vehemence, of cocksureness or rudeness, the braggadocio of the mild-mannered man safely entrenched behind his typewriter' (*TC* 14). Apology, indeed, becomes a notable feature of the later Eliot, particularly when he stands on the lecture-platform: apology for publishing the notes to *The Waste Land* (*OP* 109–10), for making a dramatic hero out of an 'insufferable prig' (above, p. 99). The later writing sometimes has the air of the confessional, and 'To Criticize the Critic' ends on the virtue of 'humility' which should inform the critic's writings as he gets older.

Whether this parade of faults appeases readers who have been put off by various aspects of Eliot's work is an open question. Might his later comment on *The Waste Land*, where 'I wasn't even bothering whether I understood what I was saying' (above, p. 42), be a comfort to readers who feel they cannot 'understand' the work, in assuring them that the poem is indeed incomprehensible? On the other hand, we must, as I remarked earlier, be careful about putting our trust in these later statements of Eliot. I have no doubt that he did come to regret his 'pontifical solemnity', but he was also aware that his writings are the product of a specific historical time and place, and that the 1950s, for example, cannot annul or rewrite the occasion of the early 1920s. Everything had changed for Eliot, personally and professionally, by the later period: the personal happiness he finally found in his second marriage, the consolidation and security of his reputation – he was awarded both the Order of Merit and the Nobel Prize in 1948 – even the notable West End success of his play *The Cocktail Party* of 1949. Of course, Eliot had become an esteemed public figure before this period, as the invitation to give the Clark Lectures at Cambridge (1926) and the various American lecture tours of the 1930s show; but he was increasingly deluged by this type of recognition, plus the chairmanship of many societies and the award of 16 honorary doctorates from British universities and elsewhere. And to judge from the tone of Eliot's later lectures – the affability, at times jocularity, of 'The Frontiers of Criticism' (1956), for example, or 'American Literature and the American Language' (1953) (*OP* 103–18, *TC* 43–60) – Eliot seemed very at home in this public role. There is nothing of the agonizing soul-searching of the 'eminent men of letters' ('East Coker' III) we had found in *Four Quartets*.

In 'To Criticize the Critic', although regretting the tone of the earlier work, he also stands by it, not only as the inevitable 'dogmatism of youth' where the ageing writer will acknowledge more reservations and qualifications, but as a necessary strategy in the literary polemics of the time, a consequence of the need to establish his own poetry by attacking prevailing tastes. Thus, 'I was writing in a context which the reader of today has either forgotten, or has never experienced' (*TC* 16). He also implies that his later doubts about *The Waste Land* notes are occasioned, as we have seen, by his worry about their subsequent effect on the practice of literary criticism, a different practice from the 'impressionistic' criticism prevailing when the poem was written. We must therefore bear in mind the historical context in approaching Eliot's critical pronouncements; over the course of a long career characterized by a high degree of self-reflexivity there will be change and doubt but no straightforward repudiation. In 'To Criticize the Critic' Eliot finds himself 'constantly irritated by having my words, perhaps written thirty or forty years ago, quoted as if I had uttered them yesterday', and insists that the date of any essay should always be borne in mind as indicating its historical occasion. He gives as an example the famous statement of 1928 about being 'classicist in literature' and so forth as one that 'has continued to dog its author long after it has ceased, in his opinion, to be a satisfactory statement of his beliefs' (*TC* 14–15).

Yet in going on to discuss that statement further in the essay, he indicates that fundamentally his viewpoint remains the same, though 'I should not be inclined to express it in quite this way' (*TC* 15). There is change, but also a conspicuous degree of consistency in Eliot's criticism. 'The Frontiers of Criticism' of 1956 is an essay that maintains much of the earlier outlook: 'the error' in responding to literature of 'mistaking explanation for understanding' (*OP* 109); the reservations about criticism based on biography (*OP* 111–12); the insistence that 'the meaning is what the poem means to different sensitive readers' (*OP* 113); the declaration that 'I do not think of *enjoyment* and *understanding* as distinct activities – one emotional and the other intellectual' (*OP* 115). This last statement resumes Eliot's key struggle throughout his work to maintain what he would see as the 'integrity' of poetry – that it is not versified religion, or morality, or philosophy, or 'belief'. As he had previously declared, it certainly has something to 'do with' morals, religion and politics

(*SW* x), and 'understanding' should be addressed to finding out what this 'something' is, otherwise 'our enjoyment will profit us no more than mere amusement and pastime' (*OP* 117). But a poem can never be fully 'explained' or its 'meaning' defined: 'there is, in all great poetry, something which must remain unaccountable . . . and . . . that is what matters most' (*OP* 112). What we ultimately have is the poem, irreducible to anything else; compare the statement from *The Use of Poetry* that 'that which is to be communicated is the poem itself, and only incidentally the experience and the thought which have gone into it' (*UP* 30). And there are comments from other late essays which sound like a resumé of 'Tradition and the Individual Talent':

> it is not that we have repudiated the past, as the obstinate enemies – and also the stupidest supporters – of any new movement like to believe; but that we have enlarged our conception of the past; and that in the light of what is new we see the past in a new pattern. ('American Literature and the American Language', *TC* 57)

The manner of expression may have been toned down, but there is a large degree of consistency throughout Eliot's critical work, just as I have argued for a consistency of outlook throughout the poetry, whatever the marked stylistic shift around the mid-1920s. Writing plays in the 1930s meant for Eliot a necessary 'simplification of language' in the interests of the audience's comprehension, and this resulted in 'the later *Quartets* . . . being much simpler and easier to understand than *The Waste Land* and "Ash-Wednesday". Sometimes the thing I'm trying to say, the subject matter, may be difficult, but it seems to me that I'm saying it in a simpler way' ('The Art of Poetry', p. 63). Whether readers today find the *Quartets* 'easier' given the increased remoteness of that (Christian) subject matter is doubtful, and even if they do, this may not lead to agreeing with Eliot's statement in the same interview that the *Quartets* are his 'best work', and get progressively better through the sequence (p. 64). As for *The Waste Land,* for those who do not experience 'now and then some direct shock of poetic intensity' as they struggle to 'decipher' it (*SE* 238), the difficulty of the poem will remain a disheartening experience, especially if it is a set text on the syllabus.

With regard to the charges of Eliot's elitism or cultural snobbery, I don't think he was writing with the principal aim of showing off, or mystifying a less lettered audience; his poetry would hardly have

survived had that been the case. We should remember that his education, both at school and university, had provided him with access to
a wide range of foreign literature, philosophy, theology and anthro-
pology, and that to write out of these interests was entirely natural.
Moreover, at the point of writing *The Waste Land*, Eliot is unlikely
to have had in mind future undergraduates and the examination systems imposed on them. I believe in effect in his poetic sincerity, that
he wrote what he *had* to, and what he had to surrender himself to; or,
in his words, that the 'struggle' to 'transmute his personal and private
agonies into something rich and strange' was genuine (*SE* 137). He
will quote in the notes to *The Waste Land* 19 lines from Ovid without
giving a translation, but why should this be a problem when any
number of translations exists on the library shelf? If Eliot's recondite
allusions have by now been disarmed by the army of commentators
producing student guides that give their sources, there remains the
distinction between explanation and understanding, as Eliot was well
aware, or, as he put it more sententiously in *The Rock*, 'Where is the
wisdom we have lost in knowledge? / Where is the knowledge we have
lost in information?' (*CP* 147). An emphasis on 'knowledge' and
information might lead us to overlook the fact that 'the experience of
a poem is the experience both of a moment and of a lifetime' (*SE*
250), and that the idea of 'mastering' a text in order to pass an exam
on it is not the end of such experience. When Eliot urges wisdom
in 'East Coker' as essentially the 'wisdom of humility', which is 'endless', perhaps he indicates a virtue – although the concept is unfash-
ionable – that we all need to accept as readers.

Eliot's poetry makes demands on its readers, but those demands
can be very fruitful – they might be the starting point of access, for
example, to writers like Dante or Baudelaire, and thus contribute
significantly to one's education. The later poetry, drawing conspicuously on a belief-system that many readers will not share, is undoubt-
edly today less read, studied and written about than the early work.
A section like 'East Coker' IV – 'The dripping blood our only drink',
and so on – may well present 'subject matter' that is insuperably alien.
This raises of course the theme of 'poetry and belief' that so exercised
Eliot himself; we have seen his part-denial that 'the reader must share
the beliefs of the poet in order to enjoy the poetry fully' (*SE* 269)
elaborated into the proposition that when the 'doctrine . . . or "view
of life" presented in a poem' has qualities such as coherence and
maturity then it need provide 'no obstacle to the reader's enjoyment'

whether the reader believes it or not (*UP* 96).[1] John Xiros Cooper has argued persuasively that the great popularity of the *Quartets* during and after World War II cannot be a result of the Christian viewpoint it offers, but derives from its other consolations, that in a time 'of cultural despair and fragmentation' the reader seeks refuge from 'history' in a deep personal 'inwardness' and in the wholeness of the aesthetic experience itself.[2] The poem proposes that 'renunciation of and detachment from history and worldly action is the only saving stratagem in difficult times' (p. 173). While many readers would not accept such renunciation on behalf of the gospel of Christian salvation, the formulation 'all shall be well' chimes with a less doctrinal stoicism and general sense of the hope and refuge needed in such times. I myself have also explored how the poem could be understood as 'patriotic' in spite of the many qualifications it attaches to patriotism (Ellis, *The English Eliot*, pp. 77–140). Perhaps a proportion of readers of the *Quartets* still responds along these lines, or simply enjoys the beauties of rhythm and image ('the future is a faded song . . . a lavender spray / Of wistful regret for those who are not yet here to regret, / Pressed between yellow leaves of a book that has never been opened'), notwithstanding Eliot's reservations about 'enjoyment' alone.

After the completion of the *Quartets*, Eliot's creative ambition focused almost entirely on writing for the theatre, resulting in the verse plays *The Cocktail Party* (first produced 1949), *The Confidential Clerk* (1953) and *The Elder Statesman* (1958). Although the first mentioned did enjoy a good deal of success, the later two have not received much attention, either in the theatrical world or among literary critics. The common judgement of a progressive decline in quality may mirror the fact that the plays become less doctrinal, in Christian terms, in turn, as if wrestling with issues of faith, sin, martyrdom and so forth in the earlier plays, whatever the problems this might cause for non-believers, was the source of their energy and power. Eliot's reaching out for a more extensive audience, and what seems his mellower disposition in his later years, conspire to produce a rather muted social comedy.

The Cocktail Party is the liveliest and funniest, despite (or because of) its retention of the theme of martyrdom, in this case the crucifying of Celia Coplestone by the natives she lives among as a missionary. This is a reported rather than enacted death, taking place offstage; the focus is rather on the more mundane protagonists who, with no such spiritual vocation, have to make of their habitual lives 'the best of a bad job', which is all 'any of us make of it – / Except, of course, the saints' (*CP* 410). The encouragement to stoicism in these lines is the teaching of the mysterious consultant in the play, Sir Henry Harcourt-Reilly, who also doubles as a priest-figure, ending his consultations by telling his patients to 'Go in peace. And work out your salvation with diligence' (*CP* 411). Eliot also takes the opportunity, in the act that is set in Sir Henry's consulting room, to continue his satire on 'psychological' explanations, in this case of so-called 'nervous breakdown' (*CP* 413, 415), rather than on the need for religious solutions to spiritual problems. But this religious context is far less in evidence in the two final plays, which are occupied with questions of identity, social role-play and the frustrations and lack of authenticity in 'playing a part' in our private and public lives (*CP* 501, 552), rather than with the search for 'salvation' as formerly understood.

These questions had always been important for Eliot since his earliest poetry, of course, where the roles in society his protagonists are confined to through their own weakness and the manipulations of others are a central preoccupation of 'Prufrock' and 'Portrait of a Lady'. This consciousness of playing a role, or rather several roles, is evident in the frequent use of the double or mirror figure in Eliot's work – 'Let us go then, you and I', 'Stetson! / You who were with me in the ships at Mylae!', the fourth tempter in *Murder* who quotes Becket's very words back to him (*CP* 245, 255–6). The idea of a dual identity representing the censoring/policing self on the one hand and the self drawn by illicit desire on the other has already been suggested (above, p. 56), and Eliot's characterization of Tennyson, 'the most instinctive rebel against the society in which he was the most perfect conformist' (*SE* 337), is really something of a self-portrait of the staid City banker who could also dress up as Dr Crippen for a party (Gordon, *T. S. Eliot*, p. 288).[3] The inability to be 'whole', the condition of being dispersed across these several selves, is doubtless one of the effects of spiritual alienation, of 'where you are' being 'where you are not', though occasionally, as with Sir Henry Harcourt-Reilly, who is also the One Eyed Riley of the comic song (*CP* 365), the double identity seems to enhance status. His role in the play, however, is that of 'Guardian', a dispenser of spiritual enlightenment rather than a searcher for it.

Rebel, conformist, murderer, saint: the different roles Eliot is drawn to in his work have, in some recent critical writing, led to a

marked rejection of the idea of him as primarily the Christian classicist; the picture of him emerging now is, in David E. Chinitz's words,
of 'a richer and more engaging figure . . . a multidimensional thinker
and artist', especially in his interest in popular culture, which is 'sup-
ple, frequently insightful, and always deeply ambivalent' (Chinitz,
T. S. Eliot and the Cultural Divide, p. 5). In emphasizing this interest,
Chinitz admits that 'I am no doubt attempting to account for, and
possibly to justify, my own responsiveness to Eliot's work,' but the
hope is that 'by bringing this element to light' Eliot will become
'more interesting and accessible to readers of my own generation'
(pp. 11–12). In this hope, Chinitz is joined by the editors of the recent
volume on *Gender, Desire, and Sexuality in T. S. Eliot*, referred to in
Chapter 2, who wish to show that a hitherto 'monolithic' and 'reactionary conception of early modernist culture' has obscured the rich
and varied 'gender phenomena' in Eliot, the volume attempting his
'resituation in the sex/gender/erotic contradictions of his own milieu'
(pp. 2–4). What this means is a fresh emphasis on things like Eliot's
troubled homoeroticism, together with, for example, claims for 'his
transgressive attitudes toward domesticity and marriage', which were
'for early women academics . . . uniquely inspiring' (p. 7). Gail
McDonald's essay on this latter topic calls attention to the following
the early poetry enjoyed in women's colleges, how it was 'undergraduate contraband' for the young of both sexes, and how Eliot's 'theory
of impersonality', for example, 'spoke persuasively to women for
whom the various attributes of the personal – emotions, vulnerabili-
ties, confidences – were, for professional reasons, best kept at bay'.[4]
Another contributor to the volume also argues that 'impersonality
undermines masculinity because it enjoins the renunciation of self-
possession and self-control'.[5]

The exploration here of 'Eliot's interaction with various public
and interior sectors of women, desire, and the feminine' (p. 5) also
results in claims that the significant roles in the later drama are female
ones, such as those of Celia and Julia in *The Cocktail Party*.[6] If we
cannot now call Eliot a feminist, certainly we have a marked shift
from the portrayal of his anti-feminism in the earlier criticism, and
some critics are likewise trying to take the anti-Semitism debate out
of the 'was he or wasn't he' territory to explore its 'resituation' in the
complexities of his own milieu.[7] This movement among a new generation of critics may result in students being offered in future a
'more engaging figure', in Chinitz's words, one who might reverse the

decline in appeal I spoke of at the outset: Eliot is sexier, or his work displays a more 'multidimensional' sexuality, just as he is cooler, not only the reader of Dante but the fan of Raymond Chandler and Groucho Marx. But when Chinitz ends his book by arguing that 'the portentous, the elitist, the mandarin Eliot' known to a previous generation of readers was once perhaps 'needed' but is so no longer – 'we who have inherited this Eliot do not need him and so reject him' – and that it is the Eliot who 'transgressed the cultural divide' who now 'matters' – 'this Eliot is needed today . . . if Eliot is to matter at all' (p. 189) – the effect is to call for the simple substitution of one Eliot by the other. This would be a great pity. If criticism is taking the trouble to excavate a more plural Eliot then to dispense with any aspect of him – the Dante-reading aspect for example – undoes the very passage towards multiplicity, and the absorbing challenges this provokes, that should be the point of the exercise. In 'Thoughts after Lambeth' Eliot warned that 'you will never attract the young by making Christianity easy' (*SE* 373), and an emphasis on 'accessibility' might not be the way to promote Eliot's attractions. And even David Chinitz, who would like to 'reposition' the 'Marie Lloyd' essay 'at the heart of Eliot's critical thinking' (p. 15), is content on page 18 to give no more than a passing reference to *Cats*.

NOTES

INTRODUCTION

[1] Ronald Schuchard, *Eliot's Dark Angel: Intersections of Life and Art* (New York: Oxford University Press, 1999), p. 52.

[2] Kenneth Asher, *T. S. Eliot and Ideology* (Cambridge: Cambridge Univ. Press, 1995), pp. 2–3.

[3] See *WLF* 2–3. The epigraph is taken from the climactic moment of Joseph Conrad's novella *Heart of Darkness* – its significance for Eliot is discussed below (pp. 66–7).

[4] The comment is taken from the synopsis of some extension lectures Eliot gave in 1916; it has been frequently quoted in the criticism, as for example in Asher, *T. S. Eliot and Ideology*, p. 38, Schuchard, *Eliot's Dark Angel*, pp. 27–8.

[5] I. A. Richards, *Science and Poetry* (London: Kegan Paul, Trench, Trubner, 1926), pp. 64–5n. The statement had previously appeared in Richards's essay 'A Background for Contemporary Poetry', *Criterion*, 3 (1924–5), 520.

[6] Preface to 1928 edition of *The Sacred Wood: Essays on Poetry and Criticism*, 7th ed. (London: Methuen, 1950) pp. viii, x.

[7] The Longman Critical Readers volume, ed. and introd. Harriet Davidson (Harlow: Longman, 1999), has the all-encompassing title *T. S. Eliot*, though it focuses almost exclusively on the early work and overwhelmingly on *The Waste Land*. *Four Quartets* merits a handful of pages, but poems like 'The Hollow Men' and 'Ash-Wednesday' none at all. Precisely the same point can be made about the contribution on Eliot by Andrew DuBois and Frank Lentricchia to *The Cambridge History of American Literature*, vol 5, *Poetry and Criticism 1900-1950*, ed. Sacvan Bercovitch (Cambridge: Cambridge University Press, 2003), pp. 97–130.

[8] 'For T. S. E.', in *T. S. Eliot: the Man and His Work*, ed. Allen Tate (1966; rpt. Harmondsworth: Penguin, 1971), p. 92.

THE EARLY POETRY AND PROSE

[1] W. B. Yeats, 'Modern Poetry: A Broadcast', *Essays and Introductions* (London: Macmillan, 1961), p. 499.

[2] *The Variorum Edition of the Poems of W. B. Yeats*, ed. Peter Allt and Russell K. Alspach (New York: Macmillan, 1957), p. 491.

[3] Eliot's own response to Yeats is an increasingly admiring one, though the Yeats broadcast came in the wake of the rather mixed judgement on him Eliot gave in *After Strange Gods* (1934). Here, in ironic antithesis to Yeats, Eliot implied his own relative isolation in attempting to 'maintain classical ideals' in what remains 'a romantic age' (*ASG* 34–5).

[4] W. B. Yeats, *A Vision*, 2nd corrected ed. (London: Macmillan, 1962), p. 300.

[5] For Wordsworth's discussion of poetry as originating in 'emotion recollected in tranquillity', see the Preface to the *Lyrical Ballads* (1802) in *William Wordsworth*, Oxford Authors, ed. Stephen Gill (Oxford: Oxford University Press, 1986), p. 611.

[6] The idea of a poet-medium through whom the dead communicate is forcefully staged for Eliot by Dante, who features a Virgil 'hoarse from long silence' speaking again at the beginning of the *Inferno* (Dante Alighieri, *La divina commedia (Inferno, Purgatorio, Paradiso)* ed. Natalino Sapegno, 3 vols (Florence: La nuova Italia, 1979), 1. 63). For another approach to Eliot's mediumship, see Tim Dean, 'T. S. Eliot, famous clairvoyante', in *Gender, Desire, and Sexuality in T. S. Eliot*, ed. Cassandra Laity and Nancy K. Gish (Cambridge: Cambridge University Press, 2004), pp. 43–65.

[7] For discussion of the title and structure of *The Sacred Wood*, and its place in the literary politics of its time see Peter White, 'New Light on *The Sacred Wood*', *RES*, 54 (2003), 497–515.

[8] Eliot reiterates the point elsewhere: 'what happens to a poet who has an original philosophy? Does he not become the victim of those who want their philosophy cheap and without thought, and is he not, like Blake, perpetually a riddle to those who seriously would estimate his greatness as a poet?' (*VMP* 224). Compare 'a poet may borrow a philosophy or he may do without one. It is when he philosophises upon his own *poetic* insight that he is apt to go wrong' (*UP* 99).

[9] Eliot discusses the relation between individualism and Protestantism, or rather, with the latter in its 'decay', in *After Strange Gods: A Primer of Modern Heresy*. The Page-Barbour Lectures at the University of Virginia 1933 (London: Faber, 1934), pp. 38–42.

[10] 'Anyone with a sense of centre and periphery must admit that the western tradition has been Latin, and Latin means Rome' (*NDC* 73). The essay most dedicated to this Latin centre is 'What is a Classic?', published in 1945, considered in Chapter 4.

[11] On this, see Steve Ellis, *The English Eliot: Design, Language and Landscape in 'Four Quartets'* (Routledge, 1991).

[12] Sanford Schwartz argues that Eliot's attack on excessive subjectivity, or a literature of 'personal expression', does not mean that he embraces the 'excessive objectivity' of nineteenth-century mimetic realism. Indeed, scepticism about any clear division between subject and object is one of the things Schwartz claims Eliot took from F. H. Bradley. See Sanford Schwartz, *The Matrix of Modernism: Pound, Eliot, and Early Twentieth-Century Thought* (Princeton: Princeton Univ. Press, 1985), chapter 4,

pp. 155–208. Of course, as Eliot noted in 'Shakespeare and the Stoicism of Seneca', 'what every poet starts from is his own emotions' (*SE* 137); the impulse to poetry has to be intensely and individually felt, even if that poetry is directed towards impersonality, the accessing of the tradition and the avoidance of confessionality. The tradition is only continued, or 'renewed', in being freshly individualized.

[13] Alfred Lord Tennyson, *The Poems of Tennyson*, ed. Christopher Ricks (London: Longman, 1969), pp. 564–6.

[14] See Ronald Schuchard, 'Did Eliot Know Hulme? Final Answer', *Journal of Modern Literature*, 27 (2003), 63–9.

[15] T. E. Hulme, *The Collected Writings of T. E. Hulme*, ed. Karen Csengeri (Oxford: Clarendon, 1994), p. 61. The Pelagian heresy is in the words of Hulme's editor one that 'denied the transmission of original sin' (p. 460).

[16] Ronald Schuchard maintains that as early as 1916 'though Eliot's formal conversion to Anglo-Catholicism was eleven years away, his *sensibility* was religious and Catholic, and his primary critical concerns were moral . . . as his reviews for that year show'. Ronald Schuchard, *Eliot's Dark Angel: Intersections of Life and Art* (New York: Oxford University Press, 1999) p. 68.

[17] T. S. Apteryx (pseud.), 'Observations', *Egoist*, 5 (1918), 69. Anthologies of Georgian poetry appeared five times between 1912 and 1922 and were regarded by more 'progressive' writers as holding to a tradition of insular pastoral escapism. One should note, however, that the Georgians can themselves be seen as in revolt against an older Victorian/Edwardian imperialistic poetry; see C. K. Stead, *The New Poetic: Yeats to Eliot* (1964; rpt. Harmondsworth: Penguin, 1967), chapter 3, pp. 68–95.

[18] John Paul Riquelme, *Harmony of Dissonances: T. S. Eliot, Romanticism, and Imagination* (Baltimore: Johns Hopkins University Press, 1991), p. 47.

[19] W. B. Yeats, *A Vision* (London: Werner Laurie, 1925). For Yeats's discussion of his contemporaries, which is much truncated in the second version of *A Vision* (1937), see pp. 210–2.

[20] 'O swarming city, city full of dreams, where ghosts accost the passers-by in broad daylight!' Charles Baudelaire, *The Complete Verse*, ed., introd. and trans. Francis Scarfe (London: Anvil, 1986), p. 177.

[21] For a fascinating account of Eliot's likely immersion in less intellectual pursuits during his year in France, see Nancy D. Hargrove, 'T. S. Eliot and Popular Entertainment in Paris, 1910–1911', *Journal of Popular Culture*, 36 (2003), 547–88.

[22] M. A. R. Habib, *The Early T. S. Eliot and Western Philosophy* (Cambridge: Cambridge Univ. Press, 1999), p. 41.

[23] The exile from the garden of Eden as punishment for eating fruit from the forbidden tree is recounted in Genesis 3.

[24] 'But ye have not so learned Christ . . . / That ye put off ... the old man, which is corrupt according to the deceitful lusts; / And be renewed in the spirit of your mind; / And that ye put on the new man, which after God is created in righteousness and true holiness' (Eph. 4. 20–4). See also Paul's instructions in Col. 3. 9–11 to 'put off the old man' and 'put on the

new man . . . Where there is neither Greek nor Jew . . . but Christ is all, and in all'.

25 Eliot first took issue with Richards over this in 'A Note on Poetry and Belief', *Enemy*, 1 (January 1927), 15–17, replying to Richards's comment in the *Criterion* (above, p. 138, n. 5). The debate is returned to in Chapters 2 and 3.

26 Ezra Pound, 'Harold Munro', *Criterion*, 11 (1931–2), 590.

27 In Craig Raine's translation of the poem, 'How dare you have experiences like me?', *T. S. Eliot* (Oxford: Oxford University Press, 2006), p. 181.

28 'The immense spiritual significance of the Greeks is due to their having been inspired with this central and happy idea of the essential character of human perfection'; 'Hellenism, and human life in the hands of Hellenism, is invested with a kind of aërial ease, clearness, and radiancy; they are full of what we call sweetness and light'. Matthew Arnold, *Culture and Anarchy: An Essay in Political and Social Criticism* (1869), in *Culture and Anarchy and Other Writings*, ed. Stefan Collini (Cambridge: Cambridge University Press, 1993), pp. 66–7, 130.

29 Walter Benjamin, 'Theses on the Philosophy of History', in *Illuminations*, ed. and introd. Hannah Arendt, trans. Harry Zorn (1970; rpt. London: Pimlico, 1999), p. 248. Yeats , *Variorum Poems*, p. 418.

30 Doris was the daughter of Oceanus and wife of Nereus, mother of the female sea-deities the Nereids.

31 Arthur Symons, *The Symbolist Movement in Literature*, introd. Richard Ellmann (1899; rpt. New York: Dutton, 1958), pp. 59–61. Eliot pays tribute to Symons's book as a 'revelation' in 'The Perfect Critic' (*SW* 5).

32 Hugh Kenner, *The Invisible Poet: T. S. Eliot* (1959; rpt. London: W. H. Allen, 1960), pp. 9–11.

33 Symons, *Symbolist Movement*, p. 61 ('Ah! You do not love me; so many others are jealous!' / And I, with an eye drawn towards the Unconscious: / 'Thank you, not bad; and you?').

34 Cited in Christopher Ricks's edition of Eliot's *Inventions of the March Hare: Poems 1909-1917* (London: Faber, 1996), p. 403.

35 Admittedly some of Eliot's women are more threatening than this: see for example the woman 'of sinister and violent eroticism', in Tony Pinkney's words, evoked in the early poem 'Circe's Palace' (*CP* 598), as also Pinkney's discussion of the prose poem 'Hysteria' (*CP* 32), featuring the speaker's 'phantasy of a voracious and cannibalistic vagina'. *Women in the Poetry of T. S. Eliot: A Psychoanalytic Approach* (Macmillan, 1984), pp. 25, 18–24.

36 Eliot's comment on Davidson is cited in Ricks, ed., *Inventions of the March Hare*, p. 398.

37 Ezra Pound, in recommending the poem to Harriet Monroe, the editor of *Poetry* (Chicago) in which it appeared in June 1915, declares 'Prufrock' to be 'the best poem I have yet had or seen from an American', admiring the way that Eliot has 'modernized himself' in the same letter. Subsequent correspondence indicates that Monroe needed some persuading of the poem's merits. See *The Letters of Ezra Pound 1907-1941*, ed. D. D. Paige (London: Faber, 1951), pp. 80, 85, 92–3, 101.

38   The title of chapter 1 of Marshall McLuhan's *Understanding Media: The Extensions of Man* (1964; rpt. Cambridge, MA: MIT Press, 1994).

39   Virginia Woolf, 'Modern Novels' (1919), in *The Essays of Virginia Woolf*, vol. 3, 1919–1924, ed. Andrew McNeillie (London: Hogarth, 1988), p. 33.

40   Eliot expressed his admiration for Ulysses (which Woolf didn't share) to her on several occasions; see *The Diary of Virginia Woolf*, vol. 2, 1920–4, ed. Anne Olivier Bell (1978; rpt. London: Penguin, 1981), pp. 189, 200, 202–3.

FROM *THE WASTE LAND* TO 'THE HOLLOW MEN'

1   *The Waste Land* first appeared without notes in the *Criterion* in October 1922, and in the USA in the *Dial* in November. It was published in book form with the notes by Boni and Liveright in New York in December 1922, and in London by Leonard and Virginia Woolf at the Hogarth Press in 1923.

2   See the interview 'The Art of Poetry I: T. S. Eliot', *Paris Review*, 21 (Spring–Summer 1959), 54, 63–4.

3   See for example Marianne Thormählen: 'it rather looks as if the cryptic Tiresias note came into being as a postscript attempt to create another fusional agent which the poem on its own is incapable of putting on display'. *'The Waste Land': A Fragmentary Wholeness* (Lund: Gleerup, 1978), p. 78.

4   As John Richardson has pointed out, the outcome of natural renewal in the fertility myths is in fact fundamentally incompatible with *The Waste Land*'s emphasis on the 'desert' as a justified punishment, in the Old Testament prophets, for religious backsliding. See 'After the Imagination of Our Own Hearts: Biblical Prophecy and *The Waste Land*', *English*, 48 (1999), 187–98.

5   On the similarities between the faith/doubt struggle in Eliot and the Victorian poets, see David Ned Tobin, *The Presence of the Past: T. S. Eliot's Victorian Inheritance* (Ann Arbor: UMI Research Press, 1983), pp. 9–23; the relation between *The Waste Land* and *In Memoriam* is discussed at pp. 135–8. In a statement of 1927, Eliot noted that 'doubt and uncertainty are merely a variety of belief', a kind of mutual reflex in those searching for commitment, given that 'the majority of people live below the level of belief or doubt' ('A Note on Poetry and Belief', *Enemy*, 1, 16–17).

6   F. R. Leavis, *New Bearings in English Poetry: A Study of the Contemporary Situation* (1932; rpt. Harmondsworth: Penguin, 1972), pp. 73–4.

7   Grover Smith, Jr., *T. S. Eliot's Poetry and Plays: A Study in Sources and Meaning* (Chicago: University of Chicago Press, 1956), pp. 72, 74.

8   Stephen Spender, *Eliot*, Fontana Modern Masters (Glasgow: Fontana, 1975), pp. 103, 96.

9   Michael H. Levenson, *A Genealogy of Modernism: A Study of English Literary Doctrine 1908–1922* (Cambridge: Cambridge University Press, 1984), pp. 191–2.

10   For another reading which stresses the role of Tiresias as unifier, see James Longenbach, *Modernist Poetics of History: Pound, Eliot, and the*

Sense of the Past (Princeton: Princeton University Press, 1987), pp. 200–37. Tiresias's central role is also discussed in John T. Mayer, *T. S. Eliot's Silent Voices* (New York: Oxford University Press, 1989), pp. 275–6.

[11] Lawrence Rainey, *Revisiting 'The Waste Land'* (New Haven: Yale Univ. Press, 2005), p. 115.

[12] Evelyn Waugh, *Brideshead Revisited: the Sacred and Profane Memories of Captain Charles Ryder*, rev. ed. (1945; rpt. Harmondsworth: Penguin, 1962), p. 34. The incident involved the Oxford aesthete Harold Acton, 'leaning out of his window in Christ Church reciting *The Waste Land* through a megaphone to a League of Nations garden party'. Selina Hastings, *Evelyn Waugh: A Biography* (London: Sinclair-Stevenson, 1994), pp. 93–4.

[13] Eliot's rejection of literature as predominantly the expression of 'ideas' is expressed in his August 1918 praise for Henry James having 'a mind so fine that no idea could violate it'. In the same tribute he goes on to complain that 'in England ideas run wild and pasture on the emotions; instead of thinking with our feelings (a very different thing), we corrupt our feelings with ideas'. *The Little Review Anthology*, ed. Margaret Anderson (New York: Hermitage House, 1953), p. 232.

[14] For the interesting argument that Eliot's notes to *The Waste Land* are trying to unify two critical traditions of philology and impressionism, see Jo Ellen Green Kaiser, 'Disciplining *The Waste Land*; or, How to Lead Critics into Temptation', *Twentieth Century Literature*, 44 (1998), 82–99. Kaiser tends to assume however that a 'poststructuralist' sensitivity to disorder is somehow a more authentic response to the poem than one that is produced in turn by its own cultural and historical determinants.

[15] Terry Eagleton, *Criticism and Ideology: A Study in Marxist Literary Theory* (1976; rpt. London: Verso, 1998), p. 150.

[16] See Michael Tratner, *Modernism and Mass Politics: Joyce, Woolf, Eliot, Yeats* (Stanford: Stanford University Press, 1995), chapter 7, pp. 166–82 and Rachel Potter, *Modernism and Democracy: Literary Culture 1900–1930* (Oxford: Oxford University Press, 2006), chapter 4, pp. 130–51.

[17] The poem's animus against the lower social orders is particularly featured in John Xiros Cooper's discussion, 'Reading the "Seduction" Fragment', from *T. S. Eliot and the Politics of Voice: The Argument of 'The Waste Land'* (Ann Arbor: UMI Research Press, 1987), pp. 27–39, rpt. Davidson (ed.), *T. S. Eliot*, pp. 117–35.

[18] Maud Ellmann, *The Poetics of Impersonality: T. S. Eliot and Ezra Pound* (Cambridge, MA: Harvard University Press, 1987), p. 98. Ellmann's chapter on *The Waste Land*, 'A Sphinx without a Secret', is reprinted in Davidson (ed.), *T. S. Eliot*, pp. 90–108.

[19] Christine Froula, 'Eliot's Grail Quest, or, the Lover, the Police, and *The Waste Land*', *Yale Review*, 78 (1989), 235–53, rpt. Davidson (ed.), *T. S. Eliot*, pp. 166–80 (quotation p. 173).

[20] Suzanne W. Churchill, 'Outing T. S. Eliot', *Criticism*, 47 (2005), 8. The titles of some of the works Churchill considers give a clear idea of their forensic approach: John Peter, 'A New Interpretation of *The Waste Land*'

(originally written in 1952) and 'Postscript' (1969), *Essays in Criticism*, 19 (1969), 140–75; James E. Miller, Jr., *T. S. Eliot's Personal Waste Land: Exorcism of the Demons* (University Park: Pennsylvania State University Press, 1978. See also Carole Seymour-Jones, *Painted Shadow: A Life of Vivienne Eliot* (London: Constable, 2001) and Sandra M. Gilbert and Susan Gubar, *No Man's Land: The Place of the Woman Writer in the Twentieth Century*, vol. 2, *Sexchanges* (New Haven: Yale University Press, 1989), pp. 310–4.

21 Cassandra Laity and Nancy K. Gish (ed.) *Gender, Desire, and Sexuality in T. S. Eliot* (Cambridge: Cambridge University Press), pp. 23–104.

22 Almost contemporary with this comment is Eliot's caustic review of the English translation of Freud's *The Future of an Illusion* (1928); see the *Criterion*, 8 (1928–9), 350–3. For Eliot, Freud's attempt to 'treat religion as illusion' is among other things 'shrewd and yet stupid' and characterized by 'verbal vagueness and inability to reason' (p. 350).

23 Of course, though Eliot may have been permissive about the existence of various readings, this doesn't mean he had to agree with them. Some he clearly disliked, as that of I. A. Richards (above, p. 6). See also 'Thoughts after Lambeth', *SE* 368: 'when I wrote a poem called *The Waste Land* some of the more approving critics said that I had expressed the "disillusionment of a generation", which is nonsense. I may have expressed for them their own illusion of being disillusioned, but that did not form part of my intention.'

24 Hugh Kenner, 'The Urban Apocalypse', in *Eliot in His Time: Essays on the Occasion of the Fiftieth Anniversary of 'The Waste Land'*, ed. A. Walton Litz (Princeton: Princeton University Press, 1973), pp. 27, 35.

25 For the argument that Eliot regarded his early poetry culminating in *The Waste Land* in terms of miscarriage or abortion, and that this is themed in the poem itself through multiple references to abortion, see Christina Hauck's densely argued essay 'Abortion and the Individual Talent', *ELH*, 70 (2003), 223–66.

26 In his *Poetry London* review of the first three of the *Four Quartets*, Orwell lamented the absence of a 'vitality and power' that had made early poems like 'Prufrock' and 'Whispers of Immortality' so memorable. See Bernard Bergonzi (ed.), *T. S. Eliot: 'Four Quartets': A Casebook* (Macmillan, 1969), pp. 84, 82.

27 Unpublished lecture cited in F. O. Matthiessen, *The Achievement of T. S. Eliot: An Essay on the Nature of Poetry*, 3rd ed. (New York: Oxford University Press, 1959), p. 90.

28 The publishing history of 'The Hollow Men' is rather complicated. The first four parts had previously appeared in various journals, sometimes in earlier versions and/or in the company of other poems that did not form part of the final 'Hollow Men'. Thus part III originally appeared as one of three poems entitled 'Doris's Dream Songs' in the *Chapbook*, 39 (November 1924), 36–7. The other two poems, clearly related to 'The Hollow Men', now appear among Eliot's 'Minor Poems' (*CP* 133–4). For further details, see Donald Gallup, *T. S. Eliot: A Bibliography*

(London: Faber, 1969) or B. C. Southam, *A Student's Guide to the 'Selected Poems' of T. S. Eliot*, 6th ed. (London: Faber, 1994), p. 260.

29 Joseph Conrad, *Heart of Darkness*, ed. Zdzislaw Najder (1902; rpt. London: Hesperus, 2002), pp. 80–1.

30 Marlow's admiration for Kurtz might be compared with the situation in another work from the period of 'The Hollow Men', Nick Carraway's elevation of the morally dubious but passionate Jay Gatsby above the trivial members of his social circle. F. Scott Fitzgerald, *The Great Gatsby* (1926; rpt. Harmondsworth: Penguin, 1950).

31 E. M. Forster, *A Passage to India* (1924; rpt. Harmondsworth: Penguin, 1961), pp. 125, 145–7.

32 Compare *The Idea of a Christian Society* (London: Faber, 1939), p. 25: 'the Anglo-Saxons display a capacity for *diluting* their religion, probably in excess of that of any other race'.

33 The motif of the terrifying eyes of divine judgement recurs in *The Family Reunion,* 'the desert is cleared, under the judicial sun / Of the final eye, and the awful evacuation / Cleanses (*CP* 335). Compare the unnerving quasi-divine eyes of Dr T. J. Eckleburg in Fitzgerald, *The Great Gatsby*, p. 152.

34 The two parts of *Sweeney Agonistes* are entitled 'Fragment of a Prologue' and 'Fragment of an Agon', an *Agon* being that section of an Aristophanic comedy involving a fierce contest between two protagonists, Sweeney being one of these (hence *Agonistes*). See Robert Crawford, *The Savage and the City in the Work of T. S. Eliot* (Oxford: Clarendon, 1987), pp. 162–3. On the vaudeville and jazz elements in *Sweeney*, see David E. Chinitz, *T. S. Eliot and the Cultural Divide* (Chicago: University of Chicago Press, 2003), chapter 4, pp. 105–27. 'Fragment of an Agon' originally had the subtitle 'From *Wanna Go Home, Baby?*' (*Criterion*, 5 (1927), 74).

35 T. S. Eliot, 'Eeldrop and Appleplex', *Little Review*, May/September 1917, rpt. *The Little Review Anthology*, ed. Anderson, p. 104.

36 Lyndall Gordon, *T. S. Eliot: An Imperfect Life* (London: Vintage, 1998), pp. 202, 206.

'ASH-WEDNESDAY' AND THE WRITING OF THE 1930S

1 In the words of St John of the Cross (see below), 'spiritual humility' is 'that virtue opposed to the first capital vice, spiritual pride'. *Selected Writings*, ed. and introd. Kieran Kavanaugh (New York: Paulist Press, 1987), I. 12. 7.

2 John of the Cross, *Selected Writings*, 1. 12. 6, 1. 3. 3.

3 The first three parts of 'Ash-Wednesday' (with individual titles) were originally published separately in periodicals between 1927–9. In an earlier typescript parts II to IV had titles taken from Dante's *Purgatorio*; part III retained this title, 'Som de L'Escalina' ('Top of the Stair', *Purgatorio*. 26. 146) for its separate appearance in 1929. The details of publication are summarized in B. C. Southam, *Student's Guide*, 6th ed. (London: Faber, 1994) pp. 261–2.

4 Dante Alighieri, *La vita nuova (Poems of Youth)* trans. and introd. Barbara Reynolds (London: Penguin, 1969), p. 31.
5 Certainly several recollections and photographs of Vivienne suggest an appearance and personality that resemble those of a child. 'A Child in Pain' (the phrase is her lover's, Bertrand Russell) is the title of one of the chapters of Carole Seymour-Jones's biography of Vivienne (see *Painted Shadow: A Life of Vivienne Eliot* (London: Constable, 2001) pp. 124–51).
6 In Andrew DuBois and Frank Lentricchia's words, 'the intention driving Eliot's later career – all that he did after he joined the Church of England in 1927 – is public, socially involved, intellectually activist'. 'T. S. Eliot', in *The Cambridge History of American Literature*, vol 5, *Poetry and Criticism 1900–1950*, ed. Sacvan Bercovitch (Cambridge: Cambridge University Press, 2003), p. 126.
7 T. S. Eliot, 'Literature, Science, and Dogma', *Dial*, 82 (Jan.–June 1927), 243.
8 The source is Jacques Maritain, *Art and Scholasticism: With Other Essays*, trans. J. F. Scanlan (London: Sheed and Ward, 1932), p. 109. On the previous page Maritain discusses 'the unconcealed and palpable influence of the devil on an important part of contemporary literature', an enquiry Eliot will pursue in *After Strange Gods.*
9 See also the apology for the book in the 1959 letter to Pound, quoted in Maud Ellmann, *The Poetics of Impersonality: T. S. Eliot and Ezra Pound* (Cambridge, MA: Harvard University Press, 1987), p. 35.
10 See Eliot's 'Prefatory Note' to *The Rock* (London: Faber, 1934).
11 The title of the play, with its 'sardonic implications', was suggested to Eliot by Henzie Raeburn, the wife of E. Martin Browne, who 'worked with Eliot from 1933 to 1958, directing the first productions of all the plays written during that time, and acting as consultant in their making'. Eliot's own original title was *Fear in the Way*. See E. Martin Browne, *The Making of T. S. Eliot's Plays* (Cambridge: Cambridge University Press, 1969), pp. ix, 55–6.
12 On the notable RSC revival of 1993, see Emrys Jones, '*Murder in the Cathedral* at Stratford', in Thormählen, ed., *T. S. Eliot at the Turn of the Century* (Lund: Lund University Press, 1994), pp. 146–61.
13 See D. F. Cheshire, 'T. S. Eliot's *Murder in the Cathedral*: A Survey of its First Performances and Some Important Revivals', *Theatrephile,* 2, no. 8 (Winter 1985), 65.
14 See also his assertion of 'the hereditary body of religious faith and moral practice' against modernizers like the (unnamed) 'eminent liberal divine' in *After Strange Gods*, p. 22.
15 Though perhaps this distinction between murdered wife and forsaken mother is an unnecessary one. Tony Pinkney argues that Harry's violence 'has bearing not on his wife but on his mother' (*Women in the Poetry of T. S. Eliot: A Psychoanalytic Approach* (London: Macmillan, 1984), p. 123), in keeping with Melanie Klein's idea of a 'ferocious sadism towards the maternal body buried deep within the archaeology of the psyche' (p. 145). Pinkney argues that with *The Waste Land* too the 'absent centre . . . is precisely an Oresteian phantasy of attack on the mother' (p. 101).

FOUR QUARTETS

1   See Eliot's interview with John Lehmann for the *New York Times Book Review* (29 November 1953), rpt. Bergonzi, ed., *T. S. Eliot: 'Four Quartets': A Casebook,* (London: Macmillan, 1969), p. 23.

2   Dante's *Paradiso* is full of imagery of mirrors and reflection connected with light and water that Eliot may be echoing here; see, for example, Dante's meeting with the blessed described at 3. 10–21.

3   Dante in the *Paradiso* was for Eliot the great exemplar in the attempt 'to find words for the inarticulate, to capture those feelings which people can hardly even feel, because they have no words for them'. To make people 'comprehend the incomprehensible . . . demands immense resources of language'. 'What Dante Means to Me', *TC* 134.

4   The children in 'Burnt Norton' also have a literary provenance, deriving in part from Kipling's short story 'They' (1904). See Helen Gardner, *The Composition of 'Four Quartets'* (London: Faber, 1978), pp. 39–40.

5   This does not mean, of course, that many suggestive echoes of the Bible cannot be traced; for a concise summary, see Cornelia Cook, 'Fire and Spirit: Scripture's Shaping Presence in T. S. Eliot's *Four Quartets*', *Literature and Theology*, 15 (2001), 85–101.

6   The significance of the lotus is explained in Paul Foster, *The Golden Lotus: Buddhist Influence in T. S. Eliot's 'Four Quartets'* (Sussex: The Book Guild, 1998), pp. 81–2.

7   Seamus Heaney has discussed the contribution of Dante to Eliot's 'classic' English, arguing that it involves some misrepresentation of the colloquial elements in Dante's style, as in the line from the 'Little Gidding' II, 'And the fullfed beast shall kick the empty pail'. Here, in a passage paying homage to Dante, Heaney notes how Eliot 'interposes the smooth and decorous and monosyllabic noun, "pail", as if to distance us from the raucous and parochial energies of the usual "bucket"', energies that are more authentically Dantesque. 'Energies and Identifications: Dante and the Modern Poet', in *Dante Readings*, ed. Eric Haywood (Dublin: Irish Academic Press, 1987), pp. 33–4.

8   The relation of Eliot's poem to 1930s art movements, including constructivism, abstraction and kinetic sculpture, and to the related arts journal *Axis*, is discussed in Steve Ellis, *The English Eliot: Design, Language and Landscape in 'Four Quartets'* (London: Routledge, 1991), especially chapter 1, pp. 8–30.

9   See Eliot's Commentaries in the *Criterion*, 17 (1937–8), 483 and 18 (1938–9), 60; also *After Strange Gods*, p. 17.

10   In this poem Yeats treats his distinguished public status as 'A sixty-year-old smiling public man' with some irony: 'Better to smile on all that smile, and show / There is a comfortable kind of old scarecrow' (*The Variorum Edition of the Poems of W. B. Yeats*, ed. Peter Allt and Russell K. Alspach (New York: Macmillan, 1957), pp. 443–4).

11   This concluding section of 'East Coker' III is based very closely on the lines included by St John of the Cross in his sketch of Mount Carmel, accompanying his spiritual treatise *The Ascent of Mount Carmel*; see

Selected Writings, ed. and introd. Kieran Kavanaugh (New York: Paulist Press, 1987), pp. 44–5.

12 Eliot noted in a letter that a friend of his had called this part of 'East Coker' 'Jansenist', Jansenism being a doctrine deriving from the writings of Cornelius Jansen (died 1638), and echoing Calvinism in its belief that humans were powerless to assist in their own salvation which had been predestined (or not) by God. The letter is quoted in Gardner, *The Composition of 'Four Quartets'* p. 109.

13 For discussion of *In Memoriam* and the *Quartets*, see David Ned Tobin, *The Presence of the Past: T. S. Eliot's Victorian Inheritance* (Ann Arbor: UMI Research Press, 1983), pp. 138–54.

14 See Claudia Milstead, 'Echoes of Krishna and Arjuna in Eliot's "Dry Salvages" and "Little Gidding"', *ELN*, 40 (2003), 62–76.

15 'The last canto of the *Paradiso* . . . is to my thinking the highest point that poetry has ever reached or ever can reach' ('Dante', *SE* 251).

16 'Chthonic': 'Dwelling in or beneath the surface of the earth', often with the suggestion of something dark, primitive, gloomy (*OED*).

17 Ferrar was a friend of George Herbert, whose poetry became increasingly important to Eliot in his later years, and on whom he was to write his final book, *George Herbert*, in 1962. See Ronald Schuchard, '"If I think, again, of this place": Eliot, Herbert and the Way to "Little Gidding"', in *Words in Time: New Essays on Eliot's 'Four Quartets'*, ed. Edward Lobb (London: Athlone, 1993), pp. 52–83.

18 This whole section of Eliot's essay on imitating Dante is of great interest (*TC* 128–9), and notably his remark that this part of 'Little Gidding' 'cost me far more time and trouble and vexation than any passage of the same length that I have ever written' (*TC* 129). A 'masculine' termination is one in which the line ends on a stressed syllable, a 'feminine' on an unstressed.

19 T. S. Eliot, 'Notes on the Way', *Time and Tide*, 5 January 1935, p. 6.

20 As noted in Chapter 1, Eliot seems to put the Greek heritage to work in his own writing to endorse a rather 'dark' sense of human behaviour; with the Roman heritage however, principally in Virgil, we have an ethic of piety, labour and self-denial which Eliot suggests was an important bequest to Christian monasticism. See 'Virgil and the Christian World' (*OP* 125–6). In the same essay he notes how 'the world of Virgil' is 'a more civilized world of dignity, reason and order' than that of Homer (p. 124).

21 'Last Words', *Criterion*, 18 (1938–9), 271, 274.

22 On this, see David A. Williams, '"Several Centers": T. S. Eliot's Wartime Agenda of Cultural Unity and Diversity', *Yeats Eliot Review*, 22 (2005), 15–23.

CONCLUSION

1 Of course, qualities like 'coherence' or 'maturity' are difficult to demonstrate – when does the latter become dessication or outmodedness for example? In 'What is a Classic?' Eliot raises this issue only to avoid it: 'to define *maturity* without assuming that the hearer already knows what it

means, is almost impossible . . . To make the meaning of maturity really apprehensible . . . to the immature, is perhaps impossible' (*OP* 55). This piece of brow beating perhaps doesn't take us very far.

2   John Xiros Cooper, *T. S. Eliot and the Ideology of 'Four Quartets'* (Cambridge: Cambridge University Press, 1995), pp. 113–4, 138–9.

3   The protagonist Eeldrop in Eliot's dialogue divides his time between renting a flat in a seedy and crime-ridden part of the city and living with 'a wife, three children, and a vegetable garden in a suburb'. 'Eeldrop and Appleplex,' *Little Review*, May/September 1917; rpt. *The Little Review Anthology*, ed. Margaret Anderson (New York: Hermitage House, 1953), p. 105.

4   'Through Schoolhouse Windows: Women, the Academy, and T. S. Eliot', in Laity and Gish (eds), *Gender, Desire, and Sexuality in T. S. Eliot* (Cambridge: Cambridge University Press, 2004) pp. 175–94 (quotations pp. 183, 186).

5   Dean, 'T. S. Eliot, famous clairvoyante', p. 59.

6   See the essays by Elisabeth Däumer, 'Vipers, Viragos and Spiritual Rebels: Women in T. S. Eliot's Christian Society Plays' (pp. 234–53) and Richard Badenhausen, 'T. S. Eliot Speaks the Body: the Privileging of Female Discourse in *Murder in the Cathedral* and *The Cocktail Party*' (pp. 195–214).

7   Bryan Cheyette, 'Neither Excuse nor Accuse: T. S. Eliot's Semitic Discourse', *Modernism/Modernity* 10 (2003), 431–7.

FURTHER READING

This section, together with the notes to individual chapters, suggests follow-up criticism relating to the main areas of discussion in the Guide, arranged in the order of that discussion.

The authoritative **biography** of Eliot is by Lyndall Gordon, *T. S. Eliot: An Imperfect Life* (London: Vintage, 1998). See also Peter Ackroyd, *T. S. Eliot* (London: Hamish Hamilton, 1984) and Herbert Howarth, *Notes on Some Figures Behind T. S. Eliot* (London: Chatto & Windus, 1965). Other useful **factual resources** include Caroline Behr, *T. S. Eliot: A Chronology of His Life and Works* (London: Macmillan, 1983) and Donald Gallup, *T. S. Eliot: A Bibliography* (London: Faber, 1969). One volume of Eliot's **letters**, by no means complete, has been published: *The Letters of T. S. Eliot*, Volume 1, 1898–1922, ed. Valerie Eliot (London: Faber, 1988). A major research project that will over the coming years produce new scholarly editions of **Eliot's poetry, plays, prose and correspondence** is being coordinated by the Institute of English Studies, University of London.

The **young Eliot's bawdy and erotic verse**, including the Bolo verses and 'The Triumph of Bullshit', is printed in Appendix A of Christopher Ricks, (ed.), *Inventions of the March Hare: Poems 1909–1917* (London: Faber, 1996), pp. 305–21. Ricks's volume includes poems from this period Eliot never published as well as earlier states of the published work. Apart from Ricks's commentary, for discussion of these poems see John T. Mayer, *T. S. Eliot's Silent Voices* (New York: Oxford University Press, 1989), and, for the bawdy verse particularly, Loretta Johnson, 'T. S. Eliot's Bawdy Verse: Lulu, Bolo and More Ties', *Journal of Modern Literature*, 27 (2003), 14–25.

Eliot's leanings towards **popular culture** are fully discussed in David E. Chinitz, *T. S. Eliot and the Cultural Divide* (Chicago: University of Chicago Press, 2003). Chinitz discusses the relation between the 'popular' and the 'primitive' at pp. 72–80. For full discussion of the ambiguities of Eliot's attraction towards **primitivism** and horror at its manifestations see Robert Crawford, *The Savage and the City in the Work of T. S. Eliot* (Oxford: Clarendon, 1987).

On Eliot's **education**, see 'Undergraduate Courses at Harvard', chapter 3 of Herbert Howarth, *Notes on Some Figures*, pp. 64–94. As Howarth suggests, the comparative literature courses in particular gave Eliot 'a sense of the interconnection of the units of the European comity and . . . prepared him for the doctrine of the unity of European culture' (p. 82). For information on Eliot's pre-Harvard schooling, see his own reminiscences in 'American Literature and the American Language' (*TC* 44–5). Gail McDonald's *Learning to be Modern: Pound, Eliot, and the American University* (Oxford: Clarendon, 1993) discusses the two poets as students, teachers and educational theorists, as well as the subsequent place of their work in the American syllabus.

Eliot's Ph.D. thesis was not published until many years later as *Knowledge and Experience in the Philosophy of F. H. Bradley* (London: Faber, 1964). There is much debate on the influence of the writing of **Bradley** on Eliot's work, ranging from claims that it underlies several of his key critical positions (Lewis Freed, *T. S. Eliot: The Critic as Philosopher* (West Lafayette, In: Purdue Univ. Press, 1979)) to scepticism that Bradley had any significant effect on Eliot at all (Richard Shusterman, *T. S. Eliot and the Philosophy of Criticism* (Duckworth, 1988)). Recent work on Eliot and Bradley includes Manju Jain, *T. S. Eliot and American Philosophy: The Harvard Years* (Cambridge: Cambridge University Press, 1992), especially chapter 7, pp. 205–43, and M. A. R. Habib, *The Early T. S. Eliot and Western Philosophy* (Cambridge: Cambridge University Press, 1999), especially chapter 5, pp. 125–60. See also Richard Wollheim, 'Eliot and F. H. Bradley: An Account', in *Eliot in Perspective: A Symposium*, ed. Graham Martin (London: Macmillan, 1970), pp. 169–93; Sanford Schwartz, *The Matrix of Modernism: Pound, Eliot, and Early Twentieth-Century Thought* (Princeton: Princeton University Press, 1985) and Jewel Spears Brooker, *T. S. Eliot and the Dialectic of Modernism* (Amherst: University of Massachusetts Press, 1994), pp. 172–206. For Eliot and **Bergson**, as well as Habib, see Nancy K. Gish, *Time in the Poetry of T. S. Eliot: A Study in Structure and Theme* (London: Macmillan, 1981), chapter 1, pp. 1–22, Schwartz, *The Matrix of Modernism*, Jain, *T. S. Eliot and American Philosophy*.

The question of Eliot's **religious affiliations**, and why he converted 'not to the Church of Rome but to the Church of England,' is discussed by Rudolph Germer, who also explains in what ways Eliot's religion was 'a reaction against the Unitarianism of his family', and offers a convenient summary of what that Unitarianism was. See 'T. S. Eliot's Religious Development', in *T. S. Eliot at the Turn of the Century*, ed. Marianne Thormählen (Lund: Lund University Press, 1994), 99, 96–7. Germer quotes (p. 92) from Gordon, *T. S. Eliot,* p. 87: 'the turning-point in Eliot's life came not at the time of his baptism in 1927, but in 1914 when he was circling, in moments of agitation, on the edge of conversion.' While Germer is doubtful that 'enough firm evidence' exists for this assertion, he accepts that 'Eliot's so-called conversion was the logical culmination of a long and painful spiritual quest' (p. 92). Eliot's family's religious background is explored in more detail in Eric Sigg, *The American T. S. Eliot: A Study of the Early Writings* (Cambridge: Cambridge University Press, 1989), chapter 1, pp. 1–35.

The question of Eliot's **anti-Semitism**, discussed at length in Christopher Ricks, *T. S. Eliot and Prejudice* (London: Faber, 1988), pp. 25–76, was forcefully developed in Anthony Julius, *T. S. Eliot, Anti-Semitism, and Literary Form* (Cambridge: Cambridge Univ. Press, 1995), which devotes a whole chapter to 'Gerontion' (pp. 41–74) and finds 'in the image of the squatting Jew' (p. 49) a summation of Eliot's racist animus: 'Gerontion's jew is ugly in full measure. Spawned, blistered, patched and peeled, he emerges as if from the swamp, diseased and disfigured' (p. 45); 'he is unclean, unwelcome even in the house that he owns, wretched yet monied. These lines are a horror picture, drawn with loathing. One recoils from them' (p. 49). While things like Eliot's friendship with individual Jews and his assistance on behalf of Jewish refugees in World War II complicate the picture of the trenchant anti-Semitism Julius maintains throughout his book, attempts to refute the prejudice evident in these lines from 'Gerontion' and similar instances elsewhere in Eliot's work seem to me unconvincing. Thus Ronald Schuchard, opening 'Eliot and Anti-Semitism: The Ongoing Debate' in *Modernism/Modernity* 10 (2003), 1–70, pictures Eliot as a philo-Semite, and amongst other defences sees the Jew in 'Gerontion' as a refugee-victim of the political displacements occasioned by World War I ('Burbank with a Baedeker, Eliot with a Cigar: American Intellectuals, Anti-Semitism, and the Idea of Culture', 8). Most of the respondents to Schuchard, including Julius himself, remain unconvinced, though Marjorie Perloff, 'A Response to Ronald Schuchard', pp. 51–6, is more sympathetic.

The importance of the debate is shown by its spilling over into a later issue of *Modernism/Modernity*, where there are four further short contributions, by no means all hostile to Eliot. Perhaps the most constructive is by Bryan Cheyette, who feels that the frequently speculative debate on Eliot's own attitudes, and the taking up of polarized positions of attack/defence, obscures the need for 'a much broader history of differentiating Jews from other human beings', and for 'a genuinely open dialogue about the complex nature of racial discourse within literary texts' ('Neither Excuse nor Accuse: T. S. Eliot's Semitic Discourse', *Modernism/Modernity* 10 (2003), 433–4). See also Daniel T. McGee, 'Dada Da Da: Sounding the Jew in Modernism', *ELH* 68 (2001), 501–27, where 'the Jew' is seen as the source of linguistic degeneration, as presented in *The Waste Land*. Craig Raine's essay 'In Defence of T. S. Eliot', in his book of the same title (London: Picador, 2000, pp. 320–32), aims at refuting the anti-Semitism charge, and is largely repeated in his 'Eliot and Anti-Semitism', in *T. S. Eliot* (Oxford: Oxford University Press, 2006), pp. 149–78. A new edition of Julius's book, 'with a preface and a response to the critics', to quote from the title-page, appeared in 2003 (London: Thames and Hudson). The 'response' is a lengthy post-script (pp. 302–35) addressed to those who rejected his argument, sometimes fiercely, on its first appearance, and although Julius is able to defend much of his thinking on Eliot he by no means addresses the issues of the omissions, argumentative sleight of hand and faulty documentation that, in Jewel Spears Brooker's words, resulted in a 'deeply flawed book'. See her 'Eliot in the Dock', in Jewel Spears Brooker, ed., *T. S. Eliot and Our Turning World* (London: Macmillan, 2001), p. 164.

Criticism on Eliot and **Laforgue** includes Hugh Kenner, *The Invisible Poet: T. S. Eliot* (1959; rpt. London: W. H. Allen, 1960), pp. 12–34; Piers Gray, *T. S. Eliot's Intellectual and Poetic Development 1908-1922* (Sussex; Harvester, 1982), especially chapter 1, pp. 1–37; Anne Holmes, *Jules Laforgue and Poetic Innovation* (Oxford: Clarendon, 1993), chapter 7, pp. 121–31; Habib, *The Early T. S. Eliot*, pp. 29–38, 61–96 and Ronald Schuchard, *Eliot's Dark Angel: Intersections of Life and Art* (New York: Oxford University Press, 1999), chapter 3, pp. 70–86. On Eliot and **Baudelaire**, see Lachlan Mackinnon, *Eliot, Auden, Lowell: Aspects of the Baudelairean Inheritance* (London: Macmillan, 1983), especially chapter 1, pp. 7–48.

For Eliot and his **late-Victorian poetic predecessors,** see Claire A. Cullerton, 'James Thomson and the Influence of *The City of Dreadful Night* on T. S. Eliot', *Yeats Eliot Review*, 12 (1992), 85–9; 'TSE on the poets of the Nineties' in *Inventions of the March Hare*, ed. Ricks, pp. 394–9. The influence of Thomson, Dowson and Davidson on Eliot's depiction of the city is discussed by Crawford, *The Savage and the City*, pp. 35–60. Ronald Bush notes that one of the 'ongoing concerns' in recent Eliot studies is to extend the investigation into Eliot's 'suppressed' debts to other 1890s writers, including Oscar Wilde and Lionel Johnson. See Bush, 'In Pursuit of Wilde Possum: Reflections on Eliot, Modernism, and the Nineties', *Modernism/Modernity*, 11 (2004), 469–85; Schuchard, *Eliot's Dark Angel*, especially pp. 3–9. For a very useful compilation of Eliot's statements on his debt to Symons, as well as on other early influences, see Appendix D of Ricks, ed., *Inventions of the March Hare*, pp. 385–414.

On linkages between Eliot and **the earlier generation of Victorian poets**, see the useful survey by Kristian Smidt, 'Eliot and the Victorians', in *T. S. Eliot at the Turn of the Century*, ed. Thormählen, pp. 181–97. For more detailed investigation see Carol T. Christ, *Victorian and Modern Poetics* (Chicago: University of Chicago Press, 1984), which includes some consideration of Eliot and Arnold, Browning and Tennyson, and especially David Ned Tobin, *The Presence of the Past: T. S. Eliot's Victorian Inheritance* (Ann Arbor: UMI Research Press, 1983), which presents very suggestive correspondences between Eliot's poetry and Arnold, Newman and particularly Tennyson, a poet Eliot increasingly came to admire.

For more on **readings of *The Waste Land*** from different political positions (all parties might agree that the poem represents social 'breakdown' while differing as to any proposed remedies it supports or inspires, from re-affirming the authority of the status quo to insisting on new beginnings), see Michael North, *The Political Aesthetic of Yeats, Eliot, and Pound* (Cambridge: Cambridge University Press, 1991), pp. 105–6. North refers to the attraction the poem had for communists in the 1930s in the diagnosis of capitalism in crisis it could be seen as offering: 'stylistic disorientation did, in such readings, figure political freedom'. See also Stephen Spender, 'Writers and Politics', *Partisan Review*, 34 (1967), 378. In a separate piece, North also notes the inspiration the jazzy elements of Eliot's 'American idiom' provided for black poets like Edward Brathwaite in their quest for a nation language that would subvert standard English.

'The Dialect in/of Modernism: Pound and Eliot's Racial Masquerade', *American Literary History*, 4 (1992), 56–76, rpt. Davidson (ed.), *T. S. Eliot*, pp. 136–55 (quotation p. 150).

For an extremely interesting **psychoanalytic approach** to the poem, see Wayne Koestenbaum, '*The Waste Land*: T. S. Eliot's and Ezra Pound's Collaboration on Hysteria', *Twentieth Century Literature*, 34 (1988), 113–39. Koestenbaum sees the poem displaying the same sorts of hysterical symptoms as those of Breuer and Freud's patients in *Studies on Hysteria* (1895), with Pound acting as the poem's healing analyst. For an interesting discussion of similarities between Eliot and Freud's diagnosis of humanity's ills, whatever their vastly different 'solutions', see Adam Phillips, 'The Soul of Man Under Psychoanalysis', *London Review of Books*, 29 November 2001, pp. 19–23. In Tony Pinkney's *Women in the Poetry of T. S. Eliot: A Psychoanalytic Approach* (London: Macmillan, 1984), post-Freudian developments in psychoanalysis in the work of Melanie Klein and D. W. Winnicott are drawn on to present a picture of Eliot's work as pervaded by the primal relationship with the mother, rather than the (Freudian) Oedipal struggle with the father: 'characteristically in Eliot the father is a dim, barely defined figure, present only at the remote fringes of consciousness'. Women, however, have a much more active and menacing force, 'ambivalently desired and threatening', which unleashes a corresponding aggression towards them: 'Eliot's texts are all strategies concerned both to do girls in and to deny the doing.' The recurring figure of the 'murdered woman' is 'never simply one's mistress, but is first and foremost recipient of unconscious phantasies pertaining to the most primitive stages of the infant-mother relationship' (pp. 22, 26, 57, 49).

The complicated issue of the order and date of composition of **The Waste Land manuscripts** is given the most detailed investigation in Lawrence Rainey, *Revisiting 'The Waste Land'* (New Haven: Yale University Press, 2005), who also gives an account of previous critical discussion in this area.

On Eliot and the **Criterion**, see Agha Shahid Ali, *T. S. Eliot as Editor* (Ann Arbor: UMI Research Press, 1986), and Jason Harding, *The Criterion: Cultural Politics and Periodical Networks in Inter-war Britain* (Oxford: Oxford University Press, 2002). For a detailed study of the **Ariel** poems see John H. Timmerman, *T. S. Eliot's Ariel Poems: The Poetics of Recovery* (Lewisburg: Bucknell University Press, 1984). For an interesting reading suggesting that the private experience that lies at the heart of **'Ash-Wednesday'** is Eliot's relationship with his mother, who died in 1929, rather than his wife, see Elisabeth Däumer, 'Charlotte Stearns Eliot and "Ash-Wednesday"'s Lady of Silences', *ELH* 65 (1998), 479–501 For an excellent study of Eliot's **later writing on social and cultural issues**, see Roger Kojecký, *T. S. Eliot's Social Criticism* (London: Faber, 1971). On Eliot and **Richards**, see John Constable, 'I. A. Richards, T. S. Eliot, and the Poetry of Belief', *Essays in Criticism*, 4 (1990), 222–43. For Eliot's **drama**, E. Martin Browne's study, based on prolonged collaboration with Eliot in staging the plays, is still one of the most valuable accounts; see *The Making of T. S. Eliot's Plays* (Cambridge: Cambridge University Press, 1969).

On *Four Quartets*, Helen Gardner, *The Composition of 'Four Quartets'* (London: Faber, 1978), is a discussion of and commentary on the poem as it evolved, giving much information about its manuscript stages, as well as quoting letters to friends Eliot wrote during its composition where he often asks for advice and response to the work in progress. Gardner also gives a good deal of information about the poem's literary and biographical sources.

On the *Quartets* and **St John of the Cross**, see Paul Murray, *T. S. Eliot and Mysticism: The Secret History of 'Four Quartets'* (Basingstoke: Macmillan, 1991), chapter 6, pp. 88–100. Murray's book surveys many aspects of the relation between Eliot's poem and the mystical tradition, from Buddhism to Kierkegaard. On Eliot's use of **Hindu and Buddhist teaching** throughout his work, as well as Paul Foster, *The Golden Lotus: Buddhist Influence in T. S. Eliot's 'Four Quartets'* (Sussex: The Book Guild, 1998), see Cleo McNelly Kearns, *T. S. Eliot and Indic Traditions: A Study in Poetry and Belief* (Cambridge: Cambridge University Press, 1987). Vinod Sena and Rajiva Verma, (eds), *The Fire and the Rose: New Essays on T. S. Eliot* (Delhi: Oxford University Press, 1992), also contains several useful essays on Eliot and Indic traditions: see particularly Vinod Sena, 'The Lotos and the Rose: *The Bhagavad Gita* and T. S. Eliot's *Four Quartets*', pp. 180–9 and, on the use of Indian scriptural sources in *The Waste Land*, Harish Trivedi, '"Ganga was sunken . . ." T. S. Eliot's Use of India', pp. 44–62.

For further discussion of Eliot's dialogue with other more picturesque versions of rural **England** in the 1930s and 40s, see Steve Ellis, *The English Eliot: Design, Language and Landscape in 'Four Quartets'*

(London: Routledge, 1991), chapter 3, pp. 77–140, and Jed Esty, *A Shrinking Island: Modernism and National Culture in England,* Princeton: Princeton University Press, 2004), chapter 3, pp. 108–62. For a discussion of *Four Quartets* that concentrates not on the spiritual assurances the poem offers, but on the 'psychological refuge and the outlines of a new kind of subjectivity' it can be seen as providing in a time of crisis, see John Xiros Cooper, *T. S. Eliot and the Ideology of 'Four Quartets'* (Cambridge: Cambridge University Press, 1995) (quotation p. 31). See also Edward Lobb, (ed.), *Words in Time: New Essays on Eliot's 'Four Quartets'* (London: Athlone, 1993).

For more on Eliot and **Dante**, see Steve Ellis, *Dante and English Poetry: Shelley to T. S. Eliot* (Cambridge: Cambridge University Press, 1983), chapter 7, pp. 210–43, and Dominic Manganiello, *T. S. Eliot and Dante* (Basingstoke: Macmillan, 1989). On **Virgil**, see Gareth Reeves, *T. S. Eliot: A Virgilian Poet* (London: Macmillan, 1989).

BIBLIOGRAPHY

Ackroyd, Peter (1984), *T. S. Eliot*, London: Hamish Hamilton.

Ali, Agha Shahid (1986), *T. S. Eliot as Editor*, Ann Arbor: UMI Research Press.

Arnold, Matthew (1993), *Culture and Anarchy and Other Writings*, ed. Stefan Collini, Cambridge: Cambridge University Press.

Asher, Kenneth (1995), *T. S. Eliot and Ideology*, Cambridge: Cambridge University Press.

Baudelaire, Charles (1986), *The Complete Verse*, ed., introd. and trans. Francis Scarfe, London: Anvil.

Behr, Caroline (1983), *T. S. Eliot: A Chronology of His Life and Works*, London: Macmillan.

Benjamin, Walter (1999), 'Theses on the Philosophy of History', in *Illuminations*, ed. and introd. Hannah Arendt, trans. Harry Zorn, 1970; rpt. London: Pimlico, pp. 245–55.

Bergonzi, Bernard (ed.) (1969), *T. S. Eliot: 'Four Quartets': A Casebook*, London: Macmillan.

Brooker, Jewel Spears (2001), 'Eliot in the Dock', in *T. S. Eliot and Our Turning World*, ed. Jewel Spears Brooker, London: Macmillan, pp. 157–64.

Brooker, Jewel Spears (1994), *T. S. Eliot and the Dialectic of Modernism*, Amherst: University of Massachusetts Press.

Browne, E. Martin (1969), *The Making of T. S. Eliot's Plays*, Cambridge: Cambridge University Press.

Bush, Ronald (2004), 'In Pursuit of Wilde Possum: Reflections on Eliot, Modernism, and the Nineties', *Modernism/Modernity*, 11, 469–85.

Cheshire, D. F. (1985), 'T. S. Eliot's *Murder in the Cathedral*: A Survey of its First Performances and Some Important Revivals', *Theatrephile*, 2, no. 8 (winter), 65–70.

Cheyette, Bryan (2003), 'Neither Excuse nor Accuse: T. S. Eliot's Semitic Discourse', *Modernism/Modernity*, 10, 431–7.

Chinitz, David E. (2003), *T. S. Eliot and the Cultural Divide*, Chicago: University of Chicago Press.

Christ, Carol T. (1984), *Victorian and Modern Poetics*, Chicago: University of Chicago Press.

Churchill, Suzanne W. (2005), 'Outing T. S. Eliot', *Criticism*, 47, 7–30.

Conrad, Joseph (2002), *Heart of Darkness*, ed. Zdzislaw Najder, 1902; rpt. London: Hesperus.

Constable, John (1990), 'I. A. Richards, T. S. Eliot, and the Poetry of Belief', *Essays in Criticism*, 4, 222–43.

Cook, Cornelia (2001), 'Fire and Spirit: Scripture's Shaping Presence in T. S. Eliot's *Four Quartets*', *Literature and Theology*, 15, 85–101.

Cooper, John Xiros (1987), 'Reading the "Seduction" Fragment', in *T. S. Eliot and the Politics of Voice: The Argument of 'The Waste Land'*, Ann Arbor: UMI Research Press, pp. 27–39, rpt. Davidson (ed.), *T. S. Eliot*, pp. 117–35.

Cooper, John Xiros (1995), *T. S. Eliot and the Ideology of 'Four Quartets'*, Cambridge: Cambridge University Press.

Crawford, Robert (1987), *The Savage and the City in the Work of T. S. Eliot*, Oxford: Clarendon.

Cullerton, Claire A. (1992), 'James Thomson and the Influence of *The City of Dreadful Night* on T. S. Eliot', *Yeats Eliot Review*, 12, 85–9.

Dante Alighieri (1979), *La divina commedia (Inferno, Purgatorio, Paradiso)* ed. Natalino Sapegno, 3 vols, Florence: La nuova Italia.

Dante Alighieri (1969), *La vita nuova (Poems of Youth)*, trans. and introd. Barbara Reynolds, London: Penguin.

Däumer, Elisabeth (1998), 'Charlotte Stearns Eliot and "Ash-Wednesday"'s Lady of Silences', *ELH*, 65, 479–501.

Davidson, Harriet (ed.) (1999), *T. S. Eliot*, Longman Critical Readers, Harlow: Longman.

DuBois, Andrew and Frank Lentricchia (2003), 'T. S. Eliot', in *The Cambridge History of American Literature*, vol 5, *Poetry and Criticism 1900–1950*, ed. Sacvan Bercovitch, Cambridge: Cambridge University Press, pp. 97–130.

Eagleton, Terry (1998), *Criticism and Ideology: A Study in Marxist Literary Theory*, 1976; rpt. London: Verso.

Eliot, T. S. (1934), *After Strange Gods: A Primer of Modern Heresy*. The Page-Barbour Lectures at the University of Virginia 1933, London: Faber.

Eliot, T. S. (1959), The Art of Poetry I: T. S. Eliot' [interview], *Paris Review*, 21, 46–70.

Eliot, T. S. (1969), *The Complete Poems and Plays*, London: Faber.

Eliot, T. S. (1953), 'Eeldrop and Appleplex', *Little Review*, May/September 1917; rpt. *The Little Review Anthology*, ed. Margaret Anderson, New York: Hermitage House, pp. 102–9.

Eliot, T. S. ([1928]1970), *For Lancelot Andrewes: Essays on Style and Order*, new ed., London: Faber.

Eliot, T. S. (1962), *George Herbert*, London: Longmans, Green.

Eliot, T. S. (1939), *The Idea of a Christian Society*, London: Faber.

Eliot, T. S. (1996), *Inventions of the March Hare: Poems 1909–1917*, ed. Christopher Ricks, London: Faber.

Eliot, T. S. (1964), *Knowledge and Experience in the Philosophy of F. H. Bradley*, London: Faber.

Eliot, T. S. (1939), 'Last Words', *Criterion*, 18, 269–75.

Eliot, T. S. (1988), *The Letters of T. S. Eliot*, vol 1, 1898–1922, ed. Valerie Eliot, London: Faber.

Eliot, T. S. (1927), 'Literature, Science, and Dogma', *Dial*, 82, 239–43.

Eliot, T. S. (1963), 'A Note of Introduction', *In Parenthesis*, by David Jones, London: Faber, pp. vii–viii.

Eliot, T. S. (1927), 'A Note on Poetry and Belief', *Enemy*, 1 (January) 15–17.

Eliot, T. S. (1935), 'Notes on the Way', *Time and Tide*, 5 January, pp. 6–7.

Eliot, T. S. ([1948]1962), *Notes Towards the Definition of Culture*, new ed., London: Faber.

Eliot, T. S. (T. S. Apteryx (pseud.)) (1918), 'Observations', *Egoist*, 5, 69–70.

Eliot, T. S. (1957), *On Poetry and Poets*, London: Faber.

Eliot, T. S. (1928), Review of Sigmund Freud, *The Future of an Illusion*, *Criterion*, 8, (1928–9) 350–3.

Eliot, T. S. (1934), *The Rock*, London: Faber.

Eliot, T. S. ([1920]1950), *The Sacred Wood: Essays on Poetry and Criticism*, 7th ed., London: Methuen.

Eliot, T. S. (1951), *Selected Essays*, 3rd ed., London: Faber.

Eliot, T. S. (1975), *Selected Prose*, ed. Frank Kermode, London: Faber.

Eliot, T. S. ([1965]1978), *To Criticize the Critic and Other Writings*, new ed., London: Faber.

Eliot, T. S. ([1933]1964), *The Use of Poetry and the Use of Criticism: Studies in the Relation of Criticism to Poetry in England*, new ed., London: Faber.

Eliot, T. S. (1993), *The Varieties of Metaphysical Poetry . . .* ed. Ronald Schuchard, London: Faber.

Eliot, T. S. (1971), *The Waste Land: A Facsimile and Transcript of the Original Drafts Including the Annotations of Ezra Pound*, ed. Valerie Eliot, London: Faber.

Ellis, Steve (1983), *Dante and English Poetry: Shelley to T. S. Eliot*, Cambridge: Cambridge University Press.

Ellis, Steve (1991), *The English Eliot: Design, Language and Landscape in 'Four Quartets'*, London: Routledge.

Ellmann, Maud (1987), *The Poetics of Impersonality: T. S. Eliot and Ezra Pound*, Cambridge, MA: Harvard University Press.

Esty, Jed (2004), *A Shrinking Island: Modernism and National Culture in England*, Princeton: Princeton University Press.

Fitzgerald, F. Scott (1950), *The Great Gatsby*, 1926; rpt. Harmondsworth: Penguin.

Forster, E. M. (1961), *A Passage to India*, 1924; rpt. Harmondsworth: Penguin.

Foster, Paul (1998), *The Golden Lotus: Buddhist Influence in T. S. Eliot's 'Four Quartets'*, Sussex: The Book Guild.

Freed, Lewis (1979), *T. S. Eliot: The Critic as Philosopher*, West Lafayette, In: Purdue University Press.

Froula, Christine (1989), 'Eliot's Grail Quest, or, the Lover, the Police, and *The Waste Land*', *Yale Review*, 78, 235–53; rpt. Davidson (ed.), *T. S. Eliot*, pp. 166–80.

Gallup, Donald (1969), *T. S. Eliot: A Bibliography*, London: Faber.

Gardner, Helen (1978), *The Composition of 'Four Quartets'*, London: Faber.

Germer, Rudolph (1994), 'T. S. Eliot's Religious Development', in *T. S. Eliot at the Turn of the Century*, ed. Thormählen, pp. 91–104.

Gilbert, Sandra M. and Susan Gubar (1989), *No Man's Land: The Place of the Woman Writer in the Twentieth Century*, vol. 2, *Sexchanges*, New Haven: Yale University Press.

Gish, Nancy K. (1981), *Time in the Poetry of T. S. Eliot: A Study in Structure and Theme*, London: Macmillan.

Gordon, Lyndall (1998), *T. S. Eliot: An Imperfect Life*, London: Vintage.

Gray, Piers (1982), *T. S. Eliot's Intellectual and Poetic Development 1908–1922*, Sussex: Harvester.

Habib, M. A. R. (1999), *The Early T. S. Eliot and Western Philosophy*, Cambridge: Cambridge University Press.

Harding, Jason (2002), *The Criterion: Cultural Politics and Periodical Networks in Inter-war Britain*, Oxford: Oxford University Press.

Hargrove, Nancy D. (2003), 'T. S. Eliot and Popular Entertainment in Paris, 1910–1911', *Journal of Popular Culture*, 36, 547–88.

Hastings, Selina (1994), *Evelyn Waugh: A Biography*, London: Sinclair-Stevenson.

Hauck, Christina (2003), 'Abortion and the Individual Talent', *ELH*, 70, 223–66.

Heaney, Seamus (1987), 'Energies and Identifications: Dante and the Modern Poet', in *Dante Readings*, ed. Eric Haywood, Dublin: Irish Academic Press, pp. 29–46.

Holmes, Anne (1993), *Jules Laforgue and Poetic Innovation*, Oxford: Clarendon.

Howarth, Herbert (1965), *Notes on Some Figures Behind T. S. Eliot*, London: Chatto & Windus.

Hulme, T. E. (1994), *The Collected Writings of T. E. Hulme*, ed. Karen Csengeri, Oxford: Clarendon.

Jain, Manju (1992), *T. S. Eliot and American Philosophy: The Harvard Years*, Cambridge: Cambridge University Press.

John of the Cross (1987), *Selected Writings*, ed. and introd. Kieran Kavanaugh, New York: Paulist Press.

Johnson, Loretta (2003), 'T. S. Eliot's Bawdy Verse: Lulu, Bolo and More Ties', *Journal of Modern Literature*, 27, 14–25.

Julius, Anthony (1995), *T. S. Eliot, Anti-Semitism, and Literary Form*, Cambridge: Cambridge University Press. New edition 2003, London: Thames and Hudson.

Kaiser, Jo Ellen Green (1998), 'Disciplining *The Waste Land*, or, How to Lead Critics into Temptation', *Twentieth Century Literature*, 44, 82–99.

Kearns, Cleo McNelly (1987), *T. S. Eliot and Indic Traditions: A Study in Poetry and Belief*, Cambridge: Cambridge University Press.

Kenner, Hugh (1960), *The Invisible Poet: T. S. Eliot*, 1959; rpt. London: W. H. Allen.

Kenner, Hugh (1973), 'The Urban Apocalypse', in *Eliot in His Time: Essays on the Occasion of the Fiftieth Anniversary of 'The Waste Land'*, ed. A. Walton Litz, Princeton: Princeton University Press, pp. 23–49.

Koestenbaum, Wayne (1988), '*The Waste Land*: T. S. Eliot's and Ezra Pound's Collaboration on Hysteria', *Twentieth Century Literature*, 34, 113–39.

Kojecký, Roger (1971), *T. S. Eliot's Social Criticism*, London: Faber.

Laity, Cassandra and Nancy K. Gish (eds) (2004), *Gender, Desire, and Sexuality in T. S. Eliot*, Cambridge: Cambridge University Press.

Leavis, F. R. (1972), *New Bearings in English Poetry: A Study of the Contemporary Situation*, 1932; rpt. Harmondsworth: Penguin.

Levenson, Michael H. (1984), *A Genealogy of Modernism: A Study of English Literary Doctrine 1908–1922*, Cambridge: Cambridge University Press.

Longenbach, James (1987), *Modernist Poetics of History: Pound, Eliot, and the Sense of the Past*, Princeton: Princeton University Press.

McDonald, Gail (1993), *Learning to be Modern: Pound, Eliot, and the American University*, Oxford: Clarendon.

McGee, Daniel T. (2001), 'Dada Da Da: Sounding the Jew in Modernism', *ELH*, 68, 501–27.

Mackinnon, Lachlan (1983), *Eliot, Auden, Lowell: Aspects of the Baudelairean Inheritance*, London: Macmillan.

McLuhan, Marshall (1994), *Understanding Media: The Extensions of Man*, 1964; rpt. Cambridge, MA: MIT Press.

Manganiello, Dominic (1989), *T. S. Eliot and Dante*, Basingstoke: Macmillan.

Maritain, Jacques (1932), *Art and Scholasticism: With Other Essays*, trans. J. F. Scanlan, London: Sheed and Ward.

Matthiessen, F. O. (1959), *The Achievement of T. S. Eliot: An Essay on the Nature of Poetry*, 3rd ed., New York: Oxford University Press.

Mayer, John T. (1989), *T. S. Eliot's Silent Voices*, New York: Oxford University Press.

Miller, James E., Jr. (1978), *T. S. Eliot's Personal Waste Land: Exorcism of the Demons*, University Park: Pennsylvania State University Press.

Milstead, Claudia (2003), 'Echoes of Krishna and Arjuna in Eliot's "Dry Salvages" and "Little Gidding"', *ELN*, 40, 62–76.

Moody, A. D. (1979), *Thomas Stearns Eliot: Poet*, Cambridge: Cambridge University Press.

Murray, Paul (1991), *T. S. Eliot and Mysticism: The Secret History of 'Four Quartets'*, Basingstoke: Macmillan.

North, Michael (1992), 'The Dialect in/of Modernism: Pound and Eliot's Racial Masquerade', *American Literary History*, 4, 56–76; rpt. Davidson (ed.), *T. S. Eliot*, pp. 136–55.

North, Michael (1991), *The Political Aesthetic of Yeats, Eliot, and Pound*, Cambridge: Cambridge University Press.

Perloff, Marjorie (2003), 'A Response to Ronald Schuchard', *Modernism/Modernity* 10, 51–6.

Peter, John (1969), 'A New Interpretation of *The Waste Land*' and 'Postscript', *Essays in Criticism*, 19, 140–75.

Phillips, Adam (2001), 'The Soul of Man Under Psychoanalysis', *London Review of Books*, 29 November, pp. 19–23.

Pinkney, Tony (1984), *Women in the Poetry of T. S. Eliot: A Psychoanalytic Approach*, London: Macmillan.

Potter, Rachel (2006), *Modernism and Democracy: Literary Culture 1900–1930*, Oxford: Oxford University Press.

Pound, Ezra (1932), 'Harold Munro', *Criterion*, 11, 581–92.

Pound, Ezra (1951), *The Letters of Ezra Pound 1907–1941*, ed. D. D. Paige, London: Faber.

Raine, Craig (2000), *In Defence of T. S. Eliot*, London: Picador.

Raine, Craig (2006), *T. S. Eliot*, Oxford: Oxford University Press.

Rainey, Lawrence (2005), *Revisiting 'The Waste Land'*, New Haven: Yale University Press.

Reeves, Gareth (1989), *T. S. Eliot: A Virgilian Poet*, London: Macmillan.

Richards, I. A. (1925), 'A Background for Contemporary Poetry', *Criterion*, 3, 511–28.

Richards, I. A. (1926), *Science and Poetry*, London: Kegan Paul, Trench, Trubner.

Richardson, John (1999), 'After the Imagination of Our Own Hearts: Biblical Prophecy and *The Waste Land*', *English*, 48, 187–98.

Ricks, Christopher (1988), *T. S. Eliot and Prejudice*, London: Faber.

Riquelme, John Paul (1991), *Harmony of Dissonances: T. S. Eliot, Romanticism, and Imagination*, Baltimore: Johns Hopkins University Press.

Schuchard, Ronald (2003), 'Burbank with a Baedeker, Eliot with a Cigar: American Intellectuals, Anti-Semitism, and the Idea of Culture', *Modernism/Modernity* 10, 1–26.

Schuchard, Ronald (2003), 'Did Eliot Know Hulme? Final Answer', *Journal of Modern Literature*, 27, 63–9.

Schuchard, Ronald (1999), *Eliot's Dark Angel: Intersections of Life and Art*, New York: Oxford University Press.

Schuchard, Ronald (1993), '"If I think, again, of this place": Eliot, Herbert and the Way to "Little Gidding"', in *Words in Time: New Essays on Eliot's 'Four Quartets'*, ed. Edward Lobb, London: Athlone, pp. 52–83.

Schwartz, Sanford (1985), *The Matrix of Modernism: Pound, Eliot, and Early Twentieth-Century Thought*, Princeton: Princeton University Press.

Sena, Vinod and Rajiva Verma, (eds) (1992), *The Fire and the Rose: New Essays on T. S. Eliot*, Delhi: Oxford University Press.

Seymour-Jones, Carole (2001), *Painted Shadow: A Life of Vivienne Eliot*, London: Constable.

Shusterman, Richard (1988), *T. S. Eliot and the Philosophy of Criticism*, London: Duckworth.

Sigg, Eric (1989), *The American T. S. Eliot: A Study of the Early Writings*, Cambridge: Cambridge University Press.

Smidt, Kristian (1994), 'Eliot and the Victorians', in *T. S. Eliot at the Turn of the Century*, ed. Thormählen, pp. 181–97

Smith, Grover, Jr. (1956), *T. S. Eliot's Poetry and Plays: A Study in Sources and Meaning*, Chicago: University of Chicago Press.

Southam, B. C. (1994), *A Student's Guide to the 'Selected Poems' of T. S. Eliot*, 6th ed., London: Faber.

Spender, Stephen (1975), *Eliot*, Fontana Modern Masters, Glasgow: Fontana.

Spender, Stephen (1967), 'Writers and Politics', *Partisan Review*, 34, 359–81.

Stead, C. K. (1967), *The New Poetic: Yeats to Eliot*, 1964; rpt. Harmondsworth: Penguin.

Symons, Arthur (1958), *The Symbolist Movement in Literature*, introd. Richard Ellmann, 1899; rpt. New York: Dutton.

Tate, Allen (ed.) (1971), *T. S. Eliot: the Man and His Work*, Harmondsworth: Penguin.

Tennyson, Alfred, Lord (1969), *The Poems of Tennyson*, ed. Christopher Ricks, London: Longman.

Thormählen, Marianne (ed.) (1994), *T. S. Eliot at the Turn of the Century*, Lund: Lund University Press.

Thormählen, Marianne (1978), *'The Waste Land': A Fragmentary Wholeness*, Lund: Gleerup.

Timmerman, John H. (1984), *T. S. Eliot's Ariel Poems: The Poetics of Recovery*, Lewisburg: Bucknell University Press.

Tobin, David Ned (1983), *The Presence of the Past: T. S. Eliot's Victorian Inheritance*, Ann Arbor: UMI Research Press.

Tratner, Michael (1995), *Modernism and Mass Politics: Joyce, Woolf, Eliot, Yeats*, Stanford: Stanford University Press.

Waugh, Evelyn ([1945]1962), *Brideshead Revisited: The Sacred and Profane Memories of Captain Charles Ryder*, rev. ed., Harmondsworth: Penguin.

White, Peter (2003), 'New Light on *The Sacred Wood*', *RES*, 54, 497–515.

Williams, David A. (2005), '"Several Centers": T. S. Eliot's Wartime Agenda of Cultural Unity and Diversity', *Yeats Eliot Review*, 22, 15–23.

Wollheim, Richard (1970), 'Eliot and F. H. Bradley: an Account', in *Eliot in Perspective: A Symposium*, ed. Graham Martin, London: Macmillan, pp. 169–93.

Woolf, Virginia (1981), *The Diary of Virginia Woolf*, vol. 2, 1920–4, ed. Anne Olivier Bell, 1978; rpt. London: Penguin.

Woolf, Virginia (1988), 'Modern Novels', *The Essays of Virginia Woolf*, vol. 3, 1919–24, ed. Andrew McNeillie, London: Hogarth, pp. 30–7.

Wordsworth, William (1986), *William Wordsworth*, Oxford Authors, ed. Stephen Gill, Oxford: Oxford University Press.

Yeats, W. B. (1961), 'Modern Poetry: a Broadcast', *Essays and Introductions*, London: Macmillan, pp. 491–508.

Yeats, W. B. (1957), *The Variorum Edition of the Poems of W. B. Yeats*, ed. Peter Allt and Russell K. Alspach, New York: Macmillan.

Yeats, W. B. (1925), *A Vision*, London: Werner Laurie, 2nd ed. (1937), 2nd corrected ed. (1962), London: Macmillan.

INDEX